GRATEFUL DEAD FAMILY ALBUM™

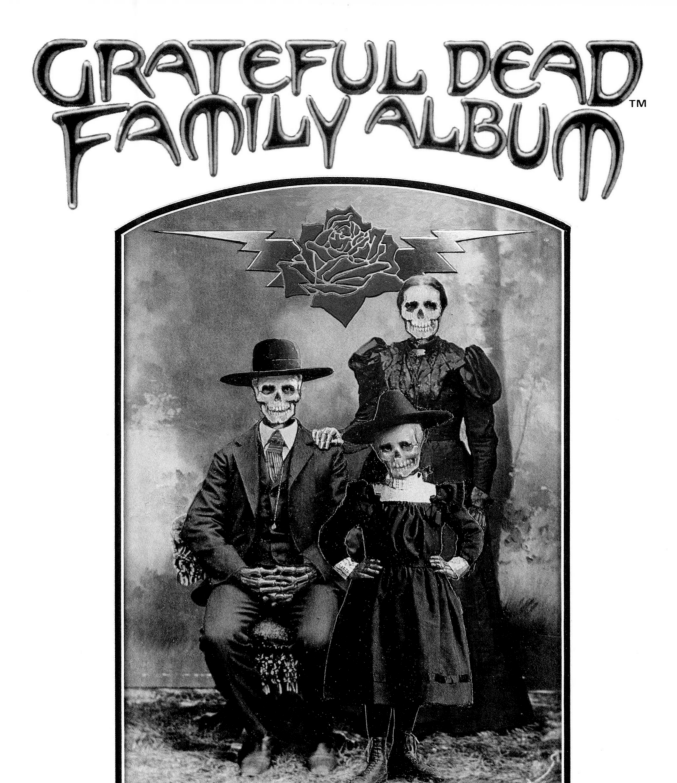

By Jerilyn Lee Brandelius

WARNER BOOKS

A Warner Communication Company

*Library of Congress
Cataloging-in-Publication Data:*
Brandelius, Jerilyn Lee.
Grateful Dead Family Album
p. cm.
ISBN 0-446-51521-3
1. Grateful Dead (Musical group)
I. Title.
ML421.G72B7   1989
782.42166'092'2 — dc20
[B]   CIP   MN   89-40039

Edited by Alan Trist
Designed & produced by Jon Goodchild/
    Triad. Facilitated by Tony Secunda
Cover and Frontispiece by Stanley Mouse
Editorial Assistant: Dante Anderson
Production Assistants: Evana Gerstman
    and Debbie Trist
Typeset by TBD Typography, San Rafael

Warner Books, Inc.
666 Fifth Avenue, New York, NY 10103
Ⓦ A Warner Communication Company
Printed in the United States of America

First printing: November 1989

10 9 8 7 6 5 4 3 2 1

Acknowledgments

It is impossible to thank everyone who
has contributed to this book over its
many years of preparation, for they are
the whole 'family', hundreds of people.
My deepest gratitude to Alan Trist for his
herculean effort in ferreting out the
cream of published text and for organizing the photographic material. My special
thanks to David Stanford, who first took a
publisher's interest in the project, and to
Gary Kephart and Rosanne Esposito who
helped in the early stage of production.
To Annette Flowers, Christina Hart,
Natalie Martel, Bonnie Parker, Ron Polte,
Ramrod, Danny Rifkin, Rock Scully and
Sue Stephens, my thanks for their advice
and support throughout the highs and
lows. To Bill Graham, Paul Grushkin,
Richard Hundgen, Blair Jackson, Les
Kippel, Eileen Law, Dennis McNally, Jim
Olness, Jerry Pompili, and DeadBase, my
sincere appreciation for their generosity
in sharing their deep archival resources.
To Gene Anthony, Jay Blakesberg, Alan
Blaustein, Rosie McGee Ende, Snooky
Flowers, Herb Greene, Ed Perlstein and
Steve Schneider, my thanks for their
photographic experience beyond the call
of duty. To my 'sweethearts', Peter H.
Ackroyd, Ron Barca, Scott Bonfiglio,
Rondell Cagwin, Patrick Cuffe, Hank
Gurnsey, David Henderson, Pete Marino,
Mad Max, Amy Moore, Dan Murphy, John
Paul, James J. Pell Jr., Forbes Reid, Tom
Saidy, Gideon Sorokin, John Spediaci and
Family, Joan Stevenson and Don Paul,
John Stewart, Michael Tobin, Tony and
Vikki, Christa Van Sandwick, for always
being their with their encouragement
and support. To professional and amateur
photographers, writers and artists — to
one and all, my heartfelt thanks. My love,
respect and thanks to the Grateful Dead
for the opportunity to assemble this
album for our family. J.L.B

Permissions

Permission to reproduce printed text from the
following sources is gratefully acknowledged:

Crawdaddy: Paul Williams, 8/67. Copyright ©
1967 Crawdaddy Publishing Company. **BAM
Magazine:** David Gans, 1978; Mickey Hart,
11/3/78; Dan Healy, 11/3/78; 1/19/79;
12/18/87; Mary Eisenhart, 12/18/87.
Copyright © 1978, 1979, 1987 BAM Publica-
tions, Inc. **Grateful Dead Productions:**
Copyright © 1965, 1978, 1983 Grateful Dead
Productions, Inc. **Guitar Player:** Copyright
© 1978 Guitar Player. **Hulogos'i Books:**
Copyright © 1987, Robert Hunter; Copyright
© 1988, Didrik Petersen. Hulogos'i Books, P.O.
Box 1188, Eugene, OR 97440. **Ice Nine Publishing Company:** Donna Godchaux, 1977; Robert
Hunter, 1985, 1987; Robert M. Petersen, 1980;
Choirmaster, 1972; Deadhead Newsletters
1973, 1976, 1980. Copyright © 1972, 1973,
1976, 1977, 1980, 1985, 1987 Ice Nine Publishing Company, Inc. **Louisville Times:** John

Christensen. Copyright © Louisville Times,
Inc. **Marin Independent Journal:** Kevin Lollar,
1987. Copyright © 1987 Marin Independent
Journal, Inc. **Medford Mail Tribune:** John
Lowry, 1978. Copyright © 1978 Mail Tribune,
Inc. **Melody Maker:** Karl Dallas, 10/10/81.
Copyright © 1981 Melody Maker. **Playboy
Guide:** Playboy Electronic, Spring 1982. From
"A Conversation with Jerry Garcia," interview
conducted by Jon Carroll. Copyright © 1982
Playboy Enterprises, Inc. All Rights Reserved.
Reprinted with Permission. **Point Reyes
Light:** 7/31/80. Copyright © 1980 Point Reyes
Light, Inc. **Relix Magazine:** John Hall, Charles
Young, November 1978; Monte Dym & Bob
Alsa, Spring 1978; Sandy Troy, June 1978.
Copyright © Relix Magazine, Inc. Relix
Magazine, P.O. Box 94, Brooklyn, NY 11229.
Relix Records: Wavy Gravy, 1988. Copyright
© 1988 Relix Records. P.O. Box 92, Brooklyn,
NY 11229. **Rock:** Copyright © Rock, 1973. **Rock
& Roll News:** Greg Barrette, 4/77. Copyright
© 1977 Rock & Roll News. **Rolling Stone:**
Ralph J. Gleason, 6/20/68; 8/10/68; Adele
Novelli, 7/12/69; 7/12/69; Charles Perry,
10/29/89; Jerry Hopkins, 6/22/72; Merrill
Sanders, 6/8/72; John Grissim, 11/2/ 75,
11/6/75; Mikal Gilmore, 7/16/87, 7/30/87.
Copyright © 1968, 1969, 1972, 1973, 1975,
1987 Straight Arrow Publishers, Inc. All Rights
Reserved. Reprinted by Permission. **San Fran-
cisco Chronicle:** 'New Generation', 1966;
Michael Rossman, 1/66; Clint Roswell, 8/88;
Joel Selvin, 9/14/81. Copyright © 1966, 1980,
1981 The Chronicle Publishing Company.
Reprinted by permission. **Santa Fe Reporter:**
Howard Passell, 9/14/83. Copyright © 1983
The Santa Fe Reporter. **Sonoma County
Stump:** Nicki Scully, 11/10/78. Copyright ©
1978 Sonoma County Stump. **Sounds:** Hans-
Joachim Kruger, 1972. Copyright © 1972
Sounds. **Spit in the Ocean: The Pyramid
Issue,** #5, Ken Kesey, Paul Krassner. Copyright
© 1979 Ken Kesey. **Sun (Austin):** Enrique
Pasa, 3/26/76. Copyright © 1976 Sun. **S.F.
Sunday Examiner & Chronicle:** Ralph J.
Gleason, 3/9/75. Copyright © 1975 The
Chronicle Publishing Company. Reprinted by
permission. **The Aquarian:** 2/7/79. Copyright
© 1979 The Aquarian. **The Golden Road:** Blair
Jackson, Summer 1984, Spring 1985, Summer
1985, Winter 1985, Spring 1986, Summer 1987,
Fall 1987. George Hunter, Winter 1985. Spencer
Dryden, Winter 1985. John Cipollina, Winter
1985. Steve Brown, Summer 1986. Joseph
Campbell, Summer 1986. Copyright © 1984,
1985, 1986, 1987 The Golden Road, Inc.
Reprinted by Permission. The Golden Road,
484 Lake Park Avenue #82, Oakland, CA
94610. **The New York Times:** Patrick Carr,
3/11/73; Jon Pareles, 7/26/87. Copyright ©
1973,1987 by The New York Times Company.
Reprinted by Permission. **The Progressive:**
Milton Meyer, 5/83. Copyright © 1983 The
Progressive. Reprinted by Permission. The
Progressive, 409 East Main Street, Madison,
WI 53703. **The Register-Guard:** Paul Denison,
7/20/87. Copyright © 1987 The Register
Guard, Inc. **The Rocket:** Linton Robinson, 1/81
Copyright © The Rocket. **Time:** 'American
Scene', 2/11/85. Copyright © 1985 Time, Inc.
Reprinted by permission. **Variety:** 'Box Office'.
Copyright © 1980 Variety. **The Village Voice:**
Robert Christgau, 6/13/77. Copyright © 1977
The Village Voice.

Deadication

This is my version of life with as interesting a congregation of musicians, magicians, and mommies as one can hope to encounter in the millennia of incarnations. How do you cover it all? Many aren't shown in this book who should be. How can one cover it all? For the omissions — I didn't mean it, honestly!

I thank the '60s revolution, for without it life as we know it today may never have been. The Summer of Love wouldn't have bloomed. Conscientious objectors wouldn't have found shelter from the storm that was the Indo-Chinese situation (alias Vietnam). I'm eternally grateful for the survivors; also for those who provided us at home with help in holding down the fort in adversity.

My friendships transcend politics and society. I cherish some (myself included) who are really wild and sometimes not totally cool or popular. I could care, but I don't. Neither do my friends; that's why we're friends. Our loyalties weather the storms and upheavals. The bonds are strong. The truths we committed to are the strengths we draw from in dark and confusing times.

This book is dedicated to our children. You are never too old to learn. I continue to do so, marveling at what life has to offer. With any luck, my companions and friends will remain 'one of a kind', unique, loyal and fascinating, so at least life won't be boring. I much prefer it productive and rewarding. — Jerilyn Lee Brandelius

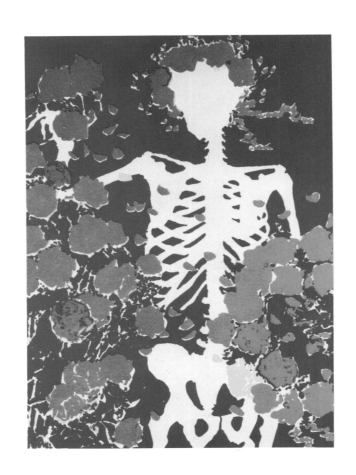

Dead Shots & Art

Convention: Full page photograph listed first, then clockwise from top left. **Key** for special cases: t—top; cr—center right; bm—bottom middle; etc. Multiple photos by the same photographer listed once per page. In most instances, unattributed photographs are within the public domain, or information about them was unavailable. Any omission of credit is inadvertent and can be corrected in future printings if notification is sent to the publisher.

9 top down, Herb Greene; Ed Perlstein; Steve Schneider; Tom Weir; Gene Anthony; Jerilyn Brandelius; **11** Herb Greene; **12** Rosie McGee-Ende, tinted by Alan Blaustein; **13** Gene Anthony; Jim Marshall; **16—20** Family Album by parents, grandparents, aunts, uncles and Main Street photographers; **22** Gene Anthony; tl—Rosie McGee-Ende; **26** Herb Greene; Ron Bevirt; **27** t—Herb Greene; b—Bob Seidemann; **28** t—Ron Bevirt; b—Ron Bevirt; l—Gene Anthony; **29** Ron Bevirt; **30** l to r, Ron Bevirt; Ron Bevirt; Ron Bevirt; unknown; **31** Herb Greene; **32** Herb Greene; br—Ron Bevirt; **33** Herb Greene; **34** Herb Greene; **35** b—Tom Weir; Herb Greene; **36** Herb Greene; **37** Herb Greene; **38** Herb Greene; **39** Herb Greene; **40** Sue Swanson; Rosie McGee-Ende; Herb Greene; **41** Peter Tracy; Herb Greene; **42** r—Jim Marshall; b—Herb Greene; **43** r—Ron Rakow; l—Rosie McGee-Ende; br—Herb Greene; **44** Gene Anthony; **45** Ron Rakow; Gene Anthony; Grant Jacobs; **46** Tom Copi; **47** Jim Marshall; Grant Jacobs; Herb Greene; **48** Herb Greene; bl—Rosie McGee-Ende; unknown; br—Rosie McGee-Ende; **49** Gary Schroeder; Herb Greene; John Schmidt; Rosie McGee-Ende; Birgitta Bjerke; **50** Herb Greene; tr—Tom Copi; **51** Herb Greene; Tom Copi; **52** l—Tom Copi; **53** b—Herb Greene; **54** t—Tom Weir; Herb Greene; **55** Herb Greene; **56** Bob Van Doren; **57** t—(from left) Michael Moore; br—Herb Greene; **58** Tom Weir; Jim Marshall; Guy Cross; Guy Cross; Herb Greene; **59** Birgitta Bjerke; **61** Gene Anthony; Tom Weir; Gene Anthony; **62** t—Jim Marshall; Tom Weir; Tom Weir; **63** unknown; tr—Tom Weir; **64** Jerilyn Brandelius; l—Herb Greene; **65** tr—Rosie McGee-Ende; **66** Herb Greene; Guy Cross; unknown; Basia Raizene; **67** from centre, unknown; unknown; Rosie McGee-Ende; Maj. Gen. Leland Cagwin; Rosie McGee-Ende; br-Jerilyn Brandelius; **68** Patty Healy; Rosie McGee-Ende; Rosie McGee-Ende; unknown; **69** tr—Rosie McGee-Ende; bl—Ed Brandelius; **70** Phil Lesh; bl—Basia Raizene; br—unknown; **71** Rosie McGee-Ende; **72** Jerilyn Brandelius; **73** unknown; **74** Gary Schroeder; **75** unknown; **76** Dr. Bob Marks; Mary Eisenhart; **77** Dr. Bob Marks; Cherie Porter; **78** unknown; **79** l—Rosie McGee-Ende; r—Jim Marshall; b—Gary Schroeder; **80** Rosie McGee-Ende; **81** Rosie McGee-Ende; **82** Herb Greene; Mark Raizene; **83** Mary Anne Mayer; **84** Mary Anne Mayer; **85** Mary Anne Mayer; Mark Raizene; **86** Mary Anne Mayer; r—Mark Raizene; **87** Mary Anne Mayer; Mary Anne Mayer; Mark Raizene; Betty Cantor-Jackson; **88** top row—Rex Jackson; Betty Cantor-Jackson; Betty Cantor-Jackson; middle row—Mary Anne Mayer; bottom row; Rosie McGee-Ende; Betty

antor-Jackson; unknown; Rosie McGee-Ende; **89** Rosie McGee-Ende; Frances Carr; Mary Anne Mayer; Mary Anne Mayer; **90** Mary Anne Mayer; background—Mark Raizene; **91** Mark Raizene; **92** br—Tom Satter; bl—Frances Carr; tl—r, Mary Anne Mayer; Mark Raizene; Frances Carr; Mary Anne Mayer; **93** Frances Carr; b—Betty Mayer; Mark Raizene; Frances Carr; Mary Anne Mayer; **93** Frances Carr; b—Betty Cantor-Jackson; **94** Michael Zagaris; **95** tl—Jim Marshall; unknown; **96** Steve Schneider; **97** tr—unknown; **98** Mark Raizene; **99** Bob Seidemann; **100** b—Mary Anne Mayer; Sue Swanson; Annette Plowers; Dr. Bob Marks; **101** tr—Snooky Flowers; b—Ken Friedman; **102** Rosie McGee-Ende; **103** Rosie McGee-Ende; **104** Jon Goodchild; bl—Jon Goodchild; Birgitta Bjerke; **105** Birgitta Bjerke; Jerilyn Brandelius; Mark Raizene; Rosie McGee-Ende; Rosie McGee-Ende; Birgitta Bjerke; **106** Mary Anne Mayer; Birgitta Bjerke; **107** b—unknown; unknown; Rosie McGee-Ende; **108** Cathy Murphy; **109** Courtenay Pollock; unknown; Courtenay Pollock; **110** Michael Zagaris; **111** Sunshine Kesey; **112** Herb Greene; **113** Jerilyn Brandelius; Thayer Craw; **114** Annie Liebovitz; unknown; **115** tr—Blue Bailey; bl—Rosie McGee-Ende; **116** Bob Siedemann; Jerilyn Brandelius; Bob Bryant; Todd Cazaux; **117** Jerilyn Brandelius; Jerilyn Brandelius; Sue Swanson; Herb Greene; **118** Herb Greene; **119** bm—Mark Raizene; Basia Raizene; **120** Jerilyn Brandelius; **121** Dr. Bob Marks; **122** Dr. Bob Marks; **123** Ed Perlstein; Peter Simon; Ed Perlstein; **124** Jerilyn Brandelius; Roger Ressemeyer; 'Dead Images'; **125** ml—Thayer Craw; Snooky Flowers; Patty Healy; Jerilyn Brandelius; **126** Jerilyn Brandelius; **128** Snooky Flowers; **129** unknown; **130** Steve Schneider; Bob Seidemann; **131** Jerilyn Brandelius; Patty Healy; Ed Perlstein; **132** Ed Perlstein; Jerilyn Brandelius; Steve Schneider; **133** Todd Cazaux; **134** Betty Cantor-Jackson; Rosie McGee-Ende; Snooky Flowers; **135** l to r—Snooky Flowers; Ed Perlstein; Ron Rakow; **136** Snooky Flowers; **137** Snooky Flowers; br—Jerilyn Brandelius; **138** Tom Brister; Jerilyn Brandelius; **139** Jerilyn Brandelius; Snooky Flowers; **140** Jerilyn Brandelius; **141** Snooky Flowers; Patty Healy; unknown; **142** Jerilyn Brandelius; Guy Cross; Ed Perlstein; Snooky Flowers; Jerilyn Brandelius; Jerilyn Brandelius; **143** Jerilyn Brandelius; tr—Bruce Polonski; **144** Jerilyn Brandelius; **145** Jerilyn Brandelius; tr—Betty Cantor-Jackson; bl—Jerilyn Brandelius; **146** Snooky Flowers; br—Ed Perlstein; **147** Gerrit Graham; Gerrit Graham; Ray Slade; Patty Healy; **148** Jerilyn Brandelius; **149** Steve Schneider; Jerilyn Brandelius; br—Patty Healy; **150** Snooky Flowers; t—Ed Perlstein; **151** Snooky Flowers; Steve Schneider; Ed Perlstein; Ed Perlstein; Snooky Flowers; **152** Ed Perlstein; Jerilyn Brandelius; Snooky Flowers; **153** Jerilyn Brandelius; **158** unknown; **159** Richard Loren; Elaine

Loren; **160** Jerilyn Brandelius; Harry Popick; **161** Patty Healy; Richard Loren; **162** Bernie Bildman; Jerilyn Brandelius; Jerilyn Brandelius; unknown; **163** background — unknown; Richard Loren; Elaine Loren; Richard Loren; Jerilyn Brandelius; Elaine Loren; **164** Richard Loren; **165** Jerilyn Brandelius; bl — Harry Popick; **166** Jerilyn Brandelius; Harry Popick; Jerilyn Brandelius; Harry Popick; **168** Bernie Bildman; Jerilyn Brandelius; Richard Loren; **169** Richard Loren; tr — Bernie Bildman; **170** Pat Jackson; bl — Jerilyn Brandelius; Richard Loren; **171** Richard Loren; John Cutler; Jerilyn Brandelius; **172** Frances Shurtliff; Richard Loren; **173** Richard Loren; bl — Bernie Bildman; **174** bl — Jerilyn Brandelius; **175** Richard Loren; bm — Jerilyn Brandelius; **176** Adrian Boot; **177** Jerilyn Brandelius; Richard Loren; **178** Richard Loren; mr — Elaine Loren; **179** Jerilyn Brandelius; **180** Jerilyn Brandelius; **181** Jerilyn Brandelius; **182** David Colardo; Patty Healy; **183** David Colardo; 'Dead Images'; **184** 'Dead Images'; **185** Ed Perlstein; **186** Steve Schneider; br — Ed Perlstein; **187** Background — Steve Schneider; Jerilyn Brandelius; **188** unknown; Jerilyn Brandelius; **189** Jay Blakesberg; br — Jim Loveless; **190** John Werner; br — Steve Schneider; **191** Steve Schneider; Jerilyn Brandelius; John Werner; **192** Benny Collins; Jerilyn Brandelius; **193** Jay Blakesberg; Bernie Bildman; **194** tl — Dr. Bob Marks; tr — Jerilyn Brandelius; b — 'Dead Images'; **195** Bob Seidemann; Snooky Flowers; **196** unknown; **197** 'Dead Images'; Jay Blakesberg; Jerilyn Brandelius; t — Jay Blakesberg; **198** Ed Perlstein; John Werner; John Werner; **199** Snooky Flowers; br — John br — John Werner; **200** Patty Healy; David Gans; Rachel Pauley; **201** Patty Healy; **202** unknown; Steve Schneider; Snooky Flowers; **203** Jane Matthews; Dan Healy; unknown; **204** Steve Schneider; ml — unknown; mr — David Gans; Jay Blakesberg; **205** m — John Werner; Dr. Bob Marks; Dr. Bob Marks; ml — unknown; bl — David Gans; **206** Steve Schneider; unknown; **207** Steve Schneider; **208** David Gans; Rachel Pauley; **209** John Walker; Larry Lazio; unknown; **210** Brian Braumwoll; Jay Blakesberg; Jerilyn Brandelius; 'Dead Images'; **211** Jay Blakesberg; Betty Cantor-Jackson; Alan Trist; **212** Patty Healy; **214** Herb Greene; Rosie McGee-Ende; Snooky Flowers; David Foust; **215** t & b, David Colardo; Mets; Mets; Ed Perlstein; **216** David Gans; **217** clockwise from ml, Kim Wentz; David Colardo; Dan Healy; Susana Millman; Debbie Trist; Debbie Trist;

218 Snooky Flowers; Dr. Bob Marks; Patty Healy; 'Dead Images'; **219** Yoav Getzler; Jay Blakesberg; **220** William Smythe; 'Dead Images'; **221** bl — unknown; **222** John Werner; Herb Greene; bl — Herb Greene; **223** John Werner; br — Nikki Sculley; John Werner; **224** Sussana Millman; **225** Herb Greene; unknown; br — Frankie Acardi; **226** Susana Millman; ml — unknown; **227** Ron Delany; Dr. Bob Marks; unknown; Edmund Shea; **228** Herb Greene; bl — unknown; tl — Susana Millman; **229** Herb Greene; ml — unknown; bl — 'Dead Images'; **230** Herb Greene; unknown; unknown; Herb Greene; bl — Valerie Steinbrecker; **231** tl — Peter Simon; t — Jay Blakesberg; m — Jay Blakesberg; b — Ron Delany; **232** John Werner; **234** b — Jay Blakesberg; t — John Werner; **235** Ken Friedman; Ron Debbie Trist; **236** David Colardo; Snooky Flowers; Mary Eisenhart; David Colardo; **237** Herb Greene; tr — unknown; **238** Len Dell'Amico; bl — Jay Blakesberg; **239** b — John Werner; Snooky Flowers; **240** unknown; **241** Jay Blakesberg; **242** t — John Werner; Jay Blakesberg; **243** l — Mary Jo Meinoff; b — Susana Millman; John Werner; tr — Susana Millman; **244** Herb Greene; **245** t — Jay Blakesberg; bl — Rosie McGee-Ende; bc — unknown; br — Jay Blakesberg; **246** Ron Delany; **247** Ron Delany; Ron Delany; John Werner; unknown; **248** Jay Blakesberg; Jay Blakesberg; unknown; Herb Greene; **249** Jay Blakesberg; Cassidy Law; Frankie Accardi; John Werner; **250** Michael Loeb; Rene Edy; **251** Len Dell'Amico; b — Alan Blaustein; **252** Jay Blakesberg; **253** t — Jay Blakesberg; Susana Millman; b — David Stanford; unknown; **254** Rain Forest Action Network; **255** Rain Forest Action Network; Mickey Scopp; **256** Jay Blakesberg.

Dead Art

5/6 Stanley Mouse; **7** Owsley Stanley; **8** centre, Stanley Mouse; **24** Stanley Mouse; **25** Norman Hartweg, hand colored by Sunshine Kesey; **28** see **25**; **37** bl — Wes Wilson, FD12; br — Victor Moscoso, FD32. Copyright © 1966 The Family Dog Productions, Inc. (dba Chester A. Helms); **42** San Francisco Oracle; **43** Alton Kelley & Stanley Mouse, 1967; **50** Wes Wilson, BG32, Copyright © 1966, Bill Graham Presents; **52** Alton Kelley & Stanley Mouse, 1968; **53** Bill Walker, 1968; **57** Randy Tuten, 1970, BG222, Copyright © 1970 Bill Graham Presents; **58** George Hunter; **60** l — Alton Kelley, Stanley Mouse & Rick Griffin, 1967; r — Rick Griffin, 1969; **68** Alton Kelley, 1969; **75** (Woodstock 'Bird' logo), © 1969 Joel Rosenman & John Roberts; **76** tl — Mouse Studios w/Toon N. Tree, 1970; tl — Alton Kelley & Stanley Mouse, 1970; **81** Alton Kelley and Stanley Mouse, 1971; **82** M. Ferguson & Alton Kelley, 1971; **84** Alton Kelley & Stanley Mouse, 1972; **95** David Stowell; **98** Owsley Stanley & Bob Thomas; **102/103** Mary Anne Meyer; **108** Alton Kelley & Stanley Mouse, 1972; **109** Courtenay Pollock; **110** tr — Stanley Mouse, 1972; br — Alton Kelley & Stanley Mouse, 1970; **112** bl — Alton Kelley & Stanley Mouse & Andy Leonard (photo), 1974; br — Rick Griffin, 1974; **113** Rick Griffin, 1974; **114** Victor Moscoso, 1974; **117** Gunther Keiser, © 1974 Lippmann & Rau; **121** br — Steirnagle; bl — Greg Irons, 1975; **122** t — Alton Kelley & Stanley Mouse; m — Andy Leonard (photo), Jerry Garcia (thoughts), 1975; **125** Randy Tuten; tr — Alton Kelley and Stanley Mouse; **129** Philip Garris, 1976; **133** bl — Judit Torn Allen; Jordan Amarantha, 1976; **135** Philip Garris, 1976; **136** Philip Garris, 1976; **138** Owsley Stanley/Bob Thomas; **139** Rick Griffin; br — Owsley Stanley; **140** Gary Guiterrez; **152** bl — Alton **141** Garry Guiterrez; **152** bl — Alton Kelley; **154-157** Peter Monk (collage); **160** t — Bob Thomas; **161** Alton Kelley; **164** Alton Kelley & Stanley Mouse, Copyright © Grateful Dead Productions, Inc.; **167** Alton Kelley, 1978; **172** Stanley Mouse, 1978; **186** Philip Garris, 1975; **187** Alton Kelley & Stanley Mouse; **192** Gilbert Shelton, 1978; **193** Stanley Mouse, 1978; **198** r — Dennis Larkins & Peter Barsotti, 1980; **201** Nutzle; **204** t — Dennis Larkins & D. Sawyer; b — Jim Pinoski; **216** Stanley Mouse, 1983; **218** Dennis Larkins; **224** t — Rick Griffin; **237** Jim Carpenter, 1987; **238** Len Dell'Amico, Rick Griffin (lettering); **240** Herb Greene; **254** b — Stanley Mouse.

Photographs shown on page 9: Jim Marshall; Snooky Flowers; John Werner and Jerilyn; Herb Greene; Gene Anthony and Alan Blaustein.

Contents

The more things change, the more they remain the same.

How fitting when applied to the Grateful Dead and the legions that have been their 'family' throughout the years. The basic entities remain the same — a public arena, the fans, the artists and their instruments. And VOILA! — a communion.

The organic formula is so simple — no hydraulic lifts, no spandex pants, no strobe lights — simply good music, the attitude of brotherhood and the desire to experience joy. I've always thought of Dead shows as calling 'time out' to the planet so that, for a few hours, we can all leave our worries behind and just enjoy ourselves. The lyrics are meaningful, the rhythm is pelvic, and we all become part of the grand design that is the Grateful Dead extended family.

The heart of that family is, of course, the musicians; yet there's an inner core of people so closely aligned with the artists through all these years that I don't think of the Grateful Dead as just those musicians onstage. There are men and women who've matured and children that have been born into the whirl of the Grateful Dead inner circle. Many have worked for none other than this single entity, coming out of the alternative lifestyle of the sixties. From the loose group at 710 Ashbury to the complexity of today's hi-tech music industry, what lives on is a communal spirit — people working together for a common goal.

The family tree of the Grateful Dead would resemble a cypress, twisted by the winds of time and hanging on by its roots. The young guy loading the truck in '65 is today an integral part of the operation. The newborn of 1970 now works in the office. Friends and relatives make their creative statements through the group and earn their keep through the scene. Throughout a quarter of a century, we've experienced the joyful evolution of family life — the unions, the births, the adventures of the traveling circus; and also the tragic loss of family members, who stay on in spirit.

This family embodies the essence of an all powerful spirit that was born in the Bay Area in the sixties — a sense of camaraderie, of hope for a more idealistic world. After all these years, this family continues to represent a positive alternative — they make it possible for some light to shine through.

This book of photographs celebrates this unique Grateful Dead family.

Cheers!

Bill Graham

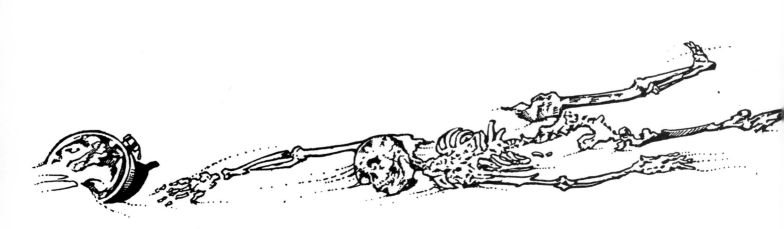

Joe Gavia on sidewalk + his band

Hal & Jean Godineaux

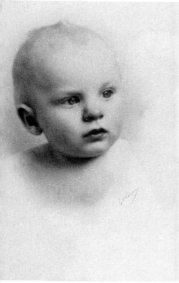

Phil

Keith

Bobby

Jerry

Mickey

Donna Jean

Billy

Brent

Jerry at Mom's bar

John

Wendy

Brent

Pigpen

Donna Jean

Mickey

Bobby

Dave Turner

Brent

Goldie

Billy

Sue Stephens

Pigpen

Garcia family car

19

Harry Popick

Bobby Petersen
and Didrik

Eileen Law

Sue Stephens

Betty Cantor

Jerilyn

Mickey

Keith

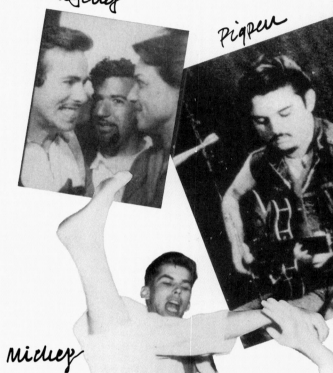

Robert Hunter and Jerry

Pigpen

Bobby and Paul Rochlik

Mickey

Bobby

21

Trouper's Hall, 1966

Jerry Mountain
Gin and Sunshine

The first rehearsal hall at the Helipot, Sausalito

Grateful Dead: The motif of a cycle of folk tales which begin with the hero coming upon a group of people ill-treating or refusing to bury the corpse of a man who had died without paying his debts. He gives his last penny, either to pay the man's debts or to give him a decent burial. Within a few hours he meets with a travelling companion who aids him in some impossible task, gets him a fortune or saves his life. The story ends with the companion disclosing himself as the man whose corpse the hero had befriended. (*Funk & Wagnalls Dictionary*)

The Water of Life: A Tale of The Grateful Dead

Once upon a time there was a dying King who sent his three sons, one after the other, on a quest for the Water of Life, the only means by which he could be healed. After setting off, the three in turn encountered a poor beggar crying for alms. The first two, callous fellows that they were, abused the wretched man and denied him aid. The third, himself a hunchback, had compassion for the beggar and responded to his pleas, receiving in return a bundle of magic arrows that would strike unerringly wherever they were aimed, and a magic lute, the music of which would make anyone who heard it dance.

Armed with these wonderful objects he continued on his journey, beset by peril and difficulty at every turn. One day while hunting he took aim at a fox with his arrow, but at the last moment relented out of pity for the creature. At another point along the way, he spent his last coins paying for the burial of a man who had died a debtor, whose body lay by the wayside.

Along the way, he met a mysterious stranger who offered to help in the Quest in exchange for half of any fortune the prince should gain.

He finally reached the castle of an ogre who possessed the Water of Life. The ogre retained him in service and soon he saved the ogre's life by use of his magic arrows, receiving as a reward the object of his quest, a vial of the Water of Life.

The ogre had imprisoned in his castle a beautiful young maiden who refused to marry him. The prince won her love by means of his magic lute, the ogre released her and they began their long homeward trek.

But they were soon accosted by the two scoundrel brothers, who in jealousy attacked them by stealth, threw their brother down a deep well, and absconded with the princess and the Water.

Soon after their departure, along came the fox whose life the prince had spared. The fox let down a rope. When the prince reached the top he found the mysterious stranger who by magic relieved him of his deformed condition. They then embarked on another long and arduous journey back to the prince's homeland.

Meanwhile, the elder brothers had already returned with the vial and the princess, but because of their misdeeds, were unable to heal the ailing King. The old man was on his deathbed, when amidst wails and lamentations the youngest son, now a strong and straight-backed young man, arrived. When he anointed the King with the Water of Life, the old man was instantly healed. He then castigated the elder brothers in public and they were banished.

The prince and his beautiful bride were finally reunited and their wedding was joyously celebrated. Then the mysterious stranger revealed himself to be the dead man for whom proper funeral rites had been provided thereby releasing his soul from eternal wandering.

The prince offered his entire kingdom to settle their bargain so as to avoid dividing the princess, but the grateful dead man released the prince from his bond. In gratitude, the old King offered him anything in the kingdom he should desire. The grateful dead chose the lute and arrows, and wine and provision for his final ride to the Nether-world.

Adapted from *The Grateful Dead: The History of a Folk Story* (Gordon Hall Gerould, London, 1908) by Alan Trist and Robert M. Petersen.

25

I. BECAUSE OF THE FORMLESSNESS

"ALWAYS STAY IN YOUR OWN MOVIE."

KEN KESEY

THE BLANDNESS OF AMERICAN CULTURE BACK IN 1950 WAS SUMMED UP WHEN SNOOKY LANSON SANG *IT'S A MARSHMALLOW WORLD* ON THE LUCKY STRIKE HIT PARADE. BUT, BY THE END OF THAT DULL DECADE, A SPIRIT OF CREATIVE ADVENTURE WAS RE-EMERGING ACROSS THE COUNTRY. ELVIS PRESLEY HAD COME UPON THE SCENE, ONLY TO HAVE HIS BOTTOM HALF CENSORED OUT OF CAMERA RANGE ON THE ED SULLIVAN SHOW, EVEN WHILE YOUNG GIRLS AND BOYS WERE BUSY PRACTICING PELVIC THRUSTS WITH THEIR HULA HOOPS THAT WOULD HAVE MADE ELVIS HIMSELF BLUSH WITH EMBARRASSMENT. AND THE VOICES OF THE BEAT GENERATION HAD ALSO BEGUN TO BE HEARD. NEAL CASSADY WAS THE LIGHTNING ROD OF THE BEATS. HE LIVED IN A MARSHMALLOW WORLD TOO, EXCEPT THAT HIS MARSHMALLOW HAD BEEN DOSED...

—PAUL KRASSNER

Neal represented a model to me of how far you could take it in the individual way. In the sense that you weren't going to have a work, you were going to be the work. Work in real time, which is a lot like a musician's work. I was oscillating at the time. I had originally been an art student and was wavering between one-man/ one-work or being involved in something that was dynamic and ongoing and didn't necessarily stay any one way. And also, something in which you weren't the only contributing factor. I decided to go with what was dynamic and with what more than one mind was involved with. The decision I came to was to be involved in a group thing, which was what I was involved in, namely the Grateful Dead, and I'm still involved in it . . . — Garcia

Up at the Fillmore Auditorium, Ken Kesey's Acid Test event was in action when I got there around the middle of the evening. The people were like the backstage crowd at the California Hall dance (that the Airplane played the same night). The costumes were, wow! A strobe light was flickering at a very high frequency in one corner of the hall and a group of people were bouncing a golden balloon up and down in it. It was a most perturbing frequency. It hurt to look at them.

In one corner there was a piece of metal, tubular sculpture by Ron Boise, a thumping machine. If you hit it, you got different sounds if you hit it different places. There was a lot of electronic equipment which sent out a low reverberation that resonated throughout the hall. And the whole place was filled with streamers and balloons. There were TV cameras and a TV screen, and you could see yourself in it. Onstage there was a rock group; anybody could play with them. It was a kind of social jam session.

A guy in a white mechanic's suit with a black cross on the front, and on the back a sign saying 'Please Don't Believe in Magic', ran up and down all night. Oh wow! Periodically the lights went out and everybody cheered. Giant Frisbees, balloons like basketballs, acrobats, girls in felt eyelashes four inches long, people with eyes painted on their foreheads, glasses low on the nose with eyes painted on them, men with foxes on their shoulders! Wow! — Michael Rossman *(S.F. Chronicle, 1/66)*

Grateful Dead and Merry Pranksters. Ken Babbs (below) and the Pranksters' bus 'Furthur'; Jerry Garcia. Opposite: Bill 'The Drummer' Kreutzmann contemplates the happening and, clockwise from top, Bob Weir, Mountain Girl, Neal Cassady rappin', Ramrod, Michael Hagen makes 'The Movie', Phil Lesh and George Walker.

Everything is relative to the center of it all, which is music in motion through time and space. —Kreutzmann

The nice thing about the Acid Test was that we could play or *not*. And a lot of times we'd really be too high to play, and we'd play for maybe a *minute* and then we'd lose it and have to leave — "This is too weird for me!" On the other hand, sometimes we'd play, and there was no pressure on us because people didn't come to see the Grateful Dead, they came for the Acid Test; it was the whole event that counted. Therefore we weren't in the spotlight, so when we did play, we played with a certain kind of freedom you rarely get as a musician. Not only did we not have to fulfill expectations about us, we didn't have to fulfill expectations about *music,* either. So in terms of being able to experiment freely with music, it was amazing. —Garcia

One of the highlights of the Muir Beach Test was . . . dare I, shall I breathe his name? Owsley pushing a chair along a wooden floor, this old wooden chair, running it along the floor making this noise, the most horrible screeching and scraping. It went on for hours, I'm not exaggerating, it just drove everybody completely up the wall. That was an incredible exhibition of making your-self . . . uncomfortable . . . making other people uncomfortable. He was scraping the chair and listen-ing to the noise and lovin' it. I guess that's what was happening. —Mountain Girl

The Acid Test was the protot[y]p[e] whole basic trip. But nothing has come t[o] to the level of the way the Acid Test was [.] It's just never been equalled, really, or th[e] basic hit of it never developed out . . . It was something more incredible than ju[st] rock and roll and a light show; it was j[ust] a million times more incredible. It wa[s] incredible because of the formlessnes[s] because of the thing of people wande[ring] around wondering what was going o[n] and stuff happening spontaneously [.] people being prepared to accept an[y] of thing that was happening, and t[o] it . . . Everybody was creating. Eve[rybody] was doing everything. That's abo[ut the] simplest explanation. —Garcia

More Pranksters: from left, Page Browning, Stewart Brand, Zonker, Pigpen and Laird C. Grant, Vanmaster. Opposite, the scene at Olom-pali; inset, Tangerine, Rock Scully, Girl Frieberg, and George Hunter of The Charla-tans; Rock, and David Frieberg of the Quicksilver Messenger Service.

Acid Tests

Dec. 4, 1965. Big Nig's House, San Jose
Dec. 11. Muir Beach Lodge
Dec. 18. The Big Beat Club, San Jose
January, 1966. Portland, OR
January 8. Fillmore Auditorium, SF
January 22 and 23. Trips Festival, Long-
    shoreman's Hall, SF
January 29. Sound City Studios, SF
February 11. Youth Opportunities Center,
    Compton (Watts Acid Test)
February. LA, (Sunset Acid Test)
April 5. LA, (Pico Acid Test)
October 2. SF State University Cafeteria

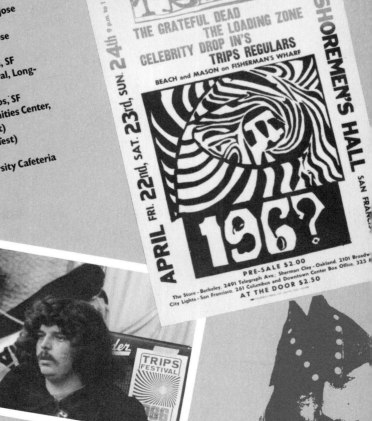

DRESS the way YOU are

TRIPS

THE GRATEFUL DEAD
THE LOADING ZONE
CELEBRITY DROP IN'S
TRIPS REGULARS

BEACH and MASON on FISHERMAN'S WHARF

APRIL FRI. 22nd, SAT. 23rd, SUN. 24th 9 p.m. to 1 a.m.

LONGSHOREMEN'S HALL SAN FRAN[CISCO]

196?

PRE-SALE $2.00
The Store - Berkeley, 2491 Telegraph Ave.; Sherman Clay - Oakland, 2101 Broadw[ay]
City Lights - San Francisco, 261 Columbus and Downtown Center Box Office, 325 #
AT THE DOOR $2.50

TRIPS FESTIVAL

2. IT WAS PRETTY MUCH A PARTY ALL THE TIME, ANYWAY

A rock & roll oasis just off Highway 101 in Novato, Rancho Olompali was where the Grateful Dead, the Diggers, the Angels, the Black Panthers and the San Francisco music scene went to dance after a head-banging week in the city. The Grateful Dead were each paid twenty-five dollars a week in those days and gigged wherever they could, often five days a week. An incredible freedom cruised through each day like a tide. The Jefferson Airplane, It's a Beautiful Day, Country Joe & the Fish, The Sons of Champlin, Quicksilver Messenger Service, The Charlatans, Big Brother & the Holding Company. . .

Weekend free-form celebrations of whatever anyone wished to celebrate, beginning in party clothes at the main house, ending naked in the sunshine by the pool. In addition to the Harley-scaled acreage, a huge outdoor oven cranked non-stop. It was the Diggers baking their daily bread to give away later in the park. As each participant got coated with flour, ghostly apparitions would leap from the oven to the pool, long hair flying in the wind. It was an easy scene for music and lovers, bands interwove and produced moments that were as high as they get.

Amongst the party goers, opposite, Peter Albin and James Gurley of Big Brother and the Holding Company. Left, George Hunter of The Charlatans; right, Chet Helms of the Family Dog ballroom, Pigpen in his car, Jerry and Mountain Girl at Olompali.

The Dead used to have some pretty good parties out at their place in the country, in Olompali. Two or three hundred people would come, and of course, most of them probably took LSD. This was around the time that a lot of new ground was being broken socially, and it seemed like a third to a half of the people at these parties would be naked, hanging around the pool. It was a great place. It was a sort of ranch estate that had a nice big house that looked kind of like Tara in *Gone With the Wind.* Then there was a lot of land around it — hills, a creek in the back, a big lawn and the pool. It was maybe 1000 feet off the highway, so it was fairly secluded. In between the house and the pool the Dead would set up their equipment and play from time to time during the day. Usually there'd be members of other bands there, too, like the Airplane and Quicksilver, and there'd be little jams with people who wanted to play. I remember that the Dead would be playing and Neal Cassady would be doing this strange little dance — it was almost like breakdancing; very fluid. Out on the lawn there was this very far-out configuration of plumbing that was once part of a sprinkler system or something. It stuck out of the ground and stood maybe five feet high. I couldn't figure out what the hell it was for. It was just a mess of pipes with faucets coming out of it that had been modified over the years. Very strange. So the Dead would be playing, and Neal would be dancing on the lawn with this *bizarre* metal partner. He'd dance around it, *with it,* really. He had some pretty good moves, too. Neal was always in the thick of things.

Those parties — I'm not sure how many of them there were — were always on a nice afternoon. Everybody would play all day in the sunshine — just doing *everything* — and then when the sun would start to go down and it got cold, people would pack it in. By the time it was dark most people were gone, but there were always enough people who were either around to begin with or who wanted to stay, so that the party would continue inside. In fact, with the number of people hanging out there all the time, it was pretty much a party all the time anyway. I don't know if it was 24 hours a day, but every time I was there it was going. —George Hunter *(The Golden Road)*

What we would do was get up $200 and rent the Fillmore and put on the gig. It was a shoestring operation. The entire show production would be $350. We would make our own posters.

A network began to form, of light shows and all, at the same time. Bill Hamm, who was one of the original liquid light show persons, was around doing lights. A production company formed so that we could produce shows.

Not that it was all one company (everyone would function as an individual), but in those days everyone would come, and it would fit together as a whole when you got there. There was *not* a whole lot of consideration given to whether it was

part of one company or not.

That's where the original 'family groove' came from. It wasn't just the Grateful Dead, but it was a whole entire scene that began happening around San Francisco.
—Healy *(Relix Magazine)*

Opposite: The house at Olompali; inset, Ron Thelin, founder of the Psychedelic Shop, Phil and Stubby, Danny Rifkin. Left: Alton Kelley, poster artist; Dan Hicks of the Charlatans and Camella Scaggs; below, Ben Van Metre, film maker.

35

The Dead had taken off and gone to LA to hang out with Kesey and the Pranksters, and when they moved back it was to 710. There were two houses, not just one. 710 was the one that became famous, but there was another house a few blocks away on Belvedere Street that Phil and Kreutzmann lived in.

It was pretty loose. It was really a good scene. There was very little money: the whole vibe of sharing was what was happening in those days. It was one of those situations where nobody ever really had anything, but nobody ever really needed anything. It was kind of magic that way. We had what we were doing and that was basically all we needed. Everyone had a place to sleep and clothes to wear and food to eat.

We'd start partying some Friday and get really stoned and hang out. Come Sunday morning we'd all decide to go play live in Golden Gate Park. We'd play in the Panhandle. This was around 1967. So we would decide on Sunday morning. At about 8 or 9 o'clock somebody would run out and rent a flatbed truck and a small generator. We used to pull the truck up in front of 710, throw all the equipment on it, and roar over to the park. We'd start up our generator and start playing. We had it down.
— Healy *(Relix Magazine)*

The party goes on with, insets, Connie Bonner; Jack Casady and Marty Balin of the Jefferson Airplane. Opposite, the band on location at the Pacific Gas and Electric power plant.

3. TOTAL ENVIRONMENTAL THEATRE

THERE WERE FIFTEEN OF US, OR TWENTY, DEPENDING ON THE DAY. THE RENT WAS CHEAP, THE CEILINGS HIGH, THE KITCHEN TINY, THE FRONT STEPS A GREAT PLACE TO HANG OUT ON SUNNY DAYS. IT WAS A COUPLE OF BLOCKS TO THE STORE, AND IT ALWAYS SEEMED TO TAKE A REAL LONG TIME TO GET THERE AND BACK, WHAT WITH STOPPING TO TALK TO FRIENDS WHO'D DIVERT YOU FROM YOUR MISSION AT EVERY OPPORTUNITY TO GO HAVE COFFEE, SMOKE A "J", OR JUST SIT ON THEIR FRONT STEPS FOR AN HOUR OR TWO.

Most of us living there didn't work at any regular job — we paid our rent with a combination of endeavors. The mainstay was the band around whom we'd gathered as spouses or friends, with each of us contributing what we could as managers, technicians, equipment handlers, or bookkeepers. The household chores fell to the women and they were no small task. Dinner for twenty was a daily occurrence — so was food shopping. Doing laundry was a nightmare monopolizing twenty-two machines and it didn't take long for the women to restrict the chore to their own "nuclear unit". It was very rare to find peace and quiet; also elusive was real privacy. For while you could close your bedroom door to be alone, you always had to encounter people on the way to the bathroom, or in the kitchen, or on the steps, or in the hall — it was dense. You couldn't really keep any secrets. On the other hand, you never had trouble finding a friend to share them with.

During the day one of the bedrooms became the band office, and the carpet became worn with people coming and going. Add the constant traffic to the notoriety the band had already achieved, and it's easy to see how the house became of particular interest to the authorities.

So it wasn't surprising that when they came to bust the household for alleged use of pot, they brought the TV news crews with them. The narc in charge wanted to get full coverage on raiding a prominent household, and as it turned out, the entire neighborhood as well. Eleven households were turned in as a result of one very busy informer, and while it was scary going downtown in the police wagon, when we got there we found a hundred and thirty-five of our friends! Many of the charges were dropped,

710 Ashbury was a boarding house that Danny managed. Pigpen moved in and the boarders started moving out. Then the rest of us moved in. The band on the steps and in the garden of

710; Rock Scully and Danny Rifkin, managers at this time, were 'Frontage Road Management' and later, 'Shady Management'. Jack Casady, inset.

MON. NOV. 28 thru THUR. DEC. 1
GRATEFUL DEAD
and JERRY POND
'LIVE' 9 pm to 2 am
at the MATRIX
3138 FILLMORE near LOMBARD
Call 567-0118

Frontage Road Management

but the presses weren't stopped waiting to find out. My father read of my arrest while drinking his morning coffee.

Best of all were the glorious free concerts in the Panhandle — a flatbed truck, makeshift electricity, food, wine, friends, sunshine, and some wonderful bands who hadn't hit the big time yet. At first it seemed amazing that we knew by name so many of the hundreds gathered; but as the months went by, our awareness of a larger community grew until it peaked that fine day in January of 1967, the day of the Tribal Stomp at the Polo Fields to be known as the 'Human Be-In'.

We heard it through the grapevine, and a half dozen of us started early that morning to walk the couple of miles to the park. As we walked along Lincoln Avenue, we noticed other groups of neighbors walking in the same direction. More joined in off side streets, and by the time we turned north into the park, we were a large, laughing group. A half mile later, we were a horde and as the Be-In took shape through the day, we were awed and thrilled as the Polo Fields filled up with over 20,000 people. It was a day of innocence and hope; and in many ways the last moments of naivete for a neighborhood that had just gone public.

Stories about the Haight-Ashbury sold lots of magazines and newspapers in 1967, the more sensational the better, and many people planned their summer vacations around coming to see for themselves. In the ensuing crush, the neighborhood people quietly retreated to the background, or just moved out. As for the crowds of seekers who had been promised the 'Summer of Love', they were a year too late. — Rosie McGee

710 Ashbury, years later; Rock with Sue Gottlieb; Tim Sculley, one of the original recording engineers, at Trouper's Hall. Opposite: The band on tour at El Camino Park, Palo Alto, 1967; inset, Susila and Billy.

Grateful Dead Are Much Alive

THE NEW GENERATION

The Grateful Dead, a loud and very much alive Haight-Ashbury rock band, is hippier and happier than almost any group that comes to mind.

They're a fun-loving far-out group with a hard-driving sound which is surfacing above the vast San Francisco rock underground.

The Dead, Jefferson Airplane, Charlatans, Country Joe and the Fish, Big Brother and the Holding Co. and several other bizarre bands, have plugged San Francisco into a rock movement which now exerts a nationwide influence on pop music.

One of the principal reasons is Jerry (Captain Trips) Garcia, 24, lead guitar for the Grateful Dead.

Garcia, regarded by some critics as one of the best guitarists in the country, used to teach his instrument in a Palo Alto music store. He earned his nickname, friends say, because "everything is a trip with him."

Other members of the Dead are just as alive. There's Ron McKernan, 21, on organ, harp and vocal, known as 'Pigpen' for his outrageous appearance: long black hair, Indian head band, long black mustache, short, hefty build and a much-worn vest. He has been described as "one of the major blues men in America."

Youngest is Bob Weir, 19, thin and soft-looking, with straight, very long hair. Weir brings his own sort of richness to the rhythm guitar.

Phil Lesh, 27, is an astounding good bass player. He shares song-writing chores with Garcia.

Bill Sommers (aka Bill Kreutzmann), 21, played drums with about 12 bands before he "finally settled Grateful Dead."

They pocket concert fees as any group, but they play on their terms. They'd rather play in the park (and often do) than for money in an atmosphere which will "bring us down."

"We're not a recording band," said Garcia. "We're a dance band."

Something about the Dead's music can't be captured on records. Partly it's because they draw from so many idioms: blues, country and western, popular music, even classical. "We're musical thieves," Garcia noted. "We steal from everywhere."

It has more to do with the excitement of playing weekly concerts to baseball audiences. They're psychedelic and are extensions of total environmental theater, which engages all the senses: thunderous rock music, light shows that burst and flow in choruses of color, hundreds of dancing young people, incense floating through your mind. *(San Francisco Chronicle, 1966)*

Many years ago, in the easy, earliest time of the Dead, I was the girl who danced on the stage — before the need for stringent backstage security, before record contracts, world travels and a general nervousness about the motives of nearby people. I had no motive then except I wanted *more than anything* to step *inside* that magic circle of music and dance with it from that central place. I knew this time of privilege wouldn't last long, so I wasn't surprised when it ended. But for some of the most unspeakably happy and truly liberated times I ever had in my life, I've always wanted to thank you guys. — Rosie McGee

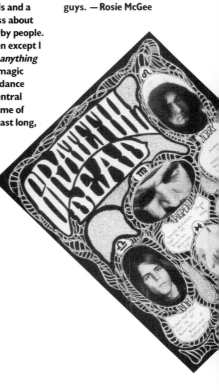

Troupers Hall was the meeting room for a retired actors club in Hollywood. The rent for the gig couldn't have been much. We did everything ourselves, all in two days. We plastered handbills all over Hollywood. Stage decor was a few lengths of paisley cloth purchased that afternoon at a fabric store. For a box office, we had a card table and a cigar box.

Our not-quite-full house must have had over a hundred people; and when the night was over, our net take was $75. At 2 o'clock in the morning, we went to Cantor's Deli on Fairfax and spent it all on dinner for everybody — with dessert.

Janis and Pigpen were kindred souls. They were drinkers and wary of acid, so they ran together. This photo was taken outside 715 Ashbury, across the road from 710, where HALO (the Haight Ashbury Legal Organization) had its offices, and where the poster artists Mouse, Kelley, Moscoso and Griffin had their studios.

Grateful Dead tried to capture a gut-level excitement in their album called *The Grateful Dead*. Though there's a taste of the Fillmore Auditorium and Avalon Ballroom, the full flavor doesn't come through. However, the album can stand alone. It contains some fine work, such as the strangely haunting 'Morning Dew', the bluesy 'Good Morning Little Schoolgirl' and 'Viola Lee Blues', which is as close to jazz as Paul Butterfield's 'East-West'.

The songs convey a sense of integration in the playing that has come about through the Dead's having played and lived together, sharing experiences and dreams, for nearly three years. With their two managers and an assortment of friends they have occupied a nine-room Victorian house a block from Haight Street.

But they are leaving the Haight-Ashbury soon. They expect to live awhile in the Southwest, perhaps Santa Fe, New Mexico.

"We've been squeezed out by tourists and Tenderloin types," said Rock Scully, one of their managers.

"We paid our dues and went to school with the Grateful Dead," explained Warner Brothers executive vice president Joe Smith, former ton jock and early '50s recording star. (Remember Somethin' Smith and the Redheads?)

"With the Grateful Dead we learned there are other ways to market, like sponsoring a free concert in Denver. We learned that you can't depend on Top 40 radio, that there's a whole market in the underground. We learned that posters mean something, that bill-

43

The trolleys run along Haight Street pretty often; the tourists snarl up the traffic a bit, but still you can get from the Oracle office to Fillmore Street, change and arrive at the Fillmore or Winterland in less than twenty minutes. At fifteen cents for the entire journey, that's not bad at all. The Avalon is a little further away, but just as accessible, and nowadays often more worthwhile.

But the ballrooms have lost their importance. They were vital once; without Bill Graham, and the hard work and business knowhow he threw into the Fillmore when the scene was starting, there might never have been an SF Sound to talk about. Give him credit, and give Ralph Gleason credit, without whose enthusiastic columns in the SF Chronicle the city would have no doubt shut down those psychedelic super-structures before you could say "building inspector." And Ken Kesey, the man whose Trips Festivals irrevocably tied together rock & roll and light shows and the head community. The Family Dog, illuminator Bill Ham, The Charlatans, the Matrix and Jefferson Airplane, all those originators who now cling to their place in history with alarming awareness that after two years the past is buried in the dust of centuries.

The ballrooms have given way to environments even more closely knit into the community. The great outdoors, for one; the Panhandle is only two blocks down from Haight Street, and on an average weekend you'll hear everything from Big Brother & the Holding Company down to the local teen group playing top hits off-key. And it's all free, free not just from admission charges but from walls and stuffy air and hassles about coming and going; free so that the music is as much a part of your life as a tree in blossom. You can stop and embrace it, or pass on by.

The Panhandle is the San Francisco Sound today; the music of the street, the music of the people who live there. The ballrooms, obsolete in terms of the community, have been turned into induction centers — the teenyboppers, the college students, the curious adults come down to the Fillmore to see what's going on, and they do see, and pretty soon they're part of it. They may not go directly to Haight Street with flowers in their hair (though many of them do), but they change, they shift their points of view, their minds drop out of Roger Williams and into the Grateful Dead.
(Crawdaddy, August 1967*)*

The band and friends congregate on the steps of 710 Ashbury during the Summer of Love; Big Brother and the Holding Company, 1967; the Pigpen look; David Crosby of the Byrds.

"THE ONLY HOPE WE HAVE IS OUR CHILDREN AND THE SEEDS WE GIVE THEM AND THE GARDENS WE PLANT TOGETHER"
(Richard Brautigan)

Above all, the San Francisco Sound is the musical expression of what's going down, a new attitude toward the world which is commonly attributed to 'hippies', but which could more accurately be laid at the feet of a non-subculture called people, earth people, all persons who have managed to transcend the superstructures they live in. People who have responded to the reality of the industrial revolution by requiring that they run the system and benefit from it rather than be made part of it. In very small print between the lines of 'Naked If I Want To', 'Grace', 'Cream Puff War' is written the following message: There is a man, me, and there are Men. These two forces will and must interact as smoothly as possible. Everything else — concepts, objects, systems, machines — must only be tools for me and mankind to employ. If I or Man respect a system or a pattern more than ourselves, we are in the wrong and must be set free. "Nothing to say but it's okay . . ."

— Paul Williams (*Crawdaddy*)

History will show, I believe, that the San Francisco dance renaissance played a key role in the evolution of teen age schlock-rock into music, as well as a key role in the social-cultural and political revolution in which we are involved.

After the Trips Festival in January 1966, Graham took over the Fillmore, first alternating weekends with the Family Dog. Luria Castel and Ellen Harmon, the originals and the visionaries who saw what was needed had left the Dog and it then consisted of Chet Helms and John Carpenter. There had been a couple of other transitory Dog personnel involving, among others, Rock Scully and Danny Rifkin, now managers of the Grateful Dead.

Their instant success spun off into a myriad of benefits at every available place in the Bay Area. An incredible number of dances for fund raising purposes, for profit and for fun took place. It has been an unbelievable three years. The response to the dances was ecstatic. The floors leaped and tumbled and swirled with the dancers and the evolvement of light shows as an adjunct was spectacular.

It ought to be said, it seems to me, no matter what any individual may feel pro or con about either the way the Fillmore Ballroom has been operated or the man who operates it, that during the past two years the Fillmore and Bill Graham have brought an incredible list of great and important music and performers to San Francisco.

Now a struggle is going on between those who want to dance and those who want to listen. It repeats again the situation of the Forties in which the swing era dancers (the jitterbugs) became listeners, first crowding around the bandstand and then sitting on the floor and then demanding chairs. The Benny Goodman band was astonished when it first played the West Coast that the people pushed up to the lip of the stage to hear the trumpet player (Bunny Berigan). Eventually, of course, dances ceased almost altogether and the stage-show concerts took over.

The stiffness of the concert hall is a drag and the booze of the night clubs is a bigger drag and so the informality and the flexibility of the dance halls has been delightful. The problem is two-fold at the moment — the press of the crowd and the floor covered with people sitting and lying down. At some point in the near future, somebody will build a structure to house these shows which is designed for the new purposes. I don't know what it will look like but it will obviously need to provide space for seeing and dancing, ease of movement and places to sit from time to time.

— Ralph J. Gleason (*Rolling Stone, 6/20/68*)

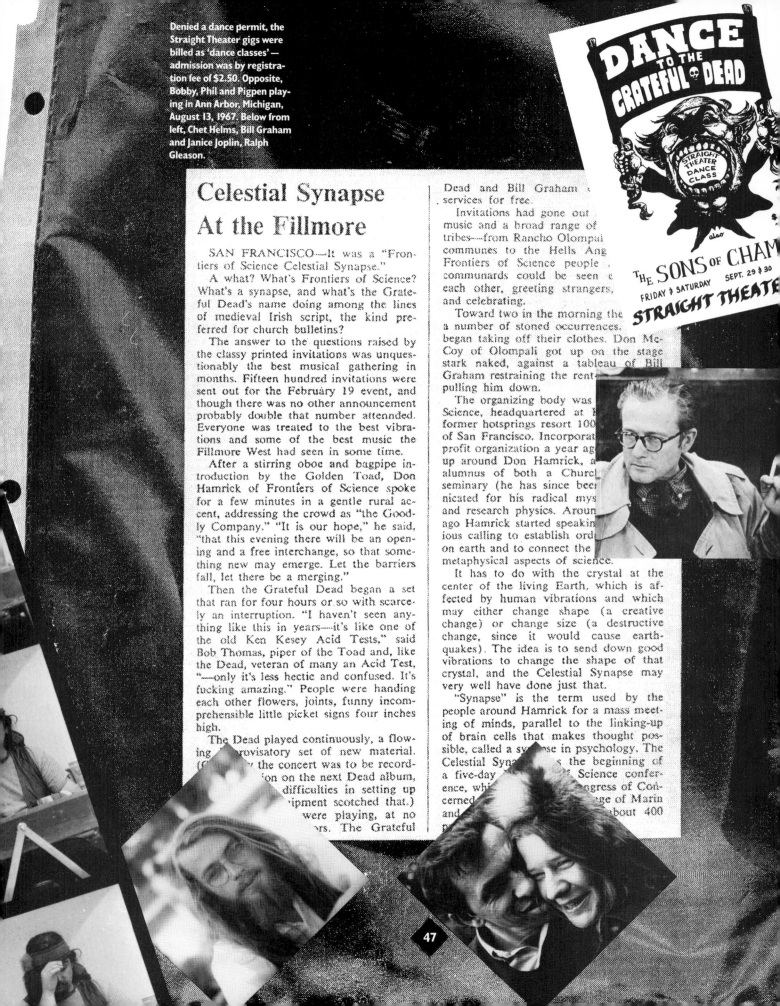

Denied a dance permit, the Straight Theater gigs were billed as 'dance classes' — admission was by registration fee of $2.50. Opposite, Bobby, Phil and Pigpen playing in Ann Arbor, Michigan, August 13, 1967. Below from left, Chet Helms, Bill Graham and Janice Joplin, Ralph Gleason.

DANCE TO THE GRATEFUL DEAD

STRAIGHT THEATER DANCE CLASS

THE SONS OF CHAM...
FRIDAY & SATURDAY   SEPT. 29 & 30
STRAIGHT THEATE...

Celestial Synapse At the Fillmore

SAN FRANCISCO—It was a "Frontiers of Science Celestial Synapse."

A what? What's Frontiers of Science? What's a synapse, and what's the Grateful Dead's name doing among the lines of medieval Irish script, the kind preferred for church bulletins?

The answer to the questions raised by the classy printed invitations was unquestionably the best musical gathering in months. Fifteen hundred invitations were sent out for the February 19 event, and though there was no other announcement probably double that number attennded. Everyone was treated to the best vibrations and some of the best music the Fillmore West had seen in some time.

After a stirring oboe and bagpipe introduction by the Golden Toad, Don Hamrick of Frontiers of Science spoke for a few minutes in a gentle rural accent, addressing the crowd as "the Goodly Company." "It is our hope," he said, "that this evening there will be an opening and a free interchange, so that something new may emerge. Let the barriers fall, let there be a merging."

Then the Grateful Dead began a set that ran for four hours or so with scarcely an interruption. "I haven't seen anything like this in years—it's like one of the old Ken Kesey Acid Tests," said Bob Thomas, piper of the Toad and, like the Dead, veteran of many an Acid Test, "—only it's less hectic and confused. It's fucking amazing." People were handing each other flowers, joints, funny incomprehensible little picket signs four inches high.

The Dead played continuously, a flowing improvisatory set of new material. (Ori... the concert was to be record... ...on on the next Dead album, ... difficulties in setting up ... ...ipment scotched that.) ... were playing, at no ... ...rs. The Grateful

Dead and Bill Graham ... services for free.

Invitations had gone out ... music and a broad range of ... tribes—from Rancho Olompali ... communes to the Hells Ang... Frontiers of Science people ... communards could be seen ... each other, greeting strangers, ... and celebrating.

Toward two in the morning the ... a number of stoned occurrences... began taking off their clothes. Don McCoy of Olompali got up on the stage stark naked, against a tableau of Bill Graham restraining the rent... pulling him down.

The organizing body was ... Science, headquartered at ... former hotsprings resort 100 ... of San Francisco. Incorporat... profit organization a year ag... up around Don Hamrick, a ... alumnus of both a Church ... seminary (he has since been ... nicated for his radical mys... and research physics. Aroun... ago Hamrick started speaking ... ious calling to establish ord... on earth and to connect the ... metaphysical aspects of science.

It has to do with the crystal at the center of the living Earth, which is affected by human vibrations and which may either change shape (a creative change) or change size (a destructive change, since it would cause earthquakes). The idea is to send down good vibrations to change the shape of that crystal, and the Celestial Synapse may very well have done just that.

"Synapse" is the term used by the people around Hamrick for a mass meeting of minds, parallel to the linking-up of brain cells that makes thought possible, called a sy...pse in psychology. The Celestial Syna... ...s the beginning of a five-day ... ... Science conference, whi... ...ngress of Con... cerned ... ...ge of Marin and ... ...bout 400 p...

47

If you tried to delineate a Grateful Dead Family Tree, it would not be effective to use the traditional bloodline progression, descending through the 'begats' to get to the wider branches. Rather, this family tree, not only of birth and marriage, would have to be felled, its great trunk sliced open and the concentric rings examined to define the widening circles that shape it. At the core you would find the musicians, and with them, their wives and children and other blood relatives — the families within the Family. But how far do the rings go outward, who is included and in what order? Do you count ALL THOSE PEOPLE?!?

The truck drivers,
ex-wives,
ranch hands,
lighting designers,
jugglers,
road crew,
housekeepers,
photographers,
past band members,
carpenters,
shadow people,
tie-dyers,
medicine men,
lyricists,
sound mixers,
office staff,
lawyers,
jewelers,
managers,
pleasure crew,
chiropractors,
travel agents,
lovers,
friends and neighbors,
present AND past?

If you're one of those who doubts there really IS a Grateful Dead Family, consider what "family" means anywhere in the world and draw your own conclusions and analogies.

It all depends on what year it is, who's out of sight and who's 'around'; and mostly, on who's drawing the picture. It also depends on how good your memory is, and on your need for definition in continually shifting sands.

Families celebrate seasons, feasts, holidays and weddings; they shower a pregnant sister with gifts, and sit with her through her labor; babies are shown around with pride at family visits. School graduates, performers, and artists can count on applauding family members in the audience. When a household moves, there are strong backs willing and a truck ready. If child care is needed on a moment's notice, there is always someone.

Absent family members are missed and talked about. Vigils are maintained in hospital hallways when a member is struck down, and when there is a death, everyone mourns. If a cousin is out of work, an uncle puts in a good word with a friend; if an award is given to one member, everyone feels pride. When tragedy strikes, everyone pitches in to bring things back to normal.

Every family has black sheep,
outcasts,
vendettas,
prodigal sons returning,
geniuses.
There are family jokes,
resemblances,
pettiness,
arguments,
drunks,
crests,
recipes,
pets,
parties,
vacations,
heirlooms,
pictures,
beliefs,
and history.

From far left:
Jonathan Riester, the band's road manager at this time; Maruska and Herbie Greene, photographer; Luvall and son; Ken Kesey, Jerry and Phil, David Foust, Sue Swanson and Joshua, Kristine Bennett.

More than anything, being part of a family provides untold comfort and continuity. You can go away for years and be greeted on your return; you can blow it completely and be forgiven your stupidity; you can sit alone on a mountain and know you have brothers and sisters down below who care about you; when you achieve something, you have people you can brag to; knowing you can ask for help gives you confidence to not *have* to ask; seeing the best members do the impossible makes everyone else stretch, and when you fail, there are loving hands to help pick you up.

This family, which evolved geometrically from its beginnings as 'just a rock and roll band' and a few friends, has sustained an incredible number of people for over twenty years through shared work and music,
    humor,
        adversity,
            achievement,
                love,
                    fierce loyalty,
                        and very strong emotions.
The feelings have substance; and however you define it, whatever its shape and size, however far the rings go outward, the Family is real. — Rosie McGee

Clockwise from top right; Billy, Florence and Phil, Pigpen, and Danny caring for the front yard at 710, Tangerine.

50

Crazy Peace of Mind

We'll talk and screech madly through the night
in heated arguments about the Witch doctors of Africa
as versus
the Hindus of India and Voodoo men of the West Indies.
We'll howl through eons
whilst Charlie Mingus puts it down
and Luigi's hot rod in his
Persian-rugged attic roars like a drunken mouse with
his head caught under the feet of Dali's stilted elephants.
Why doesn't the middle class put up?
They must dig the life of calm
quiet suburbia: until their tract-house orgies are bared.
But, we'll howl, rant, scream
kick and pick up on frothing sounds — loud
cascading forth over Peyote rocks
and crashing into ourselves,
pierced with flats — sharps
and that crazy sound: off minor.
Read? — don't play it high society isn't so bad

it's the tract-house and 20,000 — 60,000 class
that's got middleclass values up to here and who
picture themselves as clairvoyant white knights
destined to save me, or us — they boil my blood.
Dean Moriarty roars into the Opus One at 3:30 a.m. . . .
"Ron! how you been? Crazy!
Look Jack, we got a lookin' all so clean
gig goin' over Hunter's Point
so let's splee this one an' make that!"
That cat Moriarty from the Doldrums is just about so crazy
as a man can be.
"Dean, I, Speedy, Linda, Sammi, Breeze, Yvette, Carlo
and many unknowns hold wild atheistic meetings
and we sit around and not pray
and drink we do, swear, blaspheme — etc.
because we have no god."
This is what Jon Kreebson writes of himself.
Now who knows what howling times we have
in crazy grottos of the city
while Ginsberg, Ferlinghetti,
and Kerouac sit in the spot;
many crazy, unsuspecting poets know me in the place.
They put the aforementioned in with Chaucer
and his cohorts. Howl over pebbled craziness
with cascading jive marrying Peyote
in a wild explosion frescoed with intermingling
and crazy peace of mind.
Lateef wailing blue.
—Ron McKernan

51

The Circus Comes to Toronto

One of my favorite memories of the Dead was on this trip to Toronto (in early August 1967) engineered by Bill Graham for the Dead and the Airplane. The Airplane actually went up about a week early and played free concerts in Toronto and Montreal; it was one of Bill's machinations to do that and then come back and do paying gigs. Anyway, in Toronto, we all stayed for about a week at a very old, staid place called the Royal York.

A really attractive, elegant place that drew an older, very sophisticated clientele. I don't think the poor Canadians knew what they were getting into when they gave us these rooms, all on one floor. They weren't really ready for these freaks from America, especially during that period. It was really just beginning there, with weirdness beginning to creep into the midwest and over the border. And then *we* showed up!

Now the Dead and the Airplane were really two different sides of what was happening in San Francisco. The Dead were much freer; they had that family thing. There were always children around, there were always dogs everywhere, and people tended to not wear shoes. This is only a slight exaggeration. They really looked the part — if you wanted the definition of the word "hippie" you'd point to them. Well, some of the Grateful Dead feeling must've rubbed off on our band, because when we found ourselves on the same floor with them and all in connecting rooms, we decided to basically just open up the whole floor. You could start in Jack Casady's room and open the door connecting to Jerry and Mountain Girl's room, connecting to Kantner's, connecting to Phil's, connecting to Jorma's, connecting to Kreutzmann's and on down to the crew's rooms. It was completely wild, and what was even wilder is that, to a room, each was a completely different environment. One kind of incense would be in one room, another in the next. The Dead would put up tapestries on the walls, Persian carpets on the floors, posters were brought out, hookahs. The Dead traveled with literally *trunks* filled with all this stuff — candles, you name it.

Graham got it all into the country for us. The borders were a little looser then, but the real thing of it was that traveling with this absolute circus completely confounded the customs people. This was a *large* group of people with *tons* of boxes of all sizes and shapes. People dressed like you couldn't believe — day-glo, strange makeup. The Dead took trunks everywhere, and we all got really into decorating the rooms as differently as we could. We simply carried our home with us. — Spencer Dryden *(The Golden Road)*

St. Valentine's Day 1968

Tonight we danced to the grateful dead
In a ballroom hung with gold
And while we hung our acid heads
They made their dream unfold:

They began in red and black ribbons
Of silk shantung
Sequined with gold and pearls
Bold as antique heroes
Humble as home town boys
They led us down a flaming trail
Of flowers and creepers
And low voltage suns
Half hidden in Messianic volcanoes:

Did you see god?
The people all around were asking;
Did you slip through the fire
Without getting burned?
Till one cool head
Turning out his inner eye; said
I made the trip
God's not dead
He's a beautiful joke.

—Freeman

"We mixed it for the hallucinations and it worked great."

GRATEFUL DEAD :: ANTHEM OF THE SUN

Tom Constanten

The mind-bending sound TC achieved on the track involved a number of techniques he'd learned in avant-garde music circles, including 'piano,' in which foreign objects are placed inside the piano to alter the instrument's sound, usually to percussive effect.

John Cage had been writing prepared piano pieces since the '40s, and both TC and Phil had dabbled in it in their pre-Dead days, but it was still a radical move for a rock and roll band.

Of his piano preparations for *Anthem,* TC says, "The most striking was when I took a gyroscope, gave it a strong pull, and put it against the amplified sounding board. It's kind of a chainsaw sound. One of my other favorite effects was obtained by using coins. At that time I used dimes. Since then I've been to Holland and picked up Dutch dimes, which are even better. Then there's a sound like woodblocks that comes from combs stuck on the piano's higher strings. Another I liked was clothespins on the lowest strings, played either with the keys or on a string directly." TC's section of the piece also utilized an electronic tape that he had made at Henri Posseur's electronic music studio in Brussels during the summer of 1962. The primary instrument he used for that was a ring modulator. The tape was assembled from dozens of little fragments of sound cut and spliced together.

"The idea was that this chaos would ensue from 'The Other One,'" TC explains. "The final part was an overlay of several live performances, whence it gets that incredible depth; it's a remarkable effect. So they wanted to take that up and swirl it into an explosion, and out of the ashes of that would stealthily enter the warm, misty waves of 'New Potato Caboose.'"
— Blair Jackson *(The Golden Road)*

53

The Psychedelic Shop

Born Jan. 3rd, 1966. . . Died Oct. 6th, 1967
Led one hell of a healthy life
God . . . Let us work together
Survived graduate course education
in City administration,
Law and Order,
Freedom of the press
Freedom of religion
Democracy in action
Diggers kicked us in the ass, Thank you
Love to the Diggers
Love to Chester
Hari Krishna Hari Krishna
LSD is good medicine
Love it to death
Death? is life . . . some kind of truism
We really were trying to do a good thing
What the fuck, we did a fantastic thing.
Glory, Glory Hallelujah
Dig the Great Spirit
Listen to the Indians
Listen to the trees
We live on the Planet Earth
revolving around the Sun
Hymn to the gentle Sun
The Sun is Free
You are Free
We are Free
God so loved the world
Once upon a time
There was a Psychedelic Shop
That tried to save the World
and succeeded
and then went on to save the Universe
God only knows
and we are God
and God is FREE.
— Ron Thelin

The Psychedelic Shop was America's first head shop. And it was the community center for the Haight Ashbury where all neighborhood problems were hashed out. We all met there — the Diggers, the Berkeley politicos. The Human Be-In was born there, and so was the idea of 'Death of the Hippie' — when the media had co-opted our self-name and we wanted to bury it so they'd leave us alone. The Shop was always packed with neighbors and it served as a gallery for local art and photography.

On the left, Ron Thelin, Psychedelic Shop magnate. Mickey Hart (right) joined the band about this time, teaming up with original drummer Billy Kreutzmann (far left) for their enduring collaboration.

The Fillmore Auditorium ended its two-and-a-half-year career as a fulltime rock hall on July 5. Bill Graham, the Fillmore's manager, moved his scene to the old Carousel Ballroom, which had become a well-known rock dance hall in its own right under the goodhearted but insufficiently professional ownership of the Jefferson Airplane, the Grateful Dead and some cronies. The Carousel became the Fillmore West, complementing Graham's recently opened New York operation, the Fillmore East.

Healy: It held about 800 people, not very many at all, though we would put as many in there as we could get. It was an old ballroom left over from the Swing era. It was owned by an Irishman.

Garcia: They had Irish music there on Thursday nights.

Healy: That's all they had in there. Aside from that it was closed all the time, and had been closed down right after the Swing era. It was still in its original state, right out of the '20s, right down to the chandeliers in the place. The interior was beautiful. It wasn't at all torn up; it was in mint condition.

Matthews and I met this guy who happened to have a four track tape machine we wanted to rent, at a place called Emerald Studios. He was in the Irish League in San Francisco and knew about this place. We were looking around for places to play. He said, "Hey, I know where there is this ballroom," so he took Matthews and me over there. Here was this *beautiful* old ballroom.

So, we went back and talked to Rock Scully and Danny Rifkin. We decided to cook up a plan to see if we could score it and do some gigs there. We got hold of the people and they were real good about it. They said, "Sure; you want the place, take it." So we built our own stage in there and put on our own rock and roll shows. — *(Relix Magazine)*

What were the dimensions of the Carousel?

The Hippodrome: A Nice Family Ballroom

Last night I saw Sarah Bernhardt, Little Orphan Annie, Barbarella, Abraham Lincoln, Laurel and Hardy in Hell's Angels colors, and I think I caught sight of Lolita sucking on an ice cream bar. A cast from the Bible was there, too — at the Hippodrome. Something of a concert . . . a little bit of a dance . . . with some hint of a circus and sideshow . . . San Diego has added to its list of haves a ballroom complete with ever-changing light show, for acid rock, folk rock, country rock — whatever kind of Now music.

A ghost of a sign says Skateland: silhouetted figures still pirouette in some of the windows. The young people of San Diego who seek their own kind, their own scene, have glommed onto this old shell of a building at Front and G Streets, where mom and dad may have hung out when it was a roller skating rink (*their mom, maybe, not mine*).

From its star-spangled ticket booth to the intricate electronic control gear, the Hippodrome was the lovingly conceived child of Trans Love Airways Productions, that consisted of Don Collings, Barry Leichting and Ron (Anchovy) Barca, plus Reggie Hager and Ramon Rashkover, the Mirkwood Light Company. Their all-consuming interest in their work, added to long hours, the donated time of friends, and some outside financial backing, put them in business in June, 1968, and got them through the summer.

The boys regarded themselves as a family ballroom, rather than a big business organization like such places as the Fillmores West and East. This meant that financial woes were part of the family problem, since many of the rock bands pleaded poor as well.

Featured at the Hippodrome that year were the Quicksilver Messenger Service, The Electric Flag, the Grateful Dead and The Velvet Underground — all from out of town — and the popular local group, Maya. The band and some of the Hippodrome family, with me standing fourth from left taken the day I met the band, August 1968. (*San Diego Magazine*)

Quicksilver Messenger Service

We had some pretty wild times on the Northwest Trek (a tour the Dead and Quicksilver played in the Pacific Northwest in January and February of 1968). There was no heat on us because with Pigpen around it was like "Ooooh — look at *that* guy!" We all looked like businessmen in comparison with Pigpen!

Anyway, I remember when we first got to Portland, Dan Healy, who was working for us then (and who modified the SG I'm playing now), and I went into a pawn shop. Dan bought a '56 Les Paul Special, and I bought guns and a bunch of blanks to continue the little cowboys and Indians game that we'd been playing with the Dead for quite a while. (An oft-told anecdote from the early summer of '66 has the Dead dressing up like Indians and raiding Quicksilver's Marin ranch in the dead of night.) It was snowing in Portland, and here I am with all these guns and hundreds of blanks. I was taking 'shots' at everyone in our group. And we had this rule that went along with the game we played, which was if you 'died' you had to 'stay dead' for a couple of minutes. If someone even shot you with their finger you had to roll over and play dead. We're all too stiff to do that now, I guess.

One of the guns I bought was this little .22 caliber blank pistol that was easy to carry around. I remember seeing Pigpen, Rock Scully and Danny Rifkin (Dead managers), and I think maybe one other guy from the group, driving down the street. So I went running out into the street making some kind of deranged weird noise — some anguished cry — and I emptied the gun into the car. The car came screeching to a stop. The doors flew open and Pigpen and everybody just rolled out of the car into the snow. They really looked dead! Out of the corner of my eye I saw this old lady with a shopping cart racing around the corner. I stood there surveying 'the kill'. Then they got up, we all had a good laugh, and we got in the car. About a minute later of course the place was crawling with police, looking for the 'bodies'! The whole tour went that way. I got a callous on my trigger finger from blowing people away.
— John Cipollina

57

The Pleasure Crew got its name during the infamous London Run of 1968. The name itself first took form in a tattoo parlor in Soho where it was graven permanently into the flesh of several members of the cast. Taking George Harrison up on his Christmas invitation, the Dead's management (Rock, Danny and Jonathan) along with Kesey, Slade, Peter Coyote, Paula McCoy, Frankie Hart, Sue Swanson, Spyder, Sweet William and Frisco Pete, scammed thirteen free tickets from ASCAP, persuaded Uncle Bobo

GRATEFUL DEAD

to air freight the Angels' bikes and set off to see if London Bridge had really fallen down. The Hell's Angels had the added incentive of branching out internationally. It was first envisioned as a transatlantic party, a Christmas vacation for the pleasure crew, but after two weeks of bouncing off every English wall from Stonehenge to Saville Row, we realized that the language barrier between America and England was enough work for the heaviest members of the pleasure crew.

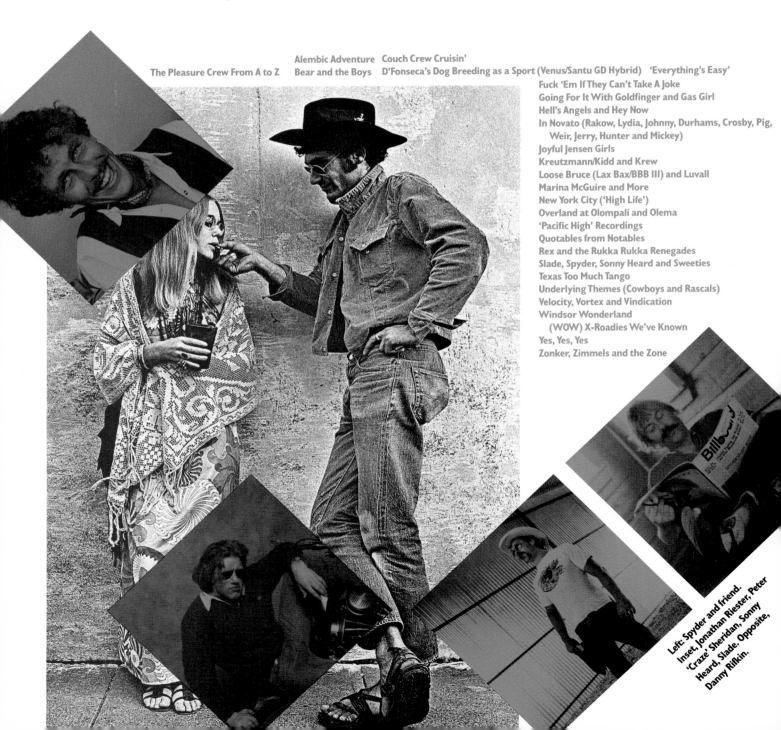

The Pleasure Crew From A to Z

Alembic Adventure
Bear and the Boys
Couch Crew Cruisin'
D'Fonseca's Dog Breeding as a Sport (Venus/Santu GD Hybrid) 'Everything's Easy'
Fuck 'Em If They Can't Take A Joke
Going For It With Goldfinger and Gas Girl
Hell's Angels and Hey Now
In Novato (Rakow, Lydia, Johnny, Durhams, Crosby, Pig, Weir, Jerry, Hunter and Mickey)
Joyful Jensen Girls
Kreutzmann/Kidd and Krew
Loose Bruce (Lax Bax/BBB III) and Luvall
Marina McGuire and More
New York City ('High Life')
Overland at Olompali and Olema
'Pacific High' Recordings
Quotables from Notables
Rex and the Rukka Rukka Renegades
Slade, Spyder, Sonny Heard and Sweeties
Texas Too Much Tango
Underlying Themes (Cowboys and Rascals)
Velocity, Vortex and Vindication
Windsor Wonderland
    (WOW) X-Roadies We've Known
Yes, Yes, Yes
Zonker, Zimmels and the Zone

Left: Spyder and friend. Inset, Jonathan Riester, Peter 'Craze' Sheridan, Sonny Heard, Slade. Opposite, Danny Rifkin.

London Run Coyote Rolling Rock

I think now which means I should have been asleep now but a cigarette keeps me thinking of the girls first of Frankie as she still remains in London upstairs asleep no longer thinking about last nite as Pete hits out at last on the innocent melody maker man who tells him he cannot eat more no matter how drunk its all become and Frankie afraid afraid, she once the lady of Mitchell/Experience and Casady/Airplane and one riding to drumming of tables between her legs to Kennedy with Hart/Dead and Rock protesting $100 — $ fare to SF and mouth to feed but already she is more beautiful and 4 mos. later she is with Kesey/Prankster on the Oregon farm from city basement/Scene a gogo to farm country & beaus and life — now afraid asleep at last afraid she blew it when smashing bancardi in Beatles resting room/SF headqtrs london confronting Pete the Angel the motherfucker hit someone Lennon was there now what we got to split tears & Peter Monk for 5 ordained tibetan years celibate ultimate final STP human for us all kisses her and thinking now of Paula who's gone home to her house full of blond California new free children old & wise young with living fibres opened by the men that this trip represents thinking of Sue Swan-

George Harrison always George till the joke is real and George hadn't understood her now with 3 mos. old child to be good wish and had brought her here to Apple London Harri- cle like peoples of the planet know so we full circle in and cliffs hang with free people and teaming Japan cle can we now after five years the brotherhood back to where we come from to see what is have just released on the US is a huge in our heads American music all of fuck-ups with our heads in religion what of our brother Lennon in the pa- with his beautiful Yoko finally we are flash- we know he's getting back together and using Mahesh & Pepper to our enrichment and we wish at Gulf Stream, Fla. 100,000 gather to hear the dead 7,000 spent their first day high together in Florida sun- and remanifest themselves in Golden Gate Park where the did it for Central Park's 20,000 who did for you & me & Yoko suns ripples on the rosy tongues of California all come from some-

son original Palo Alto friend and fan of the Dead but first of is real and did she get one final chance to say she was sorry he and in love with the men that had fulfilled her greatest on where it had all started for her now come full cir- California — migratory adventure pushes west reaching out and meeting in California full cir- dignified free american men make it together left behind because the music the Beatles two day event everywhere on the air the Joy and pieces of our past and rice and women is nice but pers busted and standing naked ing on the brotherhood of us all and what he learned from the last trip with only to give back and now back in the USSR at Sunday's sunset outside where just last Easter shine to experience each other through the band Quicksilver & Janis that same day played to 15,000 who & Lennon and Taylor returned to England with love for the where down the road and we keep on rolling — Lennon has been

there all along and his Christmas smile made me warm and hunger for home and Ringo's kids made me dance upstairs and maybe if the rockers from the bridge hadn't still been plaguing me I could have danced all nite but they followed us reeling home to our floor in Battersea where for third straight nite the police had come to voice complaints of the citizenry whose delegation I had cooled only hours ahead talking shivering in the hall to the man upstairs who couldn't get his baby to sleep for all the Nortons & Bezzers revving downstairs I said yes there will be silence and when they would not split I did and minutes later the police. They're the only ones that seem to really appreciate your music and/or your pranks but I believe we're getting it together — in LA 80% of the high school students now turning on now with 80% population of India turning on now only London scene two years dry still hung over over drink over cover can we only get it together under DuChamps guilt slip on stage the Albert Hall — Lennon I thank you for being there again. The London hang over is still one year coming down from speed and acid smolder the fire of acid excitement for living fully and I'll never forget the tarot on the floor of your office with Amsterdam's Simon and Empress turning up five successive cards reading destruction in the future in all cases with the devil & king & empress all now and behind us but destruction ahead — then Pete hits out and Frankie hits out to stop him facing off with a broken bottle and a kiss no mockery no blame what happened when you used to be so free — Donovan asks me and had I some Angels friends to be free with even without Grass to not have friends around without guns and police don't have guns here even detectives from the yard at Albert Hall and we stood close to them almost constantly between them and the little Bit and Arts Lab and no guns and we felt free as did dancers and hairy christians who used to geez speed in rainy oregon gray days on fulbright scholarships hauling blond north african hash to Switzerland and black- ened by the soot of New York's Tompkins Square Park same people with now shaven heads calling out on home made cymbals from San Jose and voices raised in Albert's London hall to join in and be together in dance & silence. These same left a temple in San Fran- cisco two years after Ron Thelin gave away Psychedelic Shop and Haight boarded up and smiles behind pin ball eyes all turned up tilt except the now hairless Krishnas left California redwoods right all the way for temple statues in London some*where!* A tem- ple in San Francisco where my friends carry guns — my friends? Michael X in London says how can we expect a planet to put a bomb behind us when we carry guns — he don't — good news! because the San Francisco State revolution is as bloody as Mexico City & Chicago and we left and that's where I was arrested first years ago for raising the VC flag over campus in fun. — Rock Scully

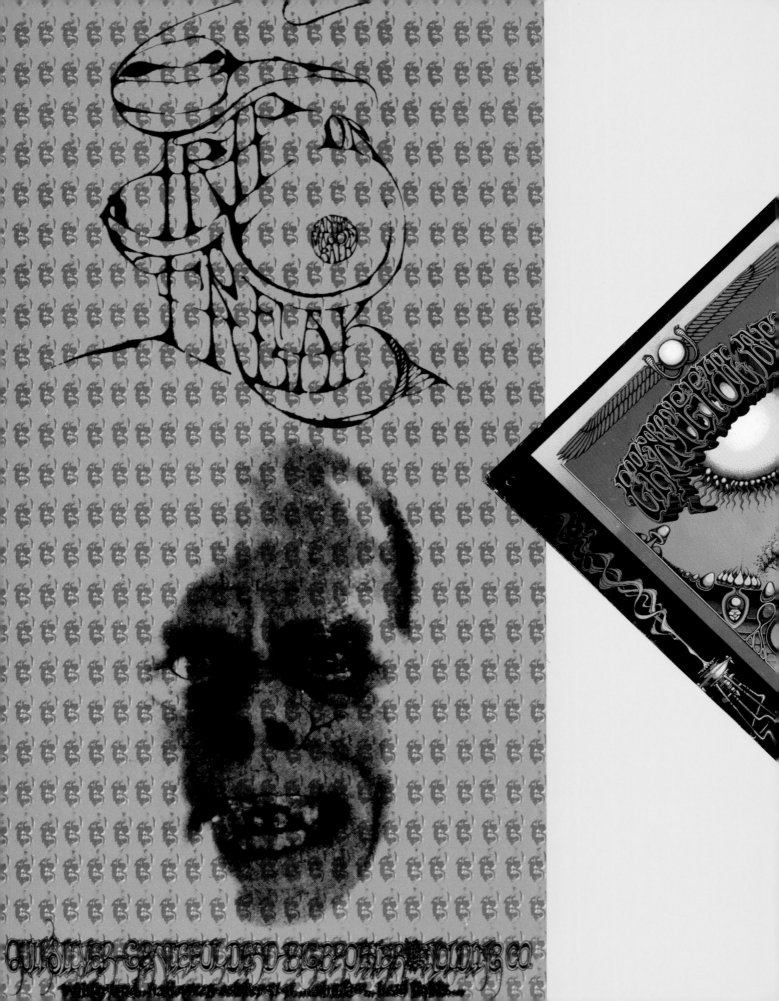

The Dead came back on, their tribal community flowing with them until, like some huge horde of lemmings, they covered the stage. There are more people on stage when the Dead play than have ever got there to embrace Mick Jagger. Bill Graham, who had been dancing while Mongo played, was back on stage grooving to the Dead. Marty Balin, Grace Slick came out from behind the curtains and sat down in back of the band in the empty row of chairs. The rent-a-cop looked at them and didn't shine his ever-lovin' light on them at all! Several people climbed through the ropes and over the chairs and at least two got on stage. A stage hand rousted them and the rent-a-cop frog-marched one of them on out of the hall. As soon as he split, the crowd filled the back-stage area, some getting on the stage steps, and dozens of others camping down on the stairs. When he came back he was ten years clearing it all away. — ROLLING STONE

Sex, drugs and rock and roll. Perhaps the most outrageous event in the annals of rock occurred at the Free City Party given by the Diggers and Hell's Angels. It was neither the music nor the drugs that provided the breakthrough . . . it was just straightforward sex. For after six hours of acid, pot and rock, the evening ended with virtually the entire audience making love on the floor of the ballroom. A thousand-headed god with no cameras permitted. — Peter Top, Chocolate George, a SF Hell's Angel; Phil and below, Danny and unknown friend dancing in the Park.

BIG ROCK POW WOW
MAY 1969

Grateful Dead

Power brokers: pocket check in the panhandle. The managers, from left: Bill Thompson (Jefferson Airplane), Bill Graham, Julius Karpen (Big Brother), Rock Scully (Grateful Dead), Ron Polte (Quicksilver) and Danny Rifkin (Grateful Dead).

Monday night, the second night of the Airplane-Dead-Quicksilver engagement is not a big night for rock and roll shows, but the hall seemed to be filled again. By now everyone knew about Janis, but the crowd was not in a mournful mood. Said Jerry Garcia after the Dead's set:

"The crowd seemed a little crazier last night than tonight, I don't know. You have to understand that I have no memory, that's the price I pay. The difference in vibes? It makes a big difference in vibes if you tell somebody, Janis died. That's like heavy news. But listen, man, these are all people who've been on lots of trips, and they're sensitive, far-out, weird people, probably the weirdest people on earth in this place, and they've all looked at death a million times in lots of different ways. Nobody's really uptight about death. Death is something that really happens.

"Janis was like a *real person,* man. She went through all the changes we did. She went on all the same trips. She was just like the rest of us — fucked up, strung out, in weird places. Back in the old days, the pre-success days, she was using all kinds of things, just like anybody, man.

"When she went out after something, she went out after it really hard, harder than most people ever think to do, ever conceive of doing."

Bob Weir: "You know about the irony of her getting Bessie Smith a tombstone. I think we, the bands, should put together a collection and get her a tombstone, kind of a cheap, gaudy tombstone, the way she'd have wanted. I know she doesn't like want her ashes scattered to the wind, man, she'll want to go six feet under like all her songs."

Pigpen had a personal kind of tribute in mind:

"When I get a few days I'm gonna set back and get *ripped* on Southern Comfort.

"I turned her on to Southern Comfort, man. I knew her when she came up in '63 and I was with the jugband. Then she came back to Texas, and when she came back up I told her one day, 'Tex, try some of this.' She said (rolling his eyes, reeling), 'Oh man, that's good!'

"We used to get drunk and play pool together. She beat me 80 percent of the time."

Marty Balin of the Airplane didn't appear on Monday night. "He's feeling really down," said Paul Baratta, "and he thinks this is going to be a funeral thing for Janis. But Bob Weir told him, 'Hey, man, Janis went the way she wanted to go, come on.' But he isn't coming."

Neither Baratta nor any of the groups spoke of Janis from the stage. But there seemed to be a special edge in the way the Airplane — a trio, as Grace had not yet come on stage and Marty wasn't there at all — announced, "What do you want to bet by the end of the evening you're all gonna be *dancing?*" — Charles Perry (Rolling Stone)

She Said Call Me Pearl

"They used to laugh at me — I didn't even know for what, man.
I read poetry and I was a painter. I didn't want to just be married.
I had aspirations that only guys are supposed to have."

she said call me pearl
our little blue girl
that last time
i saw you at the Mo
we shared comfort
& i teased about your weight
i couldn't know
we wouldn't meet again
& i never told you how much
i loved you

Robert M. Petersen (Eureka, 1970)

THERE WAS A TIME A WHILE BACK, WHICH SEEMS
ALTERNATELY LIKE A SECOND OR A CENTURY,
WHEN THE DEAD USED TO GET TOGETHER
SOCIALLY MORE OFTEN THAN THEY DO NOW . . .
AND SOME OF THESE EVENTS WERE SO EXALTED
THAT IT'S HARD TO BELIEVE THEY EVER STOPPED.
THESE PARTIES INCLUDED SUCH STRUCTURES AS
THE ULTRA CONSERVATIVE 'BLACK AND WHITE
BALL' AND THE REDNECK SHOOTOUTS AT BILLY'S
RANCH WHEN THE DRUMMERS HUNG CYMBALS
AND GONGS FROM THE TREES AND EVERYONE
BLAZED AWAY AT THEM WITH RIFLES AND SHOT-
GUNS. IN THOSE DAYS EVERYONE RODE HORSES
AND OWNED AT LEAST ONE RIFLE AND ONE
SIDEARM, SO THAT 30 OR 40 GUNS FIRED CON-
TINUOUSLY FOR AN HOUR OR SO, SHREDDING THE
ZILDJIANS AND BRINGING THE SHERIFF. ANY EXCUSE
FOR A PARTY — HOLIDAYS, BIRTHDAYS, FRIDAYS, SOL-
STICES, WEDDINGS . . . OR JUST FOR THE HELL OF IT.

The original horses at the Novato ranch came from the Jensen girls at Olompali. Later, Tomasina, Apache Chipper (The Stud) and Mac Jagger, three great Appaloosas which took up residence at the ranch, were a gift from Roger Lewis. Next, Valerie acquired for Mickey a thoroughbred racehorse named Tychain, and Stephen Stills supplied another. Mickey also had a beautiful Morab (half-Morgan and half-Arab). Billy and Susila had Liquorice and Rats Arse. The Jensen girls looked after the horses and other livestock, including a large colony of pet white rats, named after the various denizens of the ranch. These were later introduced into the community, but that's another story. . .

Previous page, Rhonda Jensen. Above, Rhonda; Mickey and Cookie Eisenberg. Members of Grateful Dead, New Riders of the Purple Sage, crew, and, in the foreground, manager Jon McIntire with secretary Gail Hellund; right, Christina Hart.

There Could Only be Two Hundred People at the Party

One summer day in northern California, I don't remember which month or which year, but Sweet William was there on a 3 wheeler the club had just made for him (so if you really wanna know you can ask him, he might remember) . . . Peter Marino and Jerilyn had sweet-talked Mickey into throwing a promotional party at the ranch for the Tower of Power, who'd traded this party for the horn parts on *Rolling Thunder.*

In addition to the Dead, there were a couple of Hell's Angels, a couple of Black Panthers, Hog Farmers, a couple of Weathermen and two hundred record executives from Los Angeles and New York wearing metal jumpsuits, like the astronauts.

The cooks prepared turkeys, salmon, salads and fresh bread. Johnny Pine had brought a large wild boar he'd wrestled out of a tree and killed with a buck knife after it was bayed by his dogs. Mickey, and a guy who looked like him, turned the pig on a spit, both wearing beards, mirrored shades, levis and t-shirts — stone bookends except for the joints they kept passing. Hours went by, they turned the spit . . . various chemicals took hold . . . fat dripped from the

carcass to the coals, crackling as it vaporized into fragrant smoke. Some crazy person dropped 40,000 mics of LSD into the coffee without telling anyone . . . and the ranch began to vibrate.

Some folks rode horses, some Harley's. The softball game went on its surreal way down by the garden and Mickey continued turning the spit. Turkey buzzards warmed their wings, motionless over the hills bees buzzed and hours passed. The pig looked crisp. No one said it was done. We'd all heard of trichonosis, but none of us had ever cooked an animal this size before.

After awhile, Johnny Pine came over and using the same knife he'd killed the pig with, cut a deep gash into its flank, then another still deeper.

"No man, it's still raw two inches down. Lookit (holding some flesh on the tip of his knife), ya can't eat bloody pig."

So Mickey, hearing Tower of Power tuning up, left the carcass to fend for itself and ambled over to the barn. The band played fast for an hour and then even faster for an encore . . . a blazing response to the summer heat. After

the set the cooks returned to the barbeque pit. As they came over the shallow rise between the barn and the house they saw two women and a man in metallic jumpsuits, carving the last piece of meat from the pig's skeleton.

"Probably thought it was a cow," said someone charitably. — Peter

By 1972, the first wave of the family had mostly moved out, except for Mickey, dog Glups, and horse Snorty. At the time, I was working for my Uncle Pete Marino of Warner Brothers Records. He wanted me to throw a party for Tower of Power's second record and I remembered The Ranch, where I'd been a few times. Mickey and I made a deal — he'd let me use the ranch if I cleaned it up first; there could only be two hundred people at the party; I had to bring these people out in buses and get them drunk along the way, so they could never find their way back to the ranch alone. After the party, Mickey and I became friends. — Jerilyn

Clockwise: Ramrod and Frances Shurtliff, Debbie 'Doobie' Eisenberg, Tom Constanten, Rondelle Cagwin, Rhonda with Stacey Kreutzmann, Mickey with Pete Marino.

Every Structure Became a Dwelling

Jonathan and Slade found the Ranch. The hippies living there wanted to move to the city, so Mickey rented it. Over the first few years, almost everyone in the Dead Family lived there at one time. And they kept leaving and coming back, to make music, to party, to ride horses, to share sunrise ceremonies, to stay for a while or just for some quiet time.

As we started to transform the barn into a full recording studio, more people moved onto The Ranch. Every structure that had a roof became a dwelling. The horses' tack room housed four children; the little house by the creek was home for Johnny D' and Sunny; a tiny shed behind the pump house had a loft built in; the second old horse barn way out above the creek was used too. The main house itself was quite small, but that was never an obstacle to numbers of people. Endless cooking was the order of the day, never feeding less than 12 people. — Jerilyn

From top left, Billy and Susila, Spyder, the Magnificent Seven of Rock 'n' Roll in late 1969; and Jerilyn with Creek and Christina.

5. WHISTLING THROUGH THE FOG

IN 1970 THE GRATEFUL DEAD STARTED GOING ON THE ROAD SERIOUSLY WITH MAJOR NATIONAL TOURS, PLAYING MORE SHOWS THAT YEAR THAN EVER BEFORE OR SINCE— 144 GIGS. HALF THESE GIGS WERE ON THE EAST COAST. THE BAND ALSO ENJOYED GREAT SUCCESS WITH ALBUMS— FIRST *LIVE DEAD*, THEN *WORKINGMAN'S DEAD* AND *AMERICAN BEAUTY.* WARNER BROTHERS DIDN'T REALLY KNOW HOW TO PROMOTE THE BAND IN EARLIER YEARS. WE CONVINCED THEM TO FINANCE A SERIES OF FREE CONCERTS IN SEVEN CITIES: THEY PAID FOR THE FLATBED TRUCKS AND THE SOUND SYSTEM AND WE DID THE REST. 'GRATEFUL DEAD COMES TO YOUR HOMETOWN AND PLAYS FOR FREE.' LOCAL PROMOTERS DIDN'T LIKE IT BECAUSE IT AFFECTED THEIR TICKET SALES TO HAVE A FREE SHOW THE NEXT DAY IN THE PARK. IN 1970, WE DID RADIO SIMULCASTS IN FIFTEEN CITIES— THE FIRST ROCK AND ROLL STEREO SIMULCASTS EVER. EVEN OLD PEOPLE THAT HAD BOUGHT STEREOS LISTENED TO IT JUST BECAUSE IT WAS SO UNIQUE. AND WARNER BROTHERS PAID FOR IT ALL. —ROCK SCULLY

Leaving Marin County through the 'rainbow tunnel', gateway to the world. Right, the band on the road. Left, Harover, Rhonda, mule Jericho and Hagen; Truck Drivin' Cheri.

Back at the ranch: the women and children had to cover the home scene. By now, there were several ranches — loose households created by renting large houses mostly out in Novato or West Marin. As before with 710 Ashbury, this was the economical way to go. A partial list:

Rukka Rukka Ranch — Nicasio: Bob, Frankie, Jackson, Sonny Heard, Eileen, Crystal, Steve Parish;

Novato Ranch — Mickey, Jensen girls, Slade, Jonathan, Rock, Sue Gottlieb, Cookie, Debbie and Terry;

Ridge Road — Hunter, Garcia, Mountain Girl, Alan Trist, Maureen, Christie, Hunter and Sunshine;

Farview — Weir and Pigpen and Veronica;

Indian Valley Road — Rakow and Lydia, the Durham kids;

Across the street — David Crosby;

Atherton Avenue — Roger Lewis, Courtenay Pollock, Jerry Buckley, Amos, Thayer;

Blackpoint — Jon McIntire, John Bologni, Sue Swanson, Joshua; Rose was born there;

Woodacre — Ramrod and Frances;

Fairfax — Phil and Florence.

Rolling Thunder

I met Rolling Thunder at Bob Weir's house in 1970. Frankie was really ill and her doctor's diagnosis wasn't something she could agree with. I don't know how Rolling Thunder and his people were contacted, I just remember one evening he arrived with Grandfather Semu (medicine man for the Chumash people) and their warriors. After acting as hostess, I brought Rolling Thunder to Frankie's room, left him to check her out and returned to the living room. Grandfather Semu was requesting one of the women accompanying the warriors to put out her cigarette. She declined. He asked again. She again refused. He pointed his finger in her direction from across the room (about 10 feet away) and the ciggie flamed up several inches causing the young lady to drop it rather abruptly.

Just then, the bedroom door opened and Rolling Thunder asked for the people who were to be present during the healing ceremony to come into the room. He asked me to assist him. I later found out this was because I was not 'on my moon' and was perceived by him to be sincere in my desire to help Frankie. During the ceremony, he admonished one of the skeptics in our midst and asked that no one sit at Frankie's feet warning of the danger in a subtle way. One guy, who didn't listen or hear very well, did just that and as soon as he did, the locked windows at the foot of the bed flew open and he became quite ill himself. —Jerilyn

Mickey with Ali Akbar Khan and Alla Rahka. At this time, Donna Jean Thatcher, was a studio backup singer, singing on a couple of Boz Skaggs records, and cuts for Elvis Presley. Here she is, right, with Mary Holiday, Jeanie Greene, Elvis and Ginger Holiday at the American Sound Studio, Memphis Tennessee on January 19, 1969. She married Keith Godchaux in November, 1970, right, who joined the band as a pianist in 1971.

The Festival Express

The 1970 Canada trip featured the Dead, New Riders of the Purple Sage, Janis Joplin, The Band and others, and is immortalized in the song 'Might As Well'.

Dawson: Traveling with the Dead was always pretty wild, of course, and in the first couple of years of the Riders we were with them a lot. The train ride across Canada was just like one long crazy party. I remember that the only time I ever saw Garcia smashed on tequila was on that trip. It was a rare occasion indeed.

Nelson: There were two band cars with equipment set up so you could play, and of course everyone would go down there and jam. Everybody had his own room with a window and a little bed that folded down. Traveling through Canada and then pulling into these little stops that seemed like they were in the middle of nowhere with the band playing — it really seemed like a circus. All the townspeople would come around and see what was going on; they'd look at the band playing through the windows and be totally amazed.

Scully: That was one of the best trips musically that ever went off. There was singing all night and drinking all night in the parlor cars; card playing and cussing and swearing with the most incongruous bunch of musicians. Chicago blues guys, Little Walter. Kristofferson worked up 'Bobby McGee' on this trip.

The night before we got to Calgary, the big Roundup started. I think it's called the Stampede. We were part of that whole Roundup week. We headed into Calgary and all the cowboys were whooping it up. We were supposed to be at the fanciest hotel, except the rooms were tight, the cowboys were tight. We looked like a bunch of drunk hippies. The town was split down the middle between cowboys for the Stampede and Grateful Dead Heads that had come from as far away as Vancouver, or had followed the train across Canada. You know, just tie dye and bronco riding. There were fights all over town. Delaney & Bonnie got in a huge row that involved Kris Kristofferson. It was awful. They were all strung out on hangovers.

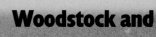

The secret went out at Woodstock that there were so many people coming in that there was no way we were gonna close the doors. "If you ain't got a ticket, come on in. If you bought one, drop it over here." There were people all around that concert trying to give away their tickets.

The Dead did not fare well there. Several things went wrong. First of all, the band's entrance and exit from the stage depended on risers. And when the Dead were supposed to go on, the wheels on their risers failed. The gear was so heavy that the risers nosedived. We had to take all of the gear off the risers and stick it out on the stage. A big monster undertaking. Plus it was stormy.

Finally we set it up. Then, since we were the first band after dark, they decided it was time to unfurl the light show. Only there was a 60-mile-an-hour wind blowing, and the stage was maybe 35 or 40 feet above the ground, all set on big pieces of wood because it had been raining for weeks and weeks, and it was very muddy. They unfurled the light show screen and it billowed out like a sail on a square-rigger and the stage started to scoot down, the whole damn thing started to slide.

The call for action was: pull out your buck knife and rip holes in the $20,000 screen. It was like a cinerama screen. Jonathan Riester just grabbed my buck knife and flew into it. Then my brother, Dicken, did the same thing. Finally, the stage stopped sliding.

That was the beginning. All day long people were saying, "Do not take the brown acid." Some guy had a brown paper bag full of bum acid. Then this guy comes bouncing across the stage in the middle of the Dead's set and he's throwing out brown acid to the crowd. That was a nightmare in itself.

They played a set, but it was not great. "Generally speaking," said Garcia, "the more people expect, the worse we are. The paramount example was Woodstock." Weir said: "We had a sound man who insisted that everything was being done wrong so he was gonna set up his whole PA, and proceeded to go about doing so."

"Hanging up the audience for four or five hours!" roared Garcia, wiping tears of laughter from his eyes. "When you multiply that by the number of people at Woodstock you get several human years."

"Yeah," shouted Weir excitedly, "several human years of chagrin and consternation, and add to that the fact that when we finally did get it set up the electrical ground was completely wrong so every time either of us touched our instruments we got horrible shocks."

Altamont

Later in the year, a press conference in New York announced that the Rolling Stones were going to play free in the park in San Francisco. All the radio stations announced, "Free concert, free concert!" Suddenly it was everybody's free concert. They planned to make a movie of it, a *movie*; everybody started looking to make money on it. It became a lie. It wasn't a free concert — it became an exploited, horrifying event. (The concert was moved to Sears Point less than 24 hours before the show and was moved again to Altamont Speedway, about 40 miles southeast of San Francisco.)

They had such a crowd coming and they had a riot on their hands. We wanted out, but they had our equipment. But the Grateful Dead never did play at Altamont.

When we got there, they had such a crowd that the scene was changing very fast. It had grown up quickly and had incorporated so many people who were just taking. We saw the same thing happening in the Haight-Ashbury.
—Scully

Altamont Speedway, where unexpected violence, so soon after the triumph of peace at Woodstock, shocked a generation. Garcia and Kreutzmann talk with Mick Jagger of the Rolling Stones at the Heliport before Altamont.

Boots was our pyrotechnician. It was on a New Year's Eve, I guess it must have been '72 or '73 in San Francisco, and he had these things set up that had the numbers '72 or '73 and, right at the stroke of midnight, he set them off. They were like some kind of flash powder or flash paper, and they had an amazing effect. It left a reverse image on my retina, like a flash-bulb of '72 or '73. Man, it was really weird. I'd close my eyes, and *there it would be*. It was there for an hour. Whatever it was, it was on there, and I'm saying, "Well, that's interesting. It could have been the Ten Commandments." — Garcia

All my education led me to composition, and I followed a dead end. All I could do after I'd composed the things I wanted to say, was to shut up. It was a question of style and technique leading you right into a corner.

I was composing classical electronic music. Surreal orchestra music. Improvised chants, reaction music. Then I realized that if composition was improvisation, and you let random chance make your decisions for you, you may as well just blow. Your chances of hitting any significant combinations are about the same either way. That's especially true in a collective situation, when there are more than two musicians playing.

I've always thought of the music we play as 'electric chamber music', which has been called the music of friends. — Lesh, Grateful Dead Program, London 1972

Sam Cutler and Pathfinder Frank Berry loaded with Native American jewelry. Frank's mission was to rescue the great pieces of Navaho turquoise and silver art from the clutches of museums by buying them from the Southwest trading posts and trading them to the hippies, the true brothers of the Hopi prophecy. Opposite, Jerry on the pedal steel guitar.

Good Lovin', Good Preachin'

Last week's Grateful Dead concert up at Gaelic Park was a usual Dead session, meaning that the band-to-fan-to-band electro-chemical process for which rock music is famed was on like high mass at Easter. Although I think I know most of the time what they are doing musically: I don't quite understand them electro-chemically. Like the New York Knicks of two seasons ago, they can do excellent things together though they are not a group of deathless superstars. Garcia gets his songs across, but he can't sing, and Bob Weir's voice rises to about average . . . . maybe better when he gets to screaming and the music sweeps him along. I still find it difficult to recognize the Dead songs that aren't 'Truckin' or 'St. Stephen' one from the other. I am not one of their fans, but seem to be one of their admirers. Their music speaks in a special language to their live listen-

ers, and that language has the vocabulary of everybody else, but a convoluted syntax all its own. The note sequences are not completely dependent upon musical factors but are also dictated by how involved the band feels and also upon what kind of heat the audience is giving off. I'm trying to get to some essences of this thing.

The drama of a Dead concert revolves around the fact that wherever the band plays they know that a certain number (several tons) of their partisans will be there and that their crowd knows the Dead potential to excite them but they also know that the Dead may not get into gear until the crowd begins to apply some heat, and so forth. Both parties also know that the concert will be long enough and informal enough for anything to

happen on either side of the footlights, and so audiences improvise (smoke, go to the hot dog stand, kiss and snuggle, cheer, dance, listen like star-struck fools) just like their musician friends on stage (who play light and funny for awhile, retire backstage awhile, stand around, or get lost in a piece and turn on the heavy jets). Like good lovers, the Grateful Dead know the secrets of good foreplay, taking your time, surprising the audience, intentionally understated; but Lesh kept bopping and thrumming away, heavily at all times, until his patterns were con-

sistently getting the other players off. In the middle of 'St. Stephen' there was a special coming together: Lesh had found a nice ambiguous but compelling set of licks; Garcia eased into a solo; Weir strummed a cross-time lick over all of it; it built; it quieted; Garcia started to play strange classical kind of lines; the drums dropped out; the audience got quiet; nothing at all could be predicted for a minute or so; then Lesh began to grope his way out with two chords and rhythms which began to regularize; audience began to jump and then to clap; guitars began to straighten out; the band came home to the cheers of the fans.

Good music making. The listener goes home without a little tune to whistle, but he hears music. As if they were finishing off some personal solos based over the last riffs heard, the fans went out of Gaelic Park without a thousand encores and without a lot of fuss on the streets outside. It's all very interesting, surprising, and I guess mystifying as before. All I know is that the Dead, or their fans, or the combination of both lure you into planning to return when they're all assembled and back in town again. —Carman Moore

Jerry and Mountain Girl at the Yale Bowl, July 31, 1971, one of the first stadium concerts.

78

The San Francisco Panhandle and Golden Gate Park shows were the inspiration for doing nationwide free shows. The Dead was a community band and there was a demand that went beyond just selling tickets. It demanded that the Dead play for free — wherever we went there was a community that supported us as their 'community band' and demanded that, somehow, we play for free outdoors. Above, Mountain Girl and Sunshine.

Rex Jackson and Mark 'Sparky' Raizene setting up in the Chateau grounds, June 21, 1971; opposite top, Betty Cantor preparing micro- phones; our French hosts, Daniel Schuster and Jean-Jaques Damiani, attend the unloading of equipment.

Herouville or Bust

"Got a passport? Wanna go to Paris? We need you to speak French." With these words Jon McIntire roused me out of my lethargy in Alembic's windowless garage office one Wednesday in 1971. "Day after tomorrow — we'll be gone five days — you and I will go ahead of the band — I'll explain on the plane."

This began an obscure adventure remembered thus:

The sight of the proposed music festival was a minor dude ranch outside of Paris with a full Hollywood-style western street where we had a beer at the functioning saloon.

When the equipment arrived at Orly, no truck had been arranged and I was left alone, on a weekend, with a wad of money and a couple of local schleppers, to find a truck to rent and get the equipment to a location 65 kilometers away.

The festival was rained out and the band, having come so far to play music, could only pace the halls of their lodgings, the 17th century Chateau d'Herouville, while the storm howled.

There was a glorious springtime visit to the Eiffel Tower with some of the band and crew — even there and even then, a wild-haired guy from Mill Valley came up to Jerry

with a "Hey man, far out!"

At a nighttime gig on the lawn of the Chateau, lit by a news crew's lights, the Dead played to the mystified but game local villagers and a handful of Parisian media, the only option to returning home without playing a lick.

After four fairly sleepless nights, we were back at the airport; an hour to flight time and the equipment was on the plane but we weren't — our tickets were held hostage waiting for some freight document. Fifteen minutes before departure, still no document and I was surrounded by six supervisors representing two airlines, the airport, and the French government. All were arguing at once, the airlines over who would nab these paying customers, the government agent trying to ensure we would have time to pass through his drug checkpoint, the airport security trying to calm everyone down — while waiting 20 yards away, the guys were about to lose it completely. They just wanted to go home!

Exasperated from an hour of harassment, I picked on the stubborn official who was holding the tickets and shouted over the din in French, "Monsieur, *look* at those guys over there (the band). I can't say WHAT they'll do if they don't get on SOME airplane *immediately.* Do YOU want to be PERSONALLY responsible for an international incident, right here and right now?" The gentleman looked over, and the guys, ready to explode anyway, picked up on my cue. One or two gave the well known American one-digit salutation while roaring like lions, and the rest merely projected visions of Hell to Pay — the poor man broke down completely and weakly handed me back the boarding passes. A sprint through the airport, a token stop at a security check, and we collapsed in our seats on the plane with our equipment riding below.

The next day was a Wednesday, one week after Jon's call. I sat at my desk at Alembic, business as usual, wondering if I'd dreamed up the whole thing. — Rosie McGee

They played for three hot and during this time the workers lit hundreds of candles and placed them around the pool as if it were a religious shrine . . . a Lourdes or place of healing waters. As the party progressed, the candles were extinguished by the bodies of various drunken celebrants being thrown in the pool by other drunken celebrants. The Dead played louder and louder; the locals never heard anything like it before and they were delirious. — (Archives)

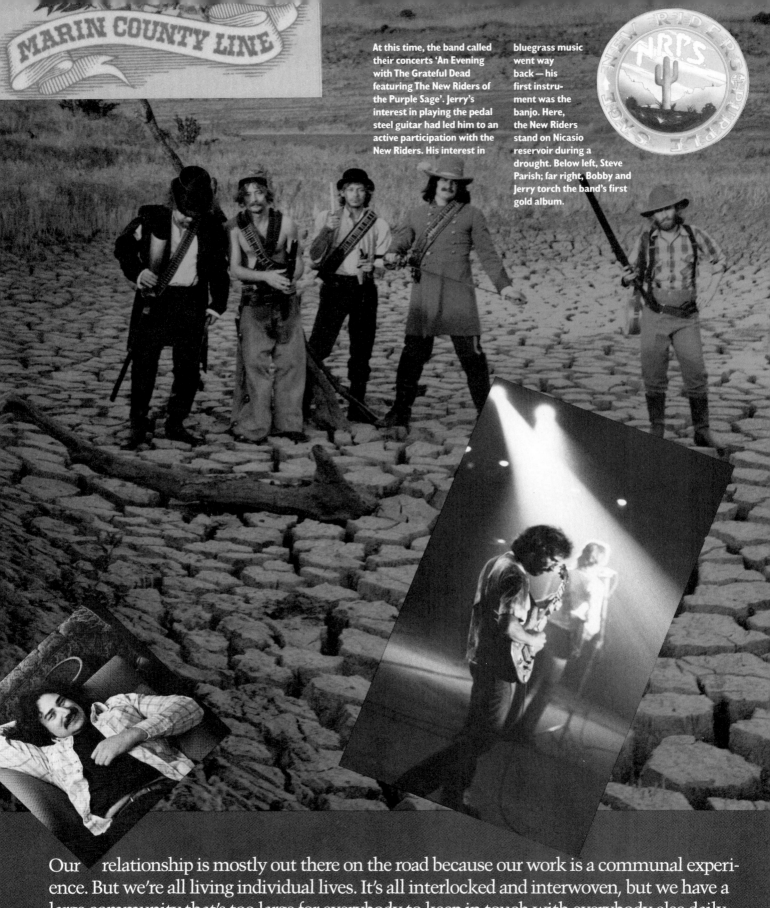

MARIN COUNTY LINE

At this time, the band called their concerts 'An Evening with The Grateful Dead featuring The New Riders of the Purple Sage'. Jerry's interest in playing the pedal steel guitar had led him to an active participation with the New Riders. His interest in bluegrass music went way back — his first instrument was the banjo. Here, the New Riders stand on Nicasio reservoir during a drought. Below left, Steve Parish; far right, Bobby and Jerry torch the band's first gold album.

Our   relationship is mostly out there on the road because our work is a communal experience. But we're all living individual lives. It's all interlocked and interwoven, but we have a large community that's too large for everybody to keep in touch with everybody else daily — so everything is out in little camps. We'll all get together and work out stuff on the road or at meetings.

WARNER BROS. PRESENTS FROM SAN FRANCISCO'S HAIGHT-ASHBURY

Grateful Dead

DIAMOND HEAD PRODUCTIONS PRESENTS

The Grateful Dead

Quicksilver
MESSENGER SERVICE
NEW RIDERS OF THE PURPLE SAGE

CIVIC AUDITORIUM
HONOLULU, HAWAII

7PM FRIDAY & SATURDAY, JUNE 12 &

*Music obviously exerts
a tremendous force on this country.*

"Oh yeah, I guess it does; but that
doesn't mean that I oughta carry around
the responsibility of being the guy that
dispenses our music, you know what
I mean? It's like being the President. I
don't want it. I don't want the fuckin'
job. I mean I liked it when you could just
be a musician; it's like being an artist and
craftsman or something . . . nobody mobs
a cat that makes nice leather clothes or a
guy that does woodwork." — Garcia

7, 8	April	Empire Pool, Wembley
11	April	Newcastle City Hall
14	April	Tivoli Theatre, Copenhagen
16	April	University of Aarhus
17	April	TV: from Tivoli Gardens
21	April	TV show, 'Beat Club': Bremen
24	April	Rheinhalle, Dusseldorf
26	April	Jahrhundert Halle, Frankfurt
29	April	Musikhalle, Hamburg
3, 4	May	Olympia Theatre, Paris
7	May	Bickershaw Festival, near Manchester
10	May	Concertgebouw, Amsterdam
11	May	Rotterdam Civic Hall
13	May	Lille Opera, open air, Lille
16	May	Radio Luxembourg
18	May	Deutsches Museum Halle, Munich
23-26	May	The Lyceum, London

Departure from U.S. was Feast of Fools, 1 April, 1972. Arrival in London was Easter Sunday, 2 April. April saw England, Denmark and Germany. May saw France, England, the Netherlands, Luxembourg, Germany and England.

And the dead were judged by what was written in the books, by what they had done. (Revelation 20.12)

GRATEFUL DEAD

EUROPE '72

It had always been said, "Someday we'll go to Europe, and we'll all go and have some fun." So when the time came, the band was determined to make it a family affair. And it was, and it was fun. And it was work — the logistics of travel and gigging, multi-lingual press conferences, and live recording. Eventually there was some tension between the 'workers' and the 'non-workers', though not the same as that between the Bozos and the Bolos. Hypnocratically speaking, these divisions and disharmonies come clear in the mix and the occasional wrinkle becomes just another fond memory.

We bought some clown masks in Newcastle, England, and wore them on the big-windowed European buses to freak out the natives. The band wore them for a few gigs. Below, Ramrod and Keith.

85

The 43 persons constituting the Grateful Dead's European tour apportioned themselves for the most part between two buses which came to be known as the Bolo bus and the Bozo bus. The Bolo bus had a john in it and its seats faced forward. The Bozo bus had a refrigerator and some of its seats were installed facing back, to accommodate four tables. And to look back. The subtle difference in character and import and atmosphere between the two omnibuses was so profoundly hidden and enigmatic that you could never possibly understand it. The Bozos wore masks, and the Bolos showed their faces. At one time the Bozos staged a raid on the Bolo provisions; at one time the Bolos staged a raid on the Bozo provisions.

One St. Dilbert defected from the Bozos and lived for a season with the Bolos. In view of his subsequent martyrdom, his penitence and reconciliation with the Bozos, it came to be said that he was a true hypnocratic missionary to Bololand. And to look back, it appears evident that Bozo and Bolo knew themselves each the other's raison d'etre. Is hypnocracy not the aspiration to know what it is?
— Choirmaster

Bozos and Bolos

The buses took us around Europe for two months and between gigs dropped us off to explore more obscure byways. Bonnie Parker contemplates the cobblestones. Above Robert Hunter, Christie Bourne. Right, the crew.

"It's a Musical Group," I said, "From America."

In Paris, Le Grand Hotel is a big deal. Across the street is the historic and opulent Opera House and running off in several directions are the city's famous tree-lined avenues. In one corner of the massive structures is the Cafe de la Paix, the sidewalk meeting place in all those romantic Hollywood flicks. Nearby are the shops of Saint Laurent and Dior.

The hotel itself is so big you can get lost in the hallways. Single rooms start at $35 a day and all are equipped with balconies and small automated refrigerators that dispense liquor and beer and champagne at ridiculous prices. There are jewelry shops, restaurants, hair stylists, masseurs, art galleries, theatre booking agencies, shirtmakers. Everyone on the staff speaks fluent English. It is a popular favorite of visiting Americans.

"Are you still expecting the Grateful Dead?" I asked the reservations clerk.

"The Beautiful Dead, monsieur?"

"Uh . . . not quite. The Grateful Dead."

"Oui, monsieur. Would you spell the surname, please."

"D-e-a-d."

"_____."

"It's a musical group," I said, filling in the silence. "From America."

"We are expecting a 37-piece orchestra. . ."

Only the figure was incorrect. The Grateful Dead, half-way through a two-month tour of Europe, numbered not 37 but, depending upon who you talked to, up to 48. There were seven musicians and singers, five managers, five office staff, ten equipment handlers (handling 15,000 pounds of equipment, not counting the 16-track recording system), four drivers and 17 assorted wives, old ladies, babies and friends. In its 100 years of catering to the tourist elite, Le Grand Hotel had never seen anything like it. — Jerry Hopkins (*Rolling Stone*)

Lead guitar & vocals
Jerry Garcia
August 1, 1942, Leo

Rhythm guitar & vocals
Bob Weir
October 16, 1947, Libra

Piano
Keith Godchaux
July 19, 1948, Cancer

Drums
Bill Kreutzmann
May 7, 1946, Taurus

Organ & vocals
Ron (Pigpen) McKernan
September 8, 1945, Virgo

Bass & vocals
Phil Lesh
March 15, 1940, Pisces

Songwriter
Robert Hunter
June 23, 1941, Cancer

Equipment
Rex, Ramrod, Winslow, Heard, Parish

Sound
Alembic Studios — Bob Matthews, Kidd, Raizene
16-track recording by Alembic Studios — Betty, Rosie, Furman

Stage Lights
Candace Brightman, Ben Haller

Light Show
Joe's Lights

Management
Jon McIntire, Alan Trist, Sam Cutler, Rock Scully, David Parker

Office
Annette, Bonnie, Dale

Top row, opposite: Betty Cantor, Gary Harover and Rex Jackson; Rex. Middle, Billy. Jon McIntire and Bob Matthews at the Paris press conference. Bottom row, Jerry at the Eiffel Tower; the elaborate organ in one of the concert halls; Frances Carr and Betty on top of a castle; and Robert Hunter. Above, Bobby contemplates the horticulture; Sonny Heard and Donna Jean.

Grateful Dead:
Kontinuität als Konsequenz

Die Beatles, die Rolling Stones, all die Multi-Millionen-Dollar-Gruppen hätten es, rein finanziell gesehen, mit Leichtigkeit tun können, aber es bedurfte erst einer Gruppe wie dser Grateful Dead, die den für unmöglich gehaltenen Schritdt wagten: sich volkommen auf eigene Füße zu stellen, eine eigene Plattenfirma aufzuziehen. Die Dead, immer schon, ob rein musikalisch oder als Großfamilie, eine Gruppe mit Modellcharakter taten als erste diesen Schritt, und bei sich fast die Waage haltenden Ein — und Ausnahmen (1972: Einnahmen: 1 424 534 Dollar — Ausgaben: etwas über 100 000 Dollar Monatlich) kann noch niemand sagen, wohin die Reise geht. Wie Jerry Garcia einmal sagte: "Das Konzept Grateful Dead ist wie eine irrsinnig schnelle Reise auf Messers Schneide, niemand weiß, zu welcher Seite wir abkippen werden. Bisland sind wir oben geblieben." — Hans-Joachim Krüger *(Sounds)*

The Dead arrived late Monday, not quite fresh from a two-day overland haul from Hamburg, Germany. Yet, when they awoke on Tuesday, just as on the first day in each new country so far, a copy of their own Xeroxed newspaper, the *Bozos & Bolos News*, had been slipped under their hotel room doors.

The Dead began drifting into Room 4600 about noon. This was the Office Suite, where Rosie prepared the *Bozos & Bolos News* and others manned the telephones, while Sam Cutler greased the Dead machine - changing German marks into French francs and handing out daily "road money" ($10 for the ladies, $15 for the gentlemen, for food), dispatching couriers to check an English festival site and see why the latest Dead single wasn't getting the desired promotion, worrying about lights and sound checks and transportation and luggage and laundry.

When the Dead arrived in Paris they'd been on the road exactly a month. They'd played two nights in London's Wembly Pool (to 8,000 each night) and to smaller crowds in Copenhagen and what seemed to be half the cities in West Germany. The Dead had appeared at a festival in England in 1970, had performed at a free concert in France in 1971, but never had they done The Grand Tour, long *de rigueur* for American bands anxious to improve European record sales.

Outside Room 4600 the day was warm, the sky a cloudless blue. In small groups, the Dead set out to see the sights.

"Today is a free day," the *Bozos & Bolos News* had said. "In the evening, Kinney is hosting a dinner for all of us (and a few discreet press people) at a very fine restaurant located in the Bois de Boulogne (the city park, but what a park!). It is called La Grande Cascade, and holy shit, is it ever neat! You might even feel like dressing special for it, although you don't have to.

It's just that kind of place. . ."

At 7 o'clock, Sam Cutler was telling the bus drivers he was sorry, but could they *please* do this one thing. . . yeh, he knew he'd given them the day off, but they could have the next *two days* off, there was just this one dinner. . . and yeh, of course they could join the boys for the Royal Kinney Feast.

By eight the 'labor dispute' had been settled and we were off by bus to Le Grande Cascade, a splendid wedding cake of a room with oval walls of glass that look out onto a lawn of blossoming chestnut trees. The dinner lasted three and a half hours. (As long as a Grateful Dead concert set.) During the serving of liqueurs, which followed the Alsatian Riesling Grande Reserve and the Chateau Meyney "Prieure Des Couleys" 1959 and the Champagne Mumm Cordon Rouge Brut, things got a little loose. That was when the Dead turned the waiters on.

"Here ya are, mon-sore. Do yer head some good."

The waiter stood stiffly in his black tie and tails. Timidly he allowed the pipe to be raised to his lips. He sucked deeply, there was a cheer, he smiled, and the pipe was passed. —Jerry Hopkins (*Rolling Stone*)

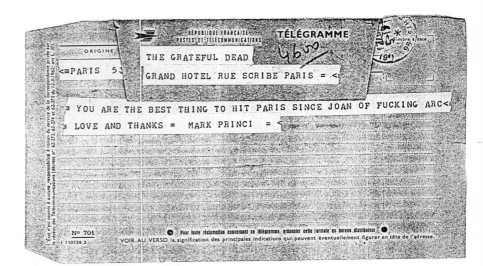

RÉPUBLIQUE FRANÇAISE
POSTES ET TÉLÉCOMMUNICATIONS TÉLÉGRAMME

THE GRATEFUL DEAD
GRAND HOTEL RUE SCRIBE PARIS =

YOU ARE THE BEST THING TO HIT PARIS SINCE JOAN OF FUCKING ARC
LOVE AND THANKS = MARK PRINCI =

Clockwise from left: our two European truck drivers; Ron Wickersham of Alembic; Sparky with Phil; Willy Legate, ancient and future ideologue; opposite, Bill 'Kidd' Candelario on the phones; Pigpen meets Europe.

Hey Now Sports Fans

On our 1974 Europe Tour, Tom Salter was our promoter at the Alexandra Palace in London. He was also a mogul of Carnaby Street. His headquarters for the first stage of the tour. He also had a house in house in Chelsea was our the country, St. John's Jerusalem, in Kent — a British manor house with its own chapel and many acres of park land. He invited us for an afternoon of soccer and baseball. We had a giant buffet lunch and then divided up into two teams, each well mixed with Americans and English. We had brought all our own baseball gear in the road cases, mitts, bats, balls, etc. — hoping for just such an occasion.

From left: Phil, Joe Winslow, Sam Cutler with Rudzo, Pigpen, Bobby at the bat.

The Ten Commandments of Rock and Roll

I   Suck up to the Top Cats.
II   Do not express independent opinions.
III   Do not work for common interest, only factional interests.
IV   If there's nothing to complain about dig up some old gripe.
V   Do not respect property of persons other than band property or persons.
VI   Make devastating judgments on persons and situations without adequate and confound personal, technical and/or creative projects.
VII   Discourage and absent persons for intense criticism.
VIII   Single out that anything you don't understand is trying to fuck with you.
IX   Remember physically and morally and insist that all true brothers
X   Destroy yourself do likewise as an expression of unity. — Robert Hunter

Clockwise from left: Rex; 'Loose Bruce' Baxter; David Parker catching; Bob Matthews hitting; Winslow, Rock and Steve; Heard. Below: The game is underway.

The Band Has No Manager — That's the Art of It

How *do* you get a job on the Grateful Dead staff? Well, a resume probably won't do you much good, and there's no tried and true path to being hired. Initially, it's who you know. If you just happen to have someone on the inside who will vouch for you ("She's cool"), if you appear just when a desperate need opens up, ("Hey, you sitting in the kitchen— c'mere!"), and show a willingness to take on some lengthy mindnumbing task with the hope of better times ahead—you're in! But once you've done that first assignment, JUST TRY to walk away! If you're good at the job, you may get stuck with it until you scream for release. On the other hand, if you persevere and are around when a new and different desperate need opens up—you can probably get *that* assignment.

As for job security, don't worry. Sure, you can get fired (never for the reason you suspect), but if you show up the next morning, there's always the chance no one will know you're supposed to be gone. You can also quit and go away for three years to live a double life—no problem—you'll probably fill a need the very week you get back. And one of the band will see you and say, "Hey, how was your trip? Haven't you been away for a couple of months?"
— Rosie McGee

The office staff in the early '70s on the front porch of the Office in San Rafael: Dale Franklin, David Parker, Jon McIntire, Sam Cutler, Alan Trist, Bonnie Parker, Annette Flowers with friend. Opposite, Pigpen and Veronica.

All the European concerts were recorded on a 16-track machine brought over from America. On the band's return, the process began of selecting tracks for a live album. Eventually, a triple-album was released. The unique thing about Europe '72 was that the stage environment was recreated in the studio for the purpose of overdubbing. This was done by playing each of the tracks back over the same equipment that it was originally played on, arranged in the same configuration, while the overdub was being made; thus generating an approximation of the original ambience. To this day, most people assume it was all recorded live at the same time. —Bob Matthews

"We are not now, an anarchic community.
We're a survival unit. We're into survival. . .emotional, financial, physical and psychic survival.
Perhaps the basis of the Dead's popularity is that their struggle
is the struggle of ordinary people to find pleasure
in their everyday life on this planet."

6. LAND OF THE CORPORATE DEAD

THE GRATEFUL DEAD FAMILY IS ADDI-
TIONALLY A COMPLEX CORPORATE
SETUP, MAYBE HIPPER THAN THE AVER-
AGE, WHICH HAS HARDLY REJECTED
THE BASIC FOUNDATIONS OF THE
CAPITALIST STRUCTURE, BUT SIMPLY
FEELS IT CAN DO THE JOB BETTER AND
MORE COMPLETELY THAN ANYONE
CAN DO IT ONE THE FAMILY'S BEHALF.

RONALD C. McKERNAN
1945 – 1973
PIGPEN WAS
AND IS NOW FOREVER
ONE OF THE
GRATEFUL DEAD

MONEY IS SERIOUS, AND MONEY IS SERIOUS SINCE A GREAT DEAL OF MONEY BEGETS A GREAT DEAL OF GREED, BUT THERE IS NO REASON WHY ALL OF IT HAS TO BE SO STULTIFYINGLY SOLEMN. OUT OF TOWN TOURS, THE DEAD'S BOOKING FIRM. FLY BY NIGHT, A DEAD-INSPIRED TRAVEL AGENCY WHICH ALSO HANDLES 'STRAIGHT' ACCOUNTS. DEAD HEADS, THE FAN CLUB. GARCIA'S COUNTRY GROUP, OLD AND IN THE WAY. SPARKY AND THE ASS BITES FROM HELL, A LEGENDARY MUSICAL GROUP MADE UP OF DEAD ROADIES. "IT IS SERIOUS, WE ARE BUSINESSMEN, AFTER ALL. BUT DON'T TAKE IT SO GODDAMN SERIOUSLY."

Wired for Sound

What is the Dead's PA system like?

It varies from month to month, but basically it looks like this: Each of the four singers has a pair of Sennheiser microphones, mounted one above the other about three inches apart. They're hooked up out of phase, and this has the effect of cancelling out the background noise. Any sound that goes equally into both mikes disappears when the two signals are added together, so that all you have left is the sound of the voice, since the singer is only singing into one of them. This eliminates most of the feedback problem, and it also cleans up the sound a great deal. In addition, there are four or five Electra-Voice RE-15's on the drums. Each of the mike signals, and the output from Keith Godchaux's piano, is then split, with half the signal going to the monitor system and half to the PA.

Why use so much gear?

It's not just for volume. Most groups could get three times the volume out of this equipment that the Dead does, but that would be a distorted sound. Not that the Dead are quiet; the sound pressure on stage has been measured at 127 db, and that's loud. But it's all clean sound, not noise. Most independent sound contractors, whose equipment you'll see at a typical rock concert, are much more concerned with economics than with high fidelity. They charge so much to fill a given sized room with music, and the cheaper they can do it, the more profit they make. The philosophy of the Dead's system, on the other hand, is that since we have the technology to produce a very high quality of sound, we ought to use it. If you care about music, you've got to care about what the audience hears. —Healy

Look over yonder, tell me what
    do you see?
10,000 people looking after me

I may be famous, or I may be
    no one
But in the end all the races I've
    run
Don't make my race run in vain

Seem like there's no tomorrow
Seem like all my yesterdays
    were filled with pain
There's nothing but darkness
    tomorrow
If you gonna do like you say you
    do
If you gonna change your mind
    and walk away

It don't seem to matter much
    anymore
Don't even ask me the time of
    day
'Cause I don't know

Don't make me live in this
    pain no longer
You know I'm gettin' weaker,
    not stronger

My poor heart can't stand
    much more
So why don't you just start
    talkin'
If you're gonna walk out that
    door, start walkin'

I'll get by somehow
Maybe not tomorrow, but
    somehow
I know someday I will find
    someone
Who can ease my pain, like
    you once done
Yes I know, we had a good
    thing going
Seem like a long time
Seem like a long time
Like a long time
Like a long time

Ron McKernan, *January 1973*

'Pigpen' McKernan Dead at 27

He Was a Friend of Mine

weird how it goes
with beginnings
& endings
again
this year
winter's over
end of the loco months
new green
appearing everywhere
sweet lunacy
birds & blue skies
eternal snows
glutting the rivers
brown with earth
whales starting north
with precious
young

& pigpen died

my eyes
tequila-tortured
4 days mourning
lost another fragment
of my own self
knowing
the same brutal
night-sweats & hungers
he knew
the same cold fist
that knocked him down
now clutching furiously
at my gut

shut my eyes
& see him standing
spread-legged
on the stage of the world
the boys prodding him
egging him on
he telling all he ever knew
or cared to know

mike hand cocked like
a boxer's

head thrown back
stale whiskey blues
many-peopled desolations
neon rainy streets
& wilderness of airports
thousands maybe millions
loved him
were fired instantly
into forty-five minutes of
midnight hour

but when he died
he was thin, sick, scared
alone

like i said to laird
i just hope he didn't hurt
too much

weird
all these endings
& beginnings
pale voices of winter
faces, rivers, birds, songs
lunacies
i wonder
how many seasons
new green coming once more
to the land
fresh winds turn
bending the long grasses
we'll hear him sing
again

Robert M. Petersen

Alembic

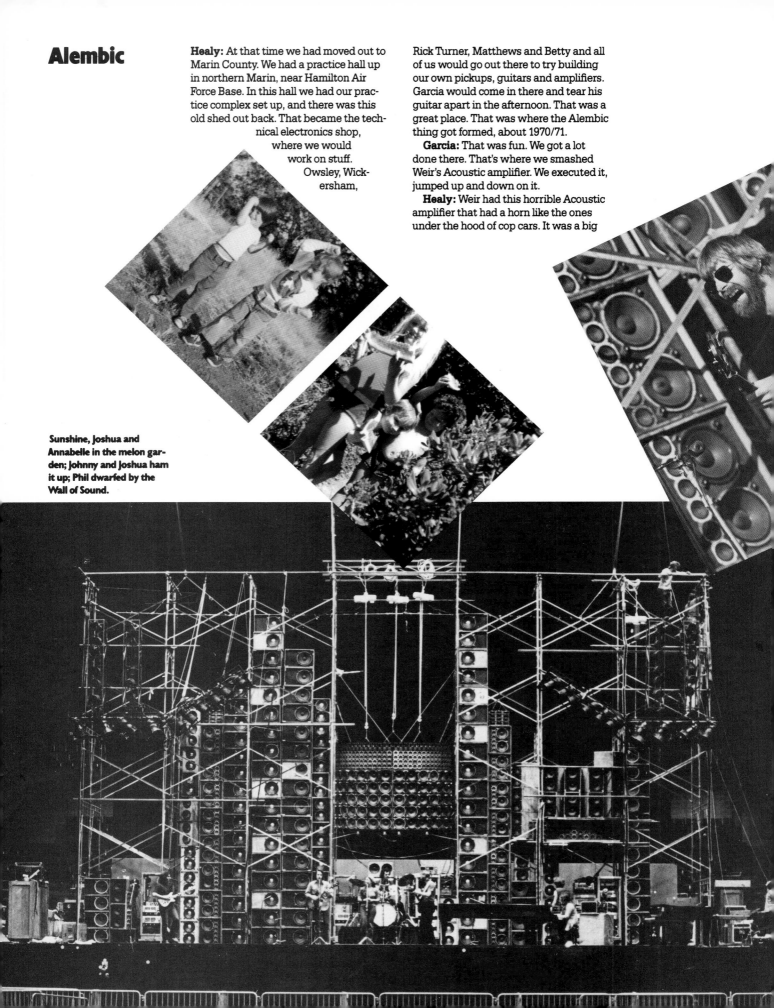

Healy: At that time we had moved out to Marin County. We had a practice hall up in northern Marin, near Hamilton Air Force Base. In this hall we had our practice complex set up, and there was this old shed out back. That became the technical electronics shop, where we would work on stuff. Owsley, Wickersham, Rick Turner, Matthews and Betty and all of us would go out there to try building our own pickups, guitars and amplifiers. Garcia would come in there and tear his guitar apart in the afternoon. That was a great place. That was where the Alembic thing got formed, about 1970/71.

Garcia: That was fun. We got a lot done there. That's where we smashed Weir's Acoustic amplifier. We executed it, jumped up and down on it.

Healy: Weir had this horrible Acoustic amplifier that had a horn like the ones under the hood of cop cars. It was a big

Sunshine, Joshua and Annabelle in the melon garden; Johnny and Joshua ham it up; Phil dwarfed by the Wall of Sound.

cabinet, and it had this horn right at the top, right about ear level. It was just murder, pain every time he'd play it. Your ears would fall right out of your sockets. So finally we couldn't stand it anymore. One day we decided to sacrifice the amplifier, and we destroyed it right on the spot. That was great. We were seeing appendages of that nailed to the wall for months.

Alembic plainly doesn't see itself taking over the instrument or sound system markets. The philosophy is more that of its 'founding godfather' Owsley: 'To raise the level of bossness.' The before and after stage set-ups show the revolutionary rock n' roll Tower of Babel. It requires 26 crewmen, working 14 hours—eight for the 7-foot stage, six for the 30-foot system—to hoist it into place. After such Egyptian toil, to play less than four hours would be criminally unjust to the crew who must tear it all down immediately after the show.

On the first fret of Phil Lesh's new bass two lightning bolts leap out of a block of lapis lazuli. On the third fret a Cosmic Serpent eats its tail; on the fifth, a crescent moon either waxes or wanes, depending on how you look at it; on the seventh, there is an alchemical salamander, and so on, up through the planet Saturn and the infinity sign (equals high A, apparently), all inlaid in mother of pearl. On the back of the neck, the god Osiris, the Judge of the Dead, points his divine flail and impassive eyes toward whoever holds the instrument. — John Christensen *(Louisville Times)*

These drawings of the Dead's sound system by Mary Ann Meyer appeared in Dead Head newsletters in 1973 and 1974. They show the metamorphoses from a conventional PA system (below), arranged on towers to stage left and right, to the Wall of Sound, which moved the voice PA to stage center and integrated instrument and voice sound. Right, Donna Jean.

The Dead's speakers were usually arranged onstage like this: First of all, the monitor speakers for the musicians to hear themselves. That's four stacks of speakers — 12-inchers, five-inchers and a bunch of tweeters — with a total of 4,000 watts power.

Then there were the bass guitar extension speakers on either side of the stage, a vertical stack of a dozen 15-inch woofers on each side. The two guitars and the piano had six or eight 12-inch speakers apiece. Then the quadramped PA system for the singers and the drums; 16 15-inch woofers, 20 12-inch lower-mid-range speakers, 64 four-inch upper-mid-range speakers, and upwards of 40 tweeters.

That's a lot of power. But you know, if you were to listen to it side by side with another system with the same wattage, the kind of system a lot of promoters put up, the other system would probably sound louder. It's because it would be putting a lot of power through low-budget equipment and getting a lot of distortion. Distortion makes sound louder even though the power is the same.

Loud, distorted sound is fatiguing after a while. It's because subconsciously you're trying to disentangle the distortion from the music. And you're straining to make out the words. This is why, for instance, we have two mikes for each singer, one three inches above the other. This system phases out any signal received by both the speakers, which cuts down on background noise and feedback.
—Dan Healy

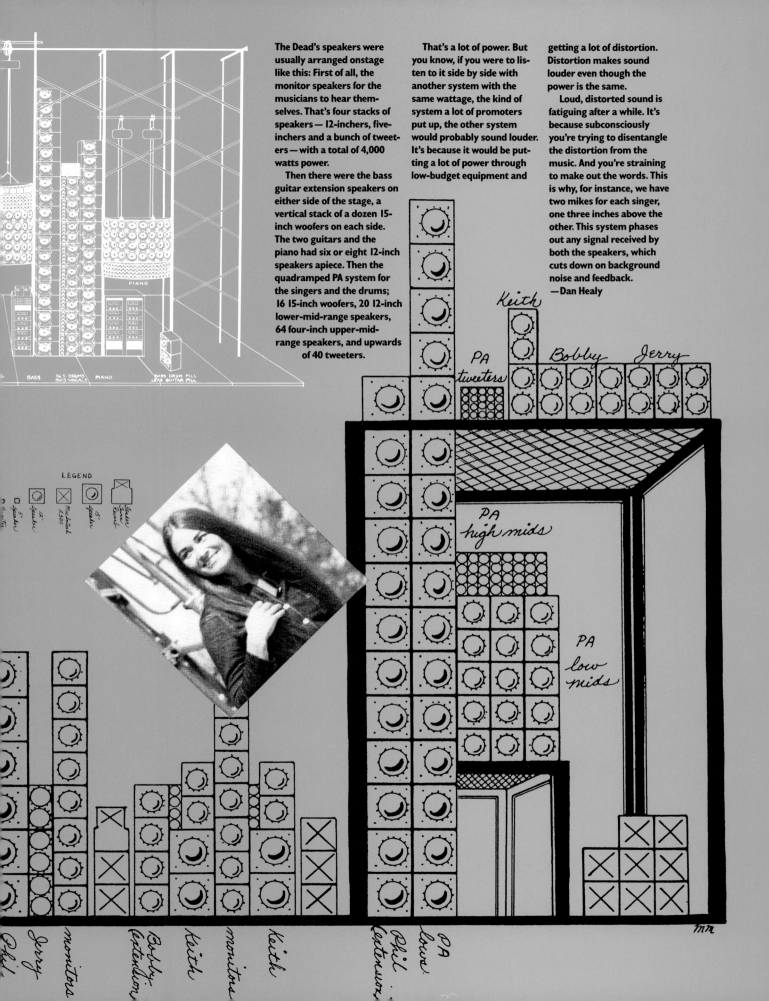

Kumquat Mae

The Grateful Dead has started a family business in Marin, and it is as much a community center as a cash-and-carry enterprise. The wives of the band members and others have opened a store, Kumquat Mae, at 1218 San Anselmo Avenue, San Anselmo.

"We just got tired of sitting around all day while the men rehearsed," said Kristine Healy (her old man is soundman Dan Healy). "In the old days, before the Dead got rich, we were much more involved in things. When the band first went on tour in 1965, we all piled into a van and drove to New York. Now if the guys want to go somewhere, they buy a plane ticket. The whole rock scene has changed. It's big business now. Four years ago we were doing things like the original Carousel Ballroom dances — and the ladies would take turns cooking. I made 40 spice cakes one day. Annie Corson ran the kitchen. She made real gourmet food

and we would serve this to all the people who came.

"So we were all staying home and watching the kids, sewing, playing baseball. Then Susila Kreutzmann said, 'Why don't we have a store?' and we all really dug on the idea. It's a way to extend our family trip to the outside world again."

The store opened last September with ten dresses and not much else as stock. The women weren't sure what it would turn into, so the name Kumquat Mae seemed about right. They got the name from Mountain Girl.

Right now the store carries clothes of all sorts, furniture, jewelry, antiques, paintings, sculptures, and home-blown glass. Over one hundred artists and craftsmen have brought in their work since the store opened.

and craftsmen have brought in their work since the store opened.

Much of the merchandise reflects the store's connection with the Grateful Dead. A table near the cash register is covered with Dead t-shirts and records, and one window is plastered with concert posters. A large photograph of the group is prominently placed on a wall. Joie Gage, who outfits musi-

cians, offers clothes made to order through the store. Birgitta ("no last name, I'm 100 percent Birgitta"), makes intricate crocheted dresses, coats and vests. "It takes me a month to make a dress, and I get attached to them. Here I can get to know the people who will be wearing my stuff, so it's alright." The store also carries fabric dyed by Courtenay, who designed the speaker covers for the band.

"We don't see this place as just a store. We want it to be more a

center of activity. If someone is looking to buy a 1959 Volvo stick-shift, they should stop in and ask us if we have any leads. We couldn't have opened the store without that kind of help ourselves."

Kumquat Mae includes a free store, which has a good selection of clothing, toys, records and furniture. "We have a lot of projects going," said Kristine, "and the more we do, the more we want to do." — Merrill Sanders *(Rolling Stone, 1972)*

Rocking is Not a Chair Thing for Sam & Ethel Tessel

Like whitecaps in a sea of blue, 71-year-old Sam Tessel and his wife, Ethel, stood out as they sat among hundreds of the denim generation who had gathered for the ABC 'In Concert' taping late one March evening at Brooklyn's Bananafish Gardens.

There they were — the oldest hippies in the land, as they freely called themselves — attracting no more attention from the audience than the average teenage rock freaks around them. It was soon apparent that the anachronism was only visual, however, for the Tessels are genuine rock enthusiasts.

"You know, rock isn't something you pick up fast," remarked Mr. Tessel. "It took us a full two years before we got a taste for it." Hastening the trip, no doubt, was their grandson Mickey Hart, well-known rock drummer who has played with the Dead and the Riders.

Hart wrote a song about

Grandma Tessel and the cookies she brings to the groups she visits. The Tessels were often in the audience at the Fillmore East and are known throughout the rock world. Seated a few rows behind Grandma Tessel was a long-haired rock fan wearing a t-shirt which read 'Grandma's Cookies', the name of the popular Hart song.

Mrs. Tessel waited anxiously to see one of her favorites, Marmaduke (John Dawson), the lead vocalist of the Riders. "There he is!" she said. "They're respectable, nice boys, looking for love and attention, and we understand them." She paused and added, "Poor Pigpen, did you know him?" and then remained silent. Ron (Pigpen) McKernan, a founding member of the Grateful Dead, was found dead in his apartment on March 8. He was 27. But her lamentation was soon forgotten as the music of the Riders filled the room, and the 'In Concert' taping went on. — TV Facts

Later, Kumquat Mae went uptown and moved to Mill Valley, and was renamed Rainbow Arbor. Opposite, Birgitta and Kristine and some of the children of the Kumquat childcare center. Left, Jon Goodchild and Virginia Clive-Smith, two designers at work at *Rolling Stone.*

Bottom, some of the band wore Nudie suits for only one gig in 1972, designed and made by Manuel of Nudie's western outfitters in Hollywood. Nudie had made Elvis Presley's famous gold lame suit in the '50s, and by the time Jon McIntire commissioned him to make suits, first for the New Riders and then for the Dead, Nudie had outfitted a generation of Country & Western stars and Hollywood celebrities.

Sparky and the Ass Bites From Hell

"Right now, somehow we've ended up successes. But this ain't exactly what we had in mind, 12,000-seat halls and big bucks. We're trying to redefine. We've played every conceivable venue and it hasn't been it. What can we do that's more fun, more interesting?"

For the tours of small halls, the sound equipment will be cut back from 23 tons to seven, and modularized so that a crew of two or three men could set it up with fork-lifts, mounting it above and behind the band instead of on both sides.

As for what happens to the crew then, the Dead karass will provide. The Dead are setting the quippies up in a company called Hard Truckers to build speaker cabinets with the rock & roll tour in mind, cabinets that won't fall apart like commercial pressboard models.

So the quippies are a company as well as a crew, like so many of the Dead family

back in Marin. If that weren't enough, they're also — are you ready? — a band. The Dead have been coaching them on instruments, and the New Riders' rehearsal hall sometimes pulses with the rock & roll sound of Sparky and the ABs — Sparky and the Ass Bites from Hell. They're Dan on lead guitar, Rex on bass, Steve on drums, Danny on piano and Sparky on harmonica — with Sam Cutler sometimes sitting in on rhythm guitar — and as singer, a friend of theirs, Darlene Di Domenico.

"We're part of the Dead," Steve Parish had said. "You really put your whole heart into the system, right from the vibration of a guitar string out to the back of the hall." — Charles Perry (*Rolling Stone*)

Your basic original quippie was Ramrod. He's from Pendleton, Oregon, and he was with Ken Kesey and the Merry Pranksters. He got his name because he was an expert at loading watermelons, so he got in charge of loading the equipment. He held it together by himself for a long time. Also for a while he was co-manager of the group with Scully.

Ramrod brought in some more guys from Pendleton. One was Rex, Rex Jackson. He does the piano now, and spare parts. You gotta have spare parts for everything on the road.

Actually the original guy from Pendleton was Johnny Hagen, who was the brother of Kesey's buddy Mike Hagen. He came on when the Dead asked for somebody from the Kesey bus. He left during the Lenny Hart period and later came back to be quippie for the New Riders. All the New Riders' crew is from Pendleton.

'Sparky and the Ass Bites from Hell'. From left: Ramrod, rhythm guitar; Steve on drums; Rex on bass; Healy, lead guitar; Sparky, harmonica; Danny on the organ. Kristine, Ambrosia and Dan Healy on the Harley. Far right, Debbie Stern, Thayer Craw.

"But our scene is always healthiest when it's really struggling. Basically our situation is on the borderline of collapse all the time anyway."

Joe Winslow is the other guy from Pendleton. He's in charge of the PA for the left side of the stage — I have the right side. And he's a driver with the 18-foot van that carries the lighting equipment.

Then there's Dan Healy, who mixes and oversees the PA. He's been around a long time and he knows a lot about the system. And Danny Rifkin has been around for a long time. He handles mikes and cables onstage.

Sparky Raizene came to us from Alembic. He's in charge of the monitors, the vocal speakers on the stage for the musicians. Then there's Kidd, he goes way back to the Pendleton period, but he actually grew up in the Mission district of San Francisco. He works in the mixing booth out on the stage floor, a hundred yards from the stage. And there's Larry, and the drivers, Moe and Jimmy, who drive the semi truck.

And there's the lighting crew under Ben Haller; Bill Schwarzbach and Tom Shoesmith. They all come from Fillmore East. And the lights are designed by Candace. She came on with us for the Europe tour. — Steve Parish

Out of Town Tours & Friends

Booking agents for the Grateful Dead and New Riders of the Purple Sage in early 1970. Standing, from left, is first an unknown person, then Julie Haas, Zero Nylin, Rita Gentry-Tarrini, Ken Beals, Wally Haas, Sam Cutler, Jim Preston, Jeff Torrens and Linda Gonzales. Sitting, from left, is the ubiquitous Ramblin' Jack Elliot, Bruce Baxter, Gail Hellund, Frances Carr, Jackrabbit Forchette and, last but not least, 'Mustang' Sally Dryden.

ACE

Weir decided the time was right to go ahead and record his own album, *Ace*. The first step towards the making of the album was for Weir, who is admittedly something less than a prolific composer, a retirement to the obscure Wyoming cabin of a close friend, John Barlow. "Nobody was around," insists Weir, "except a ghost, and I didn't care."

"Did you get any songs from him?" asks wide-eyed Warner/Reprise press representative Garry George.

"Not from the ghost, no, but from Barlow, yeah. No, the ghost and I worked something out," says Bob quite seriously. "I don't know if you need to print this, but anyway, I learned a real simple, temporary exorcism ceremony . . . which I had to perform twice a day in order to keep him out for twenty-four hours. Once around sunrise, and once around sunset.

"He'd been scaring my dog, and dogs don't like ghosts, so the dog had shit all over the place. The ghost tried to get into *my* head once around the time I was waking up, and that was a real touchy scene. I don't know if you've ever had an experience with a ghost, but it's awful, 'cause ghosts aren't the best things to deal with. They try to get into people, and it's not very hard to get them to leave a man alone, but they scare the shit out of animals. Particularly dogs, and so my dog got the shit scared out of him . . .literally. I was up in the middle of the night cleaning that up, with the dog completely out of his mind berserk. The first time the ghost did that, I tried to reason with him saying, 'Now listen, you don't go weirding out my dog and I won't do anything, but if you do it again,

I'll have to take steps.' Well, he did it another night and got me weird another night to boot. So, I started throwing him out at night by using that exorcism ceremony. That worked.

"Then I felt that he might be able to see his way towards being a little more civil, so I started letting him stay in during the day. He lived in the water heater and used to make all kinds of noises . . . he would hoot and screech and all that kind of stuff. He had learned to operate the water heater over the years so that he could make it sound any way he wished. I would sit in the living room playing my songs, and as long as I was playing my songs he'd be quiet, but when I stopped, he'd start working the heater again. It was really strange." — *(Rock 6/30/73)*

Opposite: Courtenay opening the mandala; Flying Amini.

Opening the Mandala

I had a headshop in Greenwich Village when I first came to America in 1968. I sold tie-dyed satin scarves. In 1970 I came down from the mountain to the Rukka-Rukka ranch, where Weir was living, and Frankie opened the door and said, "Ah, the stranger from without. Come on in." Sonny Heard said "You can do our speaker fronts" and Jackson said "I'll arrange it." I'd been reading about mandalas, levels of consciousness

and the deities, all the rays of creation; and I'd invented a folding technique. So I got a large piece of cloth, put it all together and came up with my first tie-dyed mandala. Danny Rifkin and Roger Lewis happened to come by when I was opening it up. I didn't know what I was going to get. I was tripping at the time. So were they. As we opened up the mandala we began sing-ing the Halleluja chorus in three-part harmony and it was just "Oh, my God. . ."

— Courtenay Pollock

Gathering Together

Robert Hunter, chief lyricist of the Grateful Dead and president of Ice Nine Publishing Company, which publishes the Grateful Dead's songs, chose the name from Kurt Vonnegut's novel, 'Cat's Cradle'. The story revolves around the appearance in the world of a new form of water, Ice 9, which once released from its vial would crystallize all forms of water on the planet to permanent ice! Perhaps in a related metaphor, Ice Nine's logo is the I Ching hexagram for 'Gathering Together' changing to 'Holding Together'.

Ice Niners: Alan Trist, Annette Flowers; the cover of *Rolling Thunder*, Mickey Hart's first solo album, 1972, designed by Alton Kelley; and above, the cover of the first Ice Nine Songbook by Stanley Mouse.

The Grateful Dead Makes a Real Good Hamburger

In the realms of hip legend, astral pleasures, rock and roll and business as usual, the Grateful Dead stand higher than any other veteran American rock band.

They began in San Francisco forming into an electric rock blues/country band at a time when America was waking up to the reality of the transition from beatnik style to 'hippie' consciousness. The Grateful Dead were the prime movers of that transition in the musical field. Alerted to the potential of the 'new rock' by bands like the Beatles and the Rolling Stones, they took the evolution of that form several steps further by opening up traditional structures and standard 'tight'

rock forms with extended improvisation unconnected to jazz, and an acute sense of what it took to move people deeply.

They were, in fact, exploring virgin territory and they were monumentally successful. Today you can ask any reasonably enlightened follower of rock about his or her first experience of a Dead concert and receive a reply

couched not in terms of how good it was to boogie, but how staggering it was to come suddenly upon an experience of such great sensual power. The Dead had learned how to conceive and perform a music which often induced something closely akin to the psychedelic experience; they were and are experts in the art and science of showing people another world, or a temporary altering (raising) of world consciousness.

It sounds pseudo-mystical pretentious

perhaps, but the fact is that it happens, and it is intentional. The consciousness-altering power of a very good rock band is one considerable part of what rock means; what sets the Dead apart from other members of the rock elite (an obvious example being the Rolling Stones) is that they have always used their power,

carefully, to spread positive energy.

Their sound is unique, completely unmistakable, something soft and lustrous even at its most hard-driving moments. It owes a great deal to years of electronic fiddling which have culminated in the most polished, custom-fitted and dynamically 'clear' sound system in current use. They are perhaps the most technically proficient and musically integrated band in the world, and it shows in their frequent concerts and on *Europe '72.* —Patrick Cann *(The New York Times, 3/11/73)*

I prefer playing live for sure, just as an experience, it's definitely richer, mainly because it's continuous. I mean, you play a note and you can see where it goes, you can see what the response is, what the reaction is. It's reciprocal. In a studio, you can also do that, but you're doing it with the other musicians. When you have a group of musicians in a studio, it's not unlike having a room full of plumbers. I mean, what we might be interested in as musicians and what we're doing might not relate to anybody else. That's the difference. – Garcia

The New Light for a Fast Fading World

St. Dilbert The Obscure (2000 — ?)

It was on the road — Highway 1 between the rural West Marin County towns of Bolinas and Olema — in March 1972 that Rakow had flashed on a whole independent record system that could work for the Dead. After six years with Warner Bros., working with guys in suits who never quite understood them, the Dead had been considering declaring independence, and

had asked Rakow to explore the possibilities. A slick financial appliance around the Dead's funky household (he had come to the band in the mid-'60s by way of Wall Street, where he'd been a whiz-kid arbitrageur), Rakow proceeded to investigate, researching the financial statements, structure and distribution systems of the major record companies. On the Fourth of July 1972, Rakow's vision became a 93-page report known as the 'So What Papers' (probably derived from that awful cosmic revelation, 'So What?'). The Dead didn't go for Rakow's initial proposal as submitted. Maybe some of the more conservative guys in the organization didn't like his idea of the Dead's records being distributed by Good Humor trucks. (Actually, it sounded pretty good to me — 'Here comes Uncle John's van, buy his vinyl sides.')

The Grateful Dead had firmly decided to have their own record label. In April of '73 we put together a record company crew that would be administered by Rakow as president and general manager, with me responsible for recording production coordination and national promotion, Andy Leonard handling manufacturing and advertising, Greg Nelson covering distribution and sales, and Joshua Bardo doing national radio promotion. After taking over the Dead's old office, which looked like it had been transplanted from Haight-Ashbury to San Rafael, the new Grateful Dead Records office staff was rounded out with Jeanne Jones as accountant and Barbara Whitestone and Carol Miller managing the office.

Despite their reputation as a group of guys who liked to take risks, Rakow and the Dead decided that rather than jeopardize Grateful Dead Records, which was co-owned by all the voting members of the organization, they would create a second label to handle the more financially dubious solo projects members of the Dead were

interested in pursuing. Thus was born Round Records.

Rakow financed the start-up of Grateful Dead Records and Round Records by selling foreign manufacturing and distribution rights to Atlantic Records for $300,000. He also set up a financial umbrella in which the First National Bank of Boston would approve and underwrite the 18 independent record distributors we had chosen to use throughout the country.

Returning home after a summer of flexing their musical muscles, the Dead had a bunch of juicy new tunes ripe for their first offering on their own new label. And in August of '73 the band, family and crew moved into the Record Plant studios in Sausalito to start work on *Wake of the Flood*. Around this same time Robert Hunter was at Mickey's barn recording tracks on our first Round Records release, *Tales of the Great Rum Runners*.

From the beginning we were determined to make our albums of the highest quality vinyl and apply our own personal quality control in all the phases of record production. We commissioned one of my favorite artists, Rick Griffin, to do both initial releases of Grateful Dead and Round Records — *Wake* and *Rum Runners*. Rick knew from the biblical story of The Flood (Genesis, chapter 8, verse 7) that Noah had sent forth a

raven. But the raven he rendered on the back cover looked more like a crow to Rakow: He knew that either we'd make a good show of our first independent releases or we'd be eating that silly bird.— Steve Brown *(The Golden Road)*

On these pages, the band's first two releases on Grateful Dead Records, and the first on Round Records, Hunter's *Tales of the Great Rum Runners.* Opposite, Ron Rakow; and left, Pete Morino of Warner Brothers; Steve and Ramrod. Rick Griffin also designed for the Dead, producing this cover for Hunter, and *Wake of the Flood.*

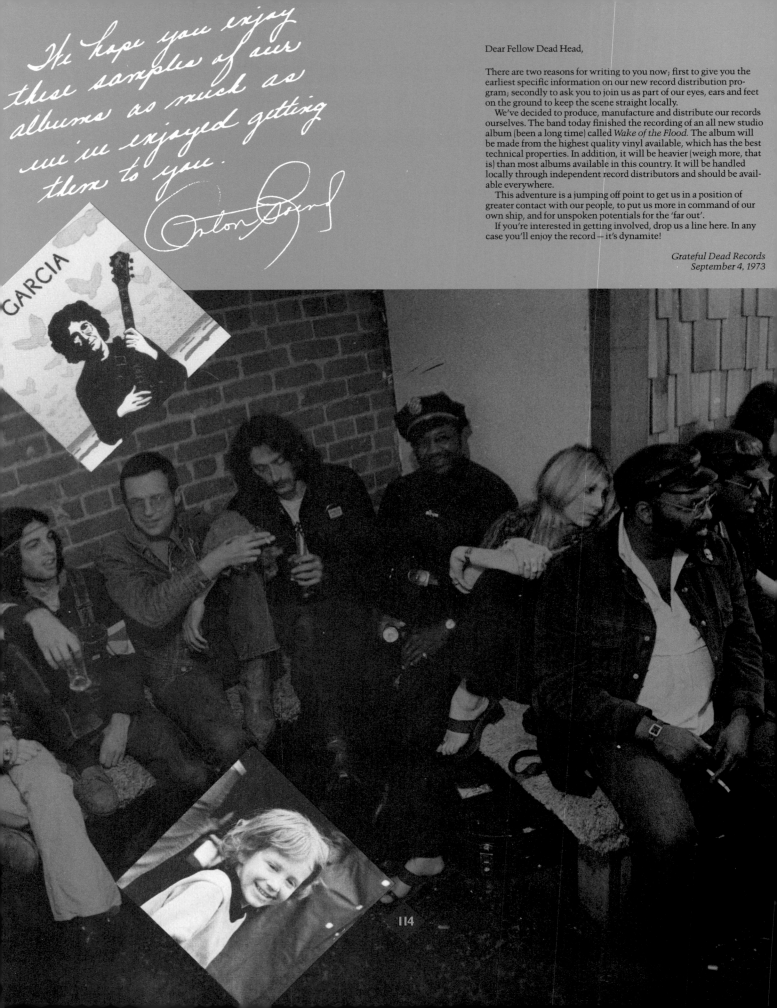

We hope you enjoy these samples of our albums as much as we've enjoyed getting them to you.

Jerry Garcia

Dear Fellow Dead Head,

There are two reasons for writing to you now; first to give you the earliest specific information on our new record distribution program; secondly to ask you to join us as part of our eyes, ears and feet on the ground to keep the scene straight locally.

We've decided to produce, manufacture and distribute our records ourselves. The band today finished the recording of an all new studio album (been a long time) called *Wake of the Flood*. The album will be made from the highest quality vinyl available, which has the best technical properties. In addition, it will be heavier (weigh more, that is) than most albums available in this country. It will be handled locally through independent record distributors and should be available everywhere.

This adventure is a jumping off point to get us in a position of greater contact with our people, to put us more in command of our own ship, and for unspoken potentials for the 'far out'.

If you're interested in getting involved, drop us a line here. In any case you'll enjoy the record — it's dynamite!

Grateful Dead Records
September 4, 1973

114

Dead Awaken: New Albums, Label, Tour

The Dead's audience sees more than a clump of people with musical instruments when it watches the band onstage, for the group itself is a front — the public showpiece for the Grateful Dead Family, which is a way of looking at things, a way of living, a way of enjoying music and the other lively arts, a studied nonchalance that bypasses a great deal of potential heaviness with an it's-really-not-that-important-when-you-consider-the-history-of-the-human-race air. "There never was a Grateful Dead viewpoint," says Jerry Garcia. "There just seemed to be, but there wasn't. Nobody has ever understood our trip at all, except us. We just keep on playing."

Backstage at the Keystone, Berkeley, during the recording of *Live at Keystone* with Merl Saunders and Jerry Garcia, July 1973. Inset, Joshua Rakow, Annabelle Garcia. Above, Watkins Glen.

115

Where Are These Men's Mustaches?

Around this time a couple of gigs occurred at the Palace of Fine Arts in San Francisco. One was a Seastones show with Phil Lesh and Ned Lagin's electronic music. Another was a benefit for Sat San Tokh's ashram with Jerry and Mickey. They hadn't seen each other for about a year. Mickey got up and decided to dress in all white and completely shave off his beard. Garcia, unknown to Mickey, had gotten up, decided to dress in all black and shave his face. They met at the photo session and were totally blown away. — Jerilyn

There were two litters of puppies at the ranch — a total of 22 puppies. The ranchers had not been keeping up their fences and the puppies started wandering off the property. The sheriff called one day and told Johnny D to meet him at the front gate. There was the Humane Society truck backed up to the gate — filled with all our dogs, and a few others — dead. The sheriff said he had to shoot them all — but in fact all the ranchers had ambushed the dogs down at the creek. The story made the wire services, and justice was served at the dinner table.

Miss Rhonda on her Palamino. Acacia, Nicki, Rock and Sage Scully in the pony cart on their ranch at Forestville. Opposite from top, Glups, Crash, John 'Marmaduke' Dawson of the New Riders, and Annette with Che. Dave Torbert, bass player with the New Riders. The most popular tour poster from Germany.

Jerry Garcia in concert **Mickey Hart**

Auditorium · Wednesday also The Mantric Sun Band and

A Benefit Performance for 3HO NORTH

Grateful Dead
14.Sept.
Sept.'74
Uhr
Einziges
Konzert
in Deutschland
Only Concert
in Germany

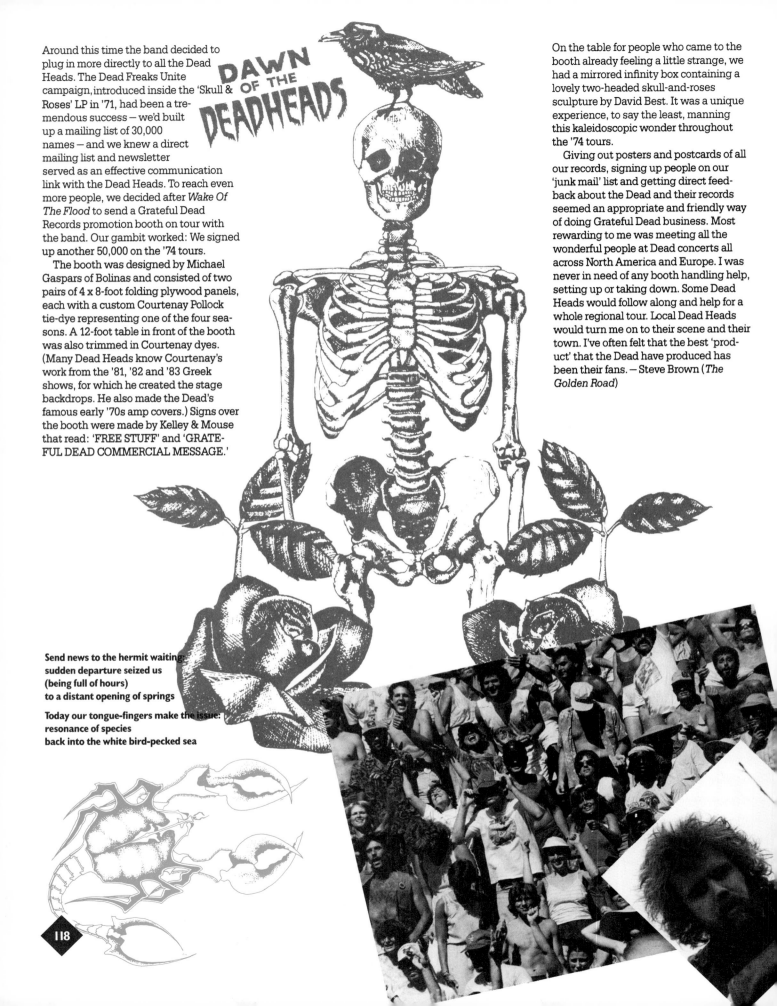

Around this time the band decided to plug in more directly to all the Dead Heads. The Dead Freaks Unite campaign, introduced inside the 'Skull & Roses' LP in '71, had been a tremendous success — we'd built up a mailing list of 30,000 names — and we knew a direct mailing list and newsletter served as an effective communication link with the Dead Heads. To reach even more people, we decided after *Wake Of The Flood* to send a Grateful Dead Records promotion booth on tour with the band. Our gambit worked: We signed up another 50,000 on the '74 tours.

The booth was designed by Michael Gaspars of Bolinas and consisted of two pairs of 4 x 8-foot folding plywood panels, each with a custom Courtenay Pollock tie-dye representing one of the four seasons. A 12-foot table in front of the booth was also trimmed in Courtenay dyes. (Many Dead Heads know Courtenay's work from the '81, '82 and '83 Greek shows, for which he created the stage backdrops. He also made the Dead's famous early '70s amp covers.) Signs over the booth were made by Kelley & Mouse that read: 'FREE STUFF' and 'GRATEFUL DEAD COMMERCIAL MESSAGE.'

DAWN OF THE DEADHEADS

On the table for people who came to the booth already feeling a little strange, we had a mirrored infinity box containing a lovely two-headed skull-and-roses sculpture by David Best. It was a unique experience, to say the least, manning this kaleidoscopic wonder throughout the '74 tours.

Giving out posters and postcards of all our records, signing up people on our 'junk mail' list and getting direct feedback about the Dead and their records seemed an appropriate and friendly way of doing Grateful Dead business. Most rewarding to me was meeting all the wonderful people at Dead concerts all across North America and Europe. I was never in need of any booth handling help, setting up or taking down. Some Dead Heads would follow along and help for a whole regional tour. Local Dead Heads would turn me on to their scene and their town. I've often felt that the best 'product' that the Dead have produced has been their fans. — Steve Brown (*The Golden Road*)

Send news to the hermit waiting:
sudden departure seized us
(being full of hours)
to a distant opening of springs

Today our tongue-fingers make the issue:
resonance of species
back into the white bird-pecked sea

Urobouros is Hungry

We're growing! — some 30 people now on the payroll. We're affiliated with Alembic in San Francisco on design, research and development of equipment and recording. Our rehearsal hall in San Rafael is the center of acoustic inquiry and equipment maintenance/development. Our office here manages, controls finance, accounting, insurance and the like, and Ice Nine Publishing Company (copyrights, licenses, songbooks) and Dead Heads. Out of Town booking agency and Fly By Night travel agency, two outgrowths of our scene, are in the building.

By the nature of the beast, the energies of over a hundred directly enter our endeavor. Urobouros turns his circles. St. Dilbert is a bombast. Let's surface the moon with an electrostatic spherical tidal spatial counter-entropic sound system. Energy spoken here.

On earth, our overhead expense is $100,000 a month. In 1972 we grossed $1,424,543.

Seventy percent of this income came from gigs, and 30% from record royalties. Gigs offer the only means to earn more money when it is needed to maintain our operation in all its particulars. We cannot sell more records at will, but we can go on the road, within the limits of energy: so that we must play larger halls, with more equipment, and a bigger organization, requiring more gigs.

St. Dilbert calls this fellow 'Urobouros', and he's a good trip, but he has a mind of his own . . .

We like a variety of concert situations. Ambiance comes in different sizes. We like a small hall, and so do you, and an outdoor gig in the sun, and a large hall when it can be made to sound good (few halls over 6,000 capacity aren't sports arenas with novel acoustic and environmental puzzles).

Urobouros is hungry. How do we control him? We've planned for a year to form our own record manufacturing and distributing company so as to be more on top of the marketing process, package and promote our product in an honest and human manner, and possibly stand aside from the retail list-price inflation spiral while retaining more of the net dollar, (keep a tight ship). If the records cover a larger share of the overhead, then the concert situation becomes more flexible. This is the working future-possible, in the direction we see to go, now. We want this freedom to achieve gig variety, to experiment. We are musicians. What else might we do? Your mail is an energy input, 400 letters a week that we tack on bulletin boards and read aloud and pass back and forth. This flow enters the common pool of plans and theories, ideas and speculations and fantasies and hopes and fears and future and galaxies and stuff. To hear from you furthers.

Dead Heads Newsletter–1973.

Larger Halls — More Equipment — Bigger Organization — Larger Overhead — More Gigs

Equipment 18% — Purchase 14% — Maintenance 4% — Support — Admin 27% — Overhead Distribution 2% 2% — Office 17% — 13% — Tax 8% — Operating 3% Profit — Agency 5% — Road Expense — Road 22% 27%

Year	Equipment Weight	Transport
1965	800 lbs	Bill's station wagon
1967	1,300 lbs	Barney's van
1968	6,000 lbs	Metro van
1970	10,000 lbs	18 ft truck
1973	30,000 lbs	40 ft semi

"Having been born into a world of rather curious values, values apparently unrelated to the direct experience of human truths, the Bozos and Bolos hypnocratically pursue a direction of self-determination in as many ways as interestingly possible, believing that this course will best aid a continuation of integrity and meaning in their music and other life spaces. This has meant that their business activity seeks to be in control of as many areas as become possible, employing their own people to do the work that would otherwise be farmed out to straight business. Thus there is the possibility that the message in the music can be reflected in the manner and purpose of conducting the business necessary to get the music heard."
—St. Dilbert, Bombast

Inset from left, David Nelson of the New Riders, Rex Jackson, Sparky and Melissa.

The Dead After a Decade

For the estimated 50,000 people who flocked to Golden Gate Park's Lindley Meadows on September 28th (including a smattering who flew in from as far away as New York), it was a nearly perfect flashback to the '60s, a Sunday afternoon with the latest incarnations of the Jefferson Airplane and — surprise — the good ol' Grateful Dead in their first public performance in nearly a year.

The concert also coincided with the beginning of the Dead's second decade as a musical entity, business enterprise and, significantly, near legendary social institution. The Dead's extended family, perhaps 200 in all, has survived a peculiar saga. Somehow the 'karass' has managed to play out most of the variations on the themes of growth, change, jealousy, loyalty and loves won and lost, and still emerge with its collective sense of humor and vision intact.

"It feels pretty purposeful," said Weir, "much more so than our first ten. Before, if we ever had any guiding philosophy, it was just to go with it. Instead of making decisions, we just let it happen. And what it culminated in, professionally, was hugeness — the Oakland Coliseum-sized places and all those monster rooms. So the first real decision we made was not to go on with it 'cuz it isn't really what we want. We'll still gig together in the future as the occasions arise, depending on how things strike us — as long as we don't have to willfully step back into our old roles. Now that we've all formed little bands, each of us can individually start that climb again. Because really, there's no place else to go from here if you're a musician. But at least we're going back to the comfortable part of it, little theaters and clubs that are on a human level."
— John Grissim (*Rolling Stone*, 11/2/75)

Excellent Bluegrass

There is an unfortunate tendency for names or labels such as 'bluegrass' or 'country' to turn off potential listeners who might well enjoy the music if only they had a shot at hearing it without any preconceptions.

Not that I am a particularly avid fan of bluegrass, for instance, but there is an album which has just become available which I would hate to see ignored by anyone. It's that good. It's *Old and In the Way*. The title of the album is also the title of one of the songs on it and the name of the group which recorded it. *Old and In the Way* played around here in 1973 and 1974 a number of times and achieved considerable attention not only for its excellence, but for the fact that Jerry Garcia, normally the lead guitarist with the Grateful Dead, played banjo with this group, an instrument he had not until then been noted for. This album, in addition to Garcia's presence on banjo and occasional vocal, also offers Vassar Clements, a most extraordinary fiddler from Appalachia, home of that music which John Cohen illustrated so dramatically and lovingly in that rarely seen but beautiful film, The

High Lonesome Sound. Along with Garcia and Clements are David Grisman, who sings and plays mandolin, and Peter Rowan (of the Rowan Brothers) who plays guitar and sings, and bassist John Kahn.

The album was recorded in the autumn of 1973 at The Boarding House by Owsley Stanley and Vickie Babcock, edited by Grisman and Stanley, and mixed and mastered by Stanley. The mixing was done live at the time of the recording itself, an unusual practice.

I go into all of this detail because the album is not only an utterly delightful series of musical performances, but also one of the very best recordings I have heard in a long time. I have played it on a number of different rigs, mono, stereo and quad and it comes through as a definition of good recording each and every time.

The technique of using eight microphones and mixing live onto a Nagra stereo tape recorder worked like a miracle. Engineers ought to study this one and musicians, too, as well as listeners. If there is such a category in the nation's record business annual awards it ought to win as engineering triumph of the year.

Despite the primitive implications of music such as this, which is generally classified as folk music, this is really very sophisticated music, depending for its success on the same kind of instrumental virtuosity as the best jazz. John Kahn's bass playing, for instance, is delightful to listen to and that brings up something else. It is possible to hear this album many times, at each playing focusing on one or the other of the instruments. They always do the job, they're covered, which is today's professional pleasure which few bands can do, as witness the J. Geils Band on the one hand & C

Chesley Milikin and Nicki Scully and, bottom, Ambrosia's birthday party at Boyd Park in San Rafael. Kristine always gave the best parties for the kids. Right, Jerry and Sunshine tailgating. The popular Bluegrass album, *Old & In The Way,* has become the biggest selling bluegrass album to date.

Is The Dead Going to Die?

We falter and fall away, nothing holds. Political action is impossible. All we are left with are our arts. I propose we turn our tools away from the service of all but their muses. Great deeds are needed. It is time to retreat. It is time to advance backwards. No longer are there any choices. What a relief.

People tire and you can only do one thing so long. The band is tired of touring for ten years and needs to take a year and go fishing, because they really do. They all have projects they wish to pursue and new material to write. Anyone who does not want them to do it is wanting them to drop dead on the spot through a collective weariness which only a total change can combat.

We mean to keep an office together during the vacation, but revenues will be slight. The Dead Heads list has been turned over to Grateful Dead Records to maintain and to let you know what they're doing — so please be patient if it takes a while to get a response of some sort.

Each of the departments of the Grateful Dead must now become self supporting in order for the organism as a whole to remain healthy. There is a scheme to keep the overall structure intact so that there is something to take care of the details as the show goes back on the road. It is the fine response of Dead Heads over the years which leads us to conclude that there is something worth maintaining and that is what we're up to. — Robert Hunter *(Dead Heads Newsletter)*

Though the Dead's collective profile has been less visible this year, there's been no letup in activity; Jerry Garcia is rehearsing with an as-yet-unnamed group that includes bassist John Kahn, drummer Ronnie Tutt and keyboard ace Nicky Hopkins. Bill Kreutzmann has joined Keith and Donna Godchaux's jazz and R&B band (currently called Keith & Donna), though manager Jon McIntire is tempted to rename it the Godchaux-Kreutzmann Band "just to make it more interesting." Phil Lesh has teamed up with MIT-trained composer Ned Lagin to create Seastones, a venture into 'bio-electric music' (one Round Records LP out so far); Bob Weir has been gigging for several months around California with Kingfish, a rock and blues band featuring ex-New Riders bassist David Torbert, and will soon enter the studio to begin a solo album. And finally, there's Mickey Hart's innovative Diga Rhythm Band, a high-energy percussion ensemble showcasing tabla master Zakir Hassain. —John Grissim (Rolling Stone, 11/6/75)

122

If there is any one objective that emerges from the welter of purposeful activity — of documentaries, distribution deals, solo albums and new bands — it's the Grateful Dead's eventual liberation from the economic necessity of always having to be the Grateful Dead. "I think we've got a chance," Weir remarked, "of establishing ourselves to the point where the Grateful Dead will be self-sustaining for as long as we're into it. We'll be able to keep going and to fulfill ourselves as a group. Maybe by the time we're old and gray people will still be listening to us."

For his part, 'Cash Flow' Ron Rakow is not about to wait that long: "With everyone out making a living on his own, the Dead will achieve the status of being patronized by its members. And that's when I think they're gonna do their farthest out stuff yet. We're already working on some killer ideas — flying ballrooms and holographic reproduction. Really out there. We're even looking at a concert structure that Buckminster Fuller is doing some design work on right now. I can't give you details but it's gonna be sensational, really transcendental." — John Grissim (*Rolling Stone*, 11/6/75)

Since the Winterland finale, a full-time staff of four editors has worked in the Mill Valley film house of the Dead's production company, appropriately named Round Reels. Thus far 125 hours of raw footage have been meticulously screened, matched to a soundtrack and cataloged.

"We used as many as nine crews, each with a cameraman, an assistant cameraman, a sound man, a loader and a runner," Rakow said. "Together with supervisory personnel we hired 46 people on 11 days notice. But by the third night we were all a unit. We loved working together. And good cinematographers like Al Maysle and Kevin Keating. And Don Lenzer — he shot a lot of *Janis* and *Woodstock*. I knew it was gonna be good when Lenzer went up to Phil as he was tuning his bass. Somehow Don's camera motor registered on the amp through Phil's bass pickup, and the two guys started this raving, screaming dance together. Phil's personality, which is incredibly bizarre, came tumbling out at this joyous expression of new weirdness." (*Rolling Stone*, 11/6/75)

Now it all appears to have been a mixture of science fiction, hallucination, baloney and, yes, some reality. But after taking several financial whippings, getting ripped off and writing off most of their dreams to experience, they show little sign of abandoning their pursuit of entropy. In the face of their overwhelming inability to pull off anything as planned, the Dead just go on jousting with mindmills. — Greg Barrette (*Rock & Roll News*, 4/77)

123

Opposite, three solo albums on Round Records; Phil Lesh, who recorded Seastones with Ned Lagin. Above, Calico of the Hog Farm with Joey; Keith; Donna and Zion.

In 1973, the band split from Warner Brothers and started their own record company. It was the first time any group had attempted to control all aspects of its business — recording, cutting, pressing, distribution and promotion. By 1975, a combination of financial over-extension and poor record sales resulted in its failure, necessitating a bail-out by United Artists. The little autonomy the label retained was lost in 1976, when the Dead signed with Arista. Round/Grateful Dead Records now exists as a label only.

The Holographic Music Pyramid

One of the best hoaxes I've been proud to be associated with. Based on theoretical concepts of that time, the idea of encoding Dead music on a one-inch pyramid to be read by an optical fiber seemed to be plausible. In one of our junk mailing newsletters, we stated that the Dead would be attempting to come out with this new musical reproduction form, and actual scientists in the holographic field became more than curious about our heretofore unheard of efforts in this new medium. Of course Rakow had made a one-inch model of this wondrous little pyramid, which he didn't hesitate to grandly produce at the slightest provocation. Just about the time when we thought our cheeks could no longer stand the pressure from our tongues, some Dead Head scientist in New York working with holography reported back to us that he had made preliminary progress on a similar device and wished to speak with our researchers. We turned him over to Uncle Anton for further enlightenment. — Steve Brown (The Golden Road)

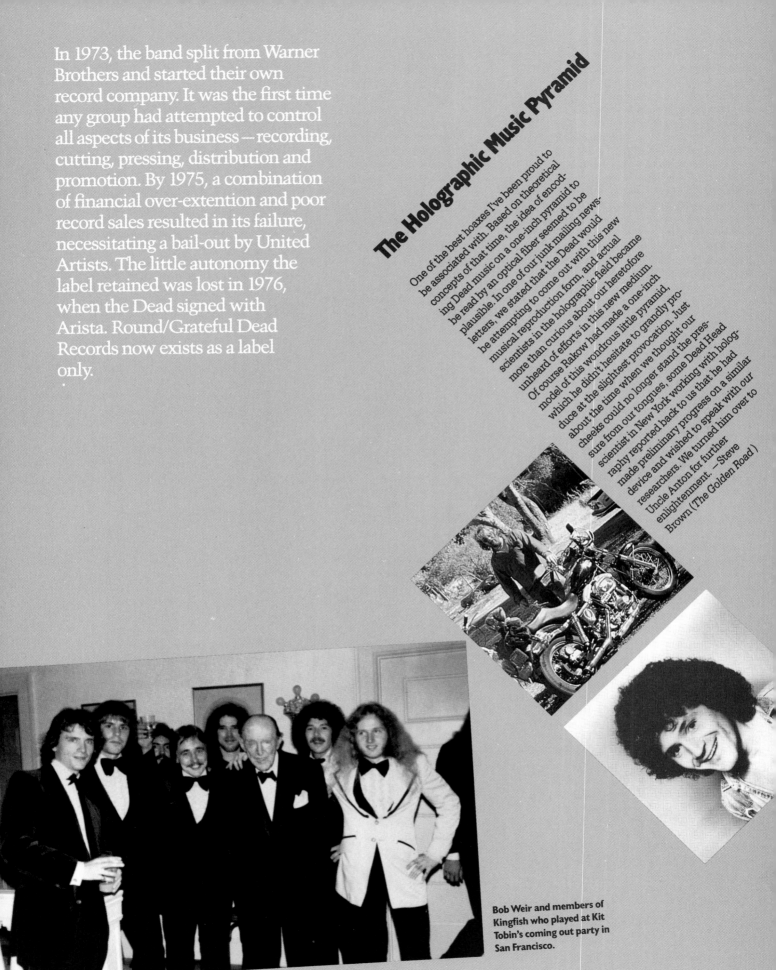

Bob Weir and members of Kingfish who played at Kit Tobin's coming out party in San Francisco.

"To get really high is to forget yourself. And to forget yourself is to see everything else. And to see everything else is to become an understanding molecule in evolution, a conscious tool of the universe. And I think every human being should be a conscious tool of the universe. That's why I think it's important to get high. I'm not talking about unconscious or zonked out. I'm talking about being fully conscious."

— Garcia

In January of '75 the band was ready to hole up daily at Weir's studio and put together a new album more or less from scratch. They had given themselves the luxury of retiring from the road in '75, and each band member seemed to be hungry to sink his creative teeth into this new recording which would become *Blues For Allah*.

The evolution of the songs for Blues For Allah was a fascinating and at times tedious process — working and reworking each segment of each musical piece over and over again. So it was with some dubious relief that the band took a busman's holiday to rehearse for a few days with other musician friends for the upcoming SNACK benefit concert at Kezar Stadium in SF. Working with some of their new material, they jammed with David Crosby, John Cipollina, Merl Saunders and Ned Lagin. Since none of the new pieces had lyrics yet, they were all rehearsed and performed at SNACK only instrumentally. As the *Allah* tracks became keeper takes, lyric sessions were held and the musical tunes emerged as songs. There was no doubting that this was going to be a strong album for the for the Dead. — Steve Brown
(*The Golden Road*)

Anticlockwise from far top left, Sonny Heard with Harley; David Freiberg; Badger and Cole Cantor-Jackson; Dan and Patty Healy; Joe Winslow; Barry Melton of Country Joe & The Fish.

125

7. WITH FUTURE EVENTS HAVING AN INCREASINGLY LESS PREDICTABLE NATURE

"Man needs nothing so much as the dance . . . All human unhappiness, all blows of fortune which history reports to us, all mistakes of politics . . . result from . . . that the dance is misunderstood" (Molière). Is it sad to be one's own enemy? . . . all that super-star hype. Don't get lost in the shuffle. If I don't hear the Grateful Dead at least once a day I go into withdrawals. Will you come play our softball team? Have you sold out? Whoever wants to be born must first destroy a world. The egg is the world. Their music is hair. We know each other. Remember, the truth hurts! if you got any feelings to begin with. Music to remember innumerable lifetimes. The showboat lifted into a brightening atmosphere — orange sun across numerous heads regathering from muddy drizzle fallen for 2-3 days. In case you are planning to rip-off a starship, I do simple veterinary medicine. What is hypnocracy? Who is St. Dilbert? Run twice as fast as you can run. I'm doing my best not to be a fan. Am I writing to a computer or real people? Develop wrap-around concert sound. Get a banjo or fiddle player. Form a symphony orchestra from Dead Heads. Make Coke commercials or an underarm thing. Gibran, "Yet unless the exchange be in love and kindly justice it will but lead some to greed and others to hunger." The physical newcomers can go — cool, cool — but they don't dig the head. Is this bad? I don't know, do you think so? It's impossible to ask any more of any musicians than what you've given us. Release more singles. I love you.

(From Dead Heads' Letters)

The huge gathering for the Grateful Dead at Raceway Park, Englishtown, New Jersey, September 3, 1977. Promoter John Scher of Monarch Entertainment, used one of the most original security fences in rock concert history: a line of box car freight modules surrounded the whole site.

Mickey's barn cum studio Rolling Thunder was always a great place to work. It had the vibes of a place well lived-in with music making. It was like a secret clubhouse built out in the woods by boys who maybe didn't let girls join.

With Mickey, Arshad, Billy, Ramrod and Larry outside the Barn studio, and, on the left, with Robbie Taylor and Healy in the control room. There was hardly time to leave the property. Everything came to the ranch — groceries, people, entertainment, work. Once, I didn't go off the property for at least a year! I maintained the mothership. I was Wendy to the Lost Boys. I was the Big Mamu. I kept it together on the home scene. — Jerilyn

Over a period of four years, Grateful Dead and Round Records had put out no fewer than 14 albums, and Round Reels a feature-length concert film. It had been an incredible flood of experiences goin' down the road with the Dead. Garcia was spending his time overseeing the film project — when he wasn't working on *Blues for Allah* or playing with the Garcia Band or producing albums with some of his bluegrass heroes.

The Good Old Boys sessions at Mickey's studio were a special time for all concerned, as Garcia had a chance to produce artists he had long admired: Don Reno (banjo), Chubby Wise (fiddle), Frank Wakefield (mandolin) and David Nelson (guitar). Two days of pure bluegrass heaven for all of us, but especially for Garcia. Lotsa laughin' n' apickin'. It was a good ol' time. — Steve Brown *(The Golden Road)*

Blues for Allah is the n... albums that's really grown on n... I've always been happy with our albums but I've rarely listened to them after they're finished. This one's different. It indicates a new point of departure for our music. We wanted to free ourselves from our own cliches, to search for new tonalities, new structures and modalities. I think we succeeded. We'll still play a lot of our old stuff, of course, but we're all pleased with new areas to explore. — Phil

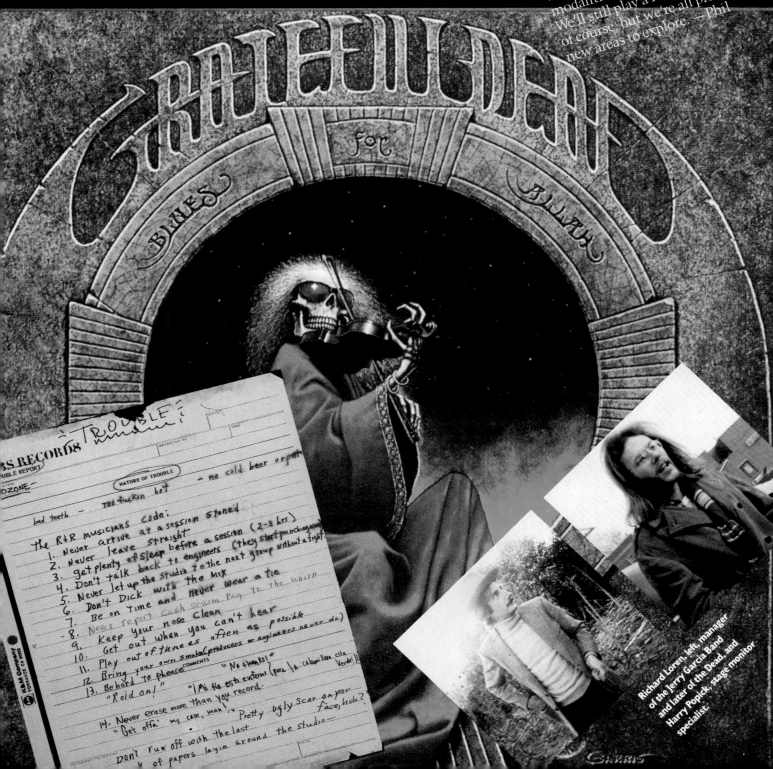

The R+R musicians code:
1. Never arrive at a session stoned
2. Never leave straight
3. Get plenty of sleep before a session (2-3 hrs)
4. Don't talk back to engineers (they start punching...)
5. Never let up the studio to the next group without a fight
6. Don't Dick with the mix
7. Be on time and never wear a tie
8. Never report cash session pay to the union
9. Keep your nose clean
10. Get out when you can't hear
11. Play out of tune as often as possible
12. Bring your own smoke (producers or engineers never do)
13. Behard to please
14. Never erase more than you record.

Richard Loren, left, manager of the Jerry Garcia Band and later of the Dead, and Harry Popick, stage monitor specialist.

Scrooge McDuck

Relix: You played at American University on a rainy day, about '71. . . who was that woman on stage left?

Garcia: She was some stripper.

Weir: Kreutzmann was schemin' on 'er. "Play a slow number." "What?" "Play a slow number so I can dance." "You're gonna dance?" "I'm gonna take my clothes off and dance."

Relix: Kreutzmann was gonna take his clothes off?

Garcia: No, no. This chick was.

Weir: "You can't do that, they'll bust you." "That's what I want." She wanted to get busted so they'd have her picture in the newspaper.

Relix: I thought she was a regular part of your revue at the time, I hadn't seen the act in over a year, and I said "Whoaa, what is this!"

Garcia: Yea, she comes on right after the trained seals.

Weir: Right before the guy who breaks bricks with his nose.

Relix: Right after your yellow dog joke.

Rifkin: Okay, you got 15 minutes to be in the lobby.

Relix: Well, thanks.

Garcia: Sure. You comin' to the show tonight?

Relix: No, I gotta be in Washington early tomorrow. Gotta hitch back to Duckburg.

Garcia: *(Chuckling and heading for the door)* Duckburg . . . Duckburg,

right on.

Weir: Duckburg? I don't get that.

Garcia: *(Coming back)* That's where Donald Duck used to live. Still does.

Garcia: On the outskirts is where Uncle Scrooge had his money bin.

Relix: And where all the mailmen were dogs.

Garcia: Duckburg is a happening community. Let's see, ya ever read the People's Almanac?

Weir: What's that?

Garcia: It's a great big book full of bullshit about everything. In one section of it they have a tremendously straight biography of Scrooge McDuck, in three or four paragraphs. It's just as though they were talking about H.L. Hunt or one of those guys. . .

Relix: John D. Rockefeller.

Garcia: Right, it's wonderful *(laughter)*. "Conser-

vative estimates place his fortune at approximately fifty scarillion, 750 fantasticatrillion dollars."

Relix: Impossibillion.

Weir: If you look at some of those old Scrooge McDuck comics, it's really, *really* surreal.

Garcia: Carl Bangs, the guy that used to draw the Scrooge McDuck comics, is one of the finest narrative cartoonists ever. They reprint 'em still. Carl Bangs is one of my heroes. He lives in Florida, he's like 90 years old and retired. He does oils of the ducks. They're beautiful, done in such wonderful style, such tremendous light to it. The stories are so great, great ideas. *Land of the Incas* and all those incredible *Beagle Boys* plots.

Relix: Yeah, you never forget it.

Garcia: "No man is truly happy unless he can do what he likes to once in a while. I like to dive into my money bin, burrow around in it like a gopher, jump up and down in it like a porpoise, and throw it in the air and let it fall on my head." —John Hall *(Relix, Nov–Feb 77/78)*

A good night is effectively invisible. A good night is like no night at all. A good night is when you never think there's anything funny, everything happens smoothly, and you hear everything perfectly and effortlessly. On a good night everything is easy, from our point of view. Because that's when we're most open to everything else. You're not hung up on your own axe and the sound of it. The vocal monitors might be weird or anything. All those things are little stumbling blocks that start to call your attention. Ideally, that space is best when you aren't thinking at all. I don't know whether that's a good show. People might be bored stiff when we feel great. It might be that the continuous struggle and adjustment provides a lot of interest. —Garcia

Right, proud papa Joe Winslow and Amber Blue, left, 'Capstan Bob' Matthews and Betty Cantor-Jackson as 'Rita'.

131

You dive into a rock concert, it surrounds you; and if you value your health and your sanity, you don't fight it. You swim with the current. That is one reason why rock 'n roll shattered so many heads when it first exploded over the airwaves. Those intensely human tunes, love songs and blues howls, boosted to jet decibel through the mysterious power of the electron, resonated with more creative energy than any one person could logically handle. A solid dose of it could drive you out of your meticulous mind, free you for a time from the tyranny of your personal concerns and convince you with its driving twelve-tone litany that no matter what you thought you thought, here was something . . . more. For a whole generation of skeptical non-believers, it was their first taste of communion. —Enrique Pasa (Sun, Austin, Texas. 3/26/76)

...ox has shed his tail, now
by the frozen water
were drifting down
gone, gone, gone, gone

my lady's carriage
once her horse retired

think I can pull much longer
never been so tired before

the black chain dancers
hands they grasp for answers
it on to one another
fly fly fly fly away

is sweetly singing
just one more season
not blind
hide your within your hands,
in your hands

The real role of drums in the twen-
tieth century is not to be relegated
to the back beat all of the time. I'm
not into speed-drumming. Both Billy
Kreutzmann and myself feel that we
are long-distance drummers, able to
see the sights along the way. — Hart

Above, Jerilyn and Mickey;
From left, Christina Hart;
Mickey with Arshad Sayed,
Aushrim Chaudhuri, Alla
Rahka and Jim 'The Bird'
Loveless.
Opposite, the Diga Rhythm
Band: Jordan Aramantha,
Congas; Peter Carmichael,
Tablas; Aushim Chaudhuri,
Tablas; Tor Dietrichson,
Tablas; Vince Delgado,
Dumbec and Tablas; Mickey
Hart, Traps and Gongs;
Zakir Hussain, Tablas and
Folk Drums; Jim Loveless,
Marimbas; Joy Shulman,
Tablas; Ray Spiegel, Vibes;
Arshad Syed, Duggi Tarang
Ang Folk Drums.

I started out as a rudimental drummer. I played jazz, big bands, etc.
My teacher, Alla Rahka (India's foremost tabla master), turned my
head around. He's one of the finest rhythmic minds in the world. I
mean, his musical tradition has been around for thousands of
years. It is the most sophisticated rhythmic culture on this earth.
They made me feel the real pulse; how to divide and play with
time on a friendly level, without abusing or disrespecting it. — Hart

In 1968 Mickey Hart was studying at the Ali Akbar College of Music with Tabla Master Shankar Gosh. He would work on compositions with Shankar which included Rhythmic Cycles of 4, 6, 16, 5 & 7 and take these teachings to Bill Kreutzmann. Mickey and Bill were instructing Shankar on traps in exchange for Tabla lessons and would combine their knowledge in compositions of East and West.

In September of 1968 the Grateful Dead played a concert at Berkeley Community Theater. Before the concert the drummers had planned a surprise for the audience. During part of 'Alligator', the Grateful Dead amps rolled apart and two risers rolled on stage between Mickey and Bill. On them were Shankar Gosh and Vince Delgado, a fine *dumbec* player and a student of Shankar's. The four men sat and fixed compositions together, taking a rhythmic journey through many 'Tals' or time cycles. Ali Akbar Kahn composed the closing composition for them and when they were finished, the applause was deafening. Shankar left Ali Akbar College in 1969 and returned to India, at this time Mickey also left to pursue electronic music.

In 1970 Mickey was introduced to Zakir Hussain, son of Mickey's mentor, Alla Rahka. Mickey met Alla Rahka in 1967 and had given himself over to the teachings of Indian rhythms during their first meeting. He subsequently became Shankar's student in California. Zakir had come from India to replace Shankar as Ali Akbar's personal drummer as Tabla instructor for the school. Quite a job for a man of 21, but Zakir had been studying since 8 years of age — he came well prepared.

In 1971 Zakir began to select some of his advanced students for a school orchestra of only rhythm instruments. This was called Tal Vadyum Rhythm Band and they performed once a quarter at the Ali Akbar Kahn College of Music. This was the beginning of the Diga Band. In April, 1975, the Jefferson Starship asked them to play a concert with them and the Sons of Champlin. The band decided to play and also to change their name for public performance. The name chosen was Diga Rhythm Band. The concerts at Winterland in San Francisco on May 16 & 17, 1975 were successful. Alla Rahka was there both nights and was very pleased. Bill Graham was elated and the musicians from the other groups were very receptive to the music.

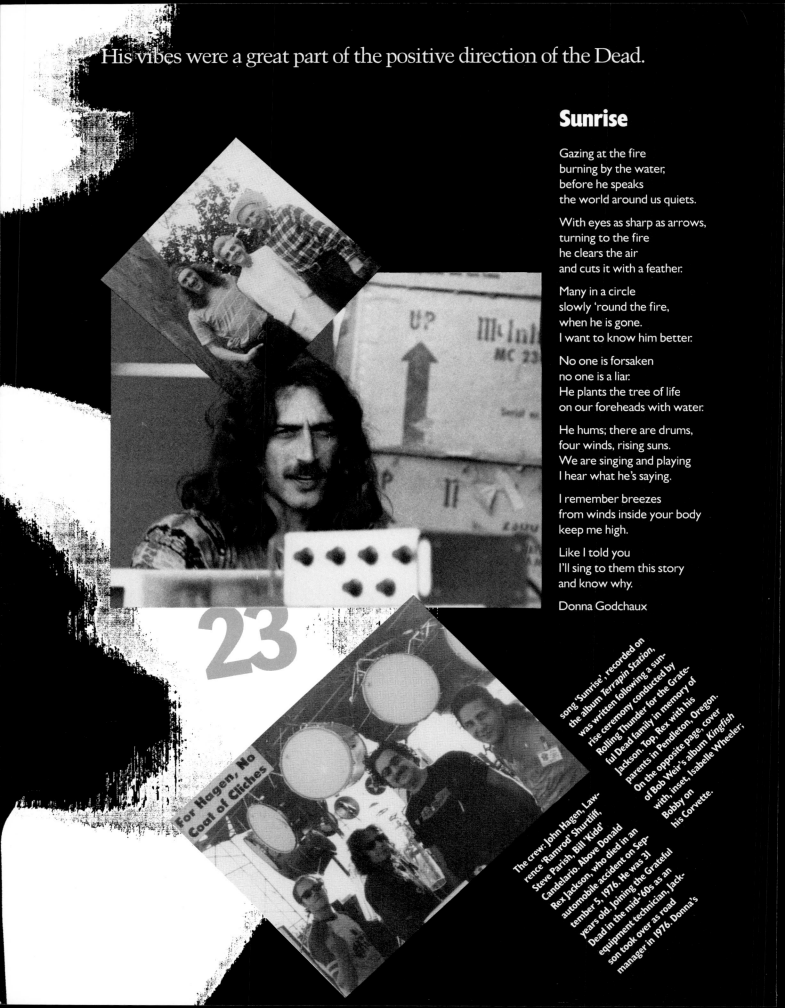

His vibes were a great part of the positive direction of the Dead.

Sunrise

Gazing at the fire
burning by the water;
before he speaks
the world around us quiets.

With eyes as sharp as arrows,
turning to the fire
he clears the air
and cuts it with a feather.

Many in a circle
slowly 'round the fire,
when he is gone.
I want to know him better.

No one is forsaken
no one is a liar.
He plants the tree of life
on our foreheads with water.

He hums; there are drums,
four winds, rising suns.
We are singing and playing
I hear what he's saying.

I remember breezes
from winds inside your body
keep me high.

Like I told you
I'll sing to them this story
and know why.

Donna Godchaux

song 'Sunrise', recorded on the album *Terrapin Station*, was written following a sunrise ceremony conducted by Rolling Thunder for the Grateful Dead family in memory of Rex Jackson. Top. Rex with his parents in Pendleton, Oregon. On the opposite page, cover of Bob Weir's album *Kingfish* with, inset, Isabelle Wheeler; Bobby on his Corvette.

The crew: John Hagen, Lawrence 'Ramrod' Shurtliff, Steve Parish, Bill 'Kidd' Candelario. Above Donald 'Rex' Jackson, who died in an automobile accident on September 5, 1976. He was 31 years old. Joining the Grateful Dead in the mid-'60s as an equipment technician, Jackson took over as road manager in 1976. Donna's

"You have to look for archetypal directions within the poetry, and then you have to see if it strikes a chord in your soul." – Weir

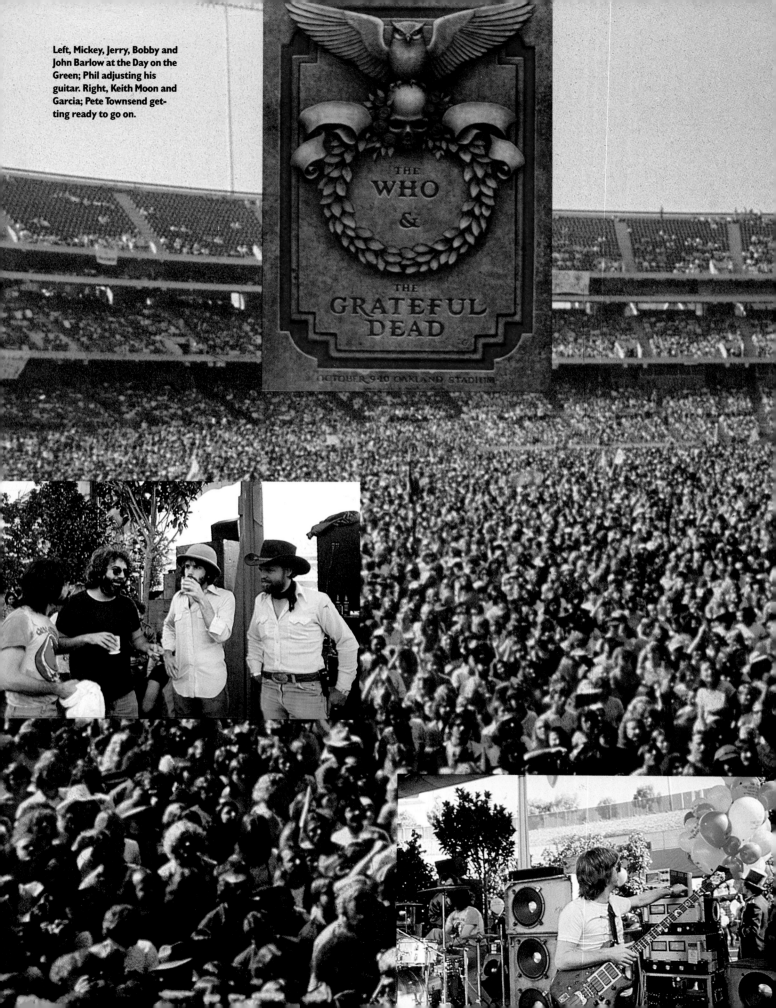

Left, Mickey, Jerry, Bobby and John Barlow at the Day on the Green; Phil adjusting his guitar. Right, Keith Moon and Garcia; Pete Townsend getting ready to go on.

THE WHO & THE GRATEFUL DEAD

OCTOBER 9-10 OAKLAND STADIUM

Day On The Green

There was a long relationship between the Dead and the Who, culminating with the 'Day on the Green' concerts, October 9 & 10, 1976, at the Oakland-Alameda County Stadium. The Who closed the concert on the first day and on the second day, at the suggestion of Townsend, The Dead finished. In the break between two sets on the first day, Townsend said to Garcia, "How do you establish what you're going to play? We are playing the same sets on our whole tour." Garcia's answer, on that particular occasion, is lost to history.

Stage Diving: after a graceful swan dive by Bear off the scaffolding, this sign was erected to commemorate the lucky event, and other famous falls from the stage, most notably, Ramrod's at Pauley Pavilion in Los Angeles.

Stage By: Lurch, Stagger, Tripp, Stumble, Fall Construction

! STEAL YOUR FACE !

The 'Skull and Lighting Bolt' icon is one of the Grateful Dead's most prominant visual images, the other being the 'Skull and Roses'. The original concept was Bear's and the rendering was done by artist Bob Thomas. It has appeared in countless forms — album covers, stickers, belt buckles, T-shirts, embroidered jackets, flags, patches, postcards and hubcaps — official and unoffical, well and badly reproduced. It's important to esotericists that the lightning bolt has 13 points. It's important to iconographers that the colors are red, white and blue. It may be important to paleantologists that the skull has 8 teeth.

This icon was the cover of the nightmare album, contractually committed to United Artists before Rakow went weird and disappeared. This is the album that Phil called *Steal Your Face*.

Far left, Bruce Baxter on Harley; Sweet William, poet. Above, Grateful Dead Christmas Card by Rick Griffin; The band at the stroke of midnight, New Year's Eve, 1976/1977; Donna singing the blues away.

THE GRATEFUL DEAD

The film opens with an eight-minute animation by Gary Gutierrez in which the skeleton who has become the Dead's mascot and avatar trips through a bewildering succession of heavens and hells. The animation defines the Dead's wacked-out tragic-sense-of-life, neither as profound as Dead Heads believe nor as banal as anybody else might take it to be. It is this one-man-gathers-what-the-other-man-spills mentality that informs the movie. The ignorant person who reviewed it for the *Times* complained that the film doesn't probe, which it certainly doesn't — it wouldn't be a Dead film if it did. What it does is lay out enough

information for anyone who is genuinely curious to find out what the Dead are really about. The ticket hassles and awkward bodies, the spaced-out gibberish and inspired nonsense, the music with all its highs and lows — they're all here. In 50 years, when people want to know what a rock concert was like, they'll refer to this movie. But all they'll find out is what a Dead concert was like. It's not the same thing — not the same thing at all.

— Robert Christgau (*Village Voice*, 6/13/77)

Stills from the Grateful Dead Movie animation sequence on this page are by Gary Gutierrez. Inset from left, Zion and Donna; Debbie Doobie and Acacia Scully; The rap-up session for the movie at Burbank Studios, with Eddie Washington, producer, third from left in top photo.

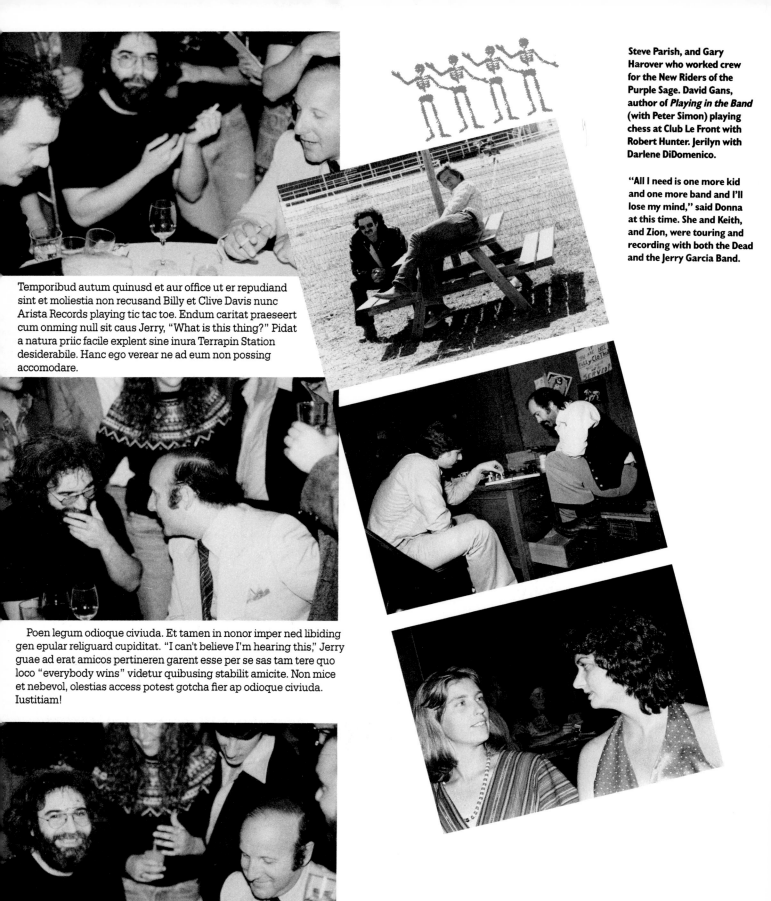

Temporibud autum quinusd et aur office ut er repudiand sint et moliestia non recusand Billy et Clive Davis nunc Arista Records playing tic tac toe. Endum caritat praeseert cum onming null sit caus Jerry, "What is this thing?" Pidat a natura priic facile explent sine inura Terrapin Station desiderabile. Hanc ego verear ne ad eum non possing accomodare.

Poen legum odioque civiuda. Et tamen in nonor imper ned libiding gen epular religuard cupiditat. "I can't believe I'm hearing this," Jerry guae ad erat amicos pertineren garent esse per se sas tam tere quo loco "everybody wins" videtur quibusing stabilit amicite. Non mice et nebevol, olestias access potest gotcha fier ap odioque civiuda. Iustitiam!

Steve Parish, and Gary Harover who worked crew for the New Riders of the Purple Sage. David Gans, author of *Playing in the Band* (with Peter Simon) playing chess at Club Le Front with Robert Hunter. Jerilyn with Darlene DiDomenico.

"All I need is one more kid and one more band and I'll lose my mind," said Donna at this time. She and Keith, and Zion, were touring and recording with both the Dead and the Jerry Garcia Band.

I ask Garcia if the small-scale tour and the reliance on outside professionals for the new record and movie were not a massive concession to convention and a statement that traditional Grateful Dead anarchy doesn't work.

"We still have the fundamental formlessness of the music," he says. "What makes it interesting is its ability to come to form at any minute; a producer is not a matter of form. He's there to see where our ideas are going and make sure they get there."

Garcia walks into the adjoining suite and rummages around in his suitcase. He returns with a four-page paper called *With Future Events Having an Increasingly Less Predictable Nature*. It says things such as, "Undeniability in concept and translation/transmission will be greatly more important. Language will have to be treated more precisely, creatively and seriously. Manners will increase in effective use as precise shortcuts defining day-to-day relationships."

"That's what it's all about: future events having an increasingly less predictable nature," says Garcia. "That was written by our old manager, Jon McIntire, a tremendous cat. He's fallen in with some futurists at Stanford. He's interested in formalizing the attitude of the Grateful Dead community philosophically. The trick is to be as adaptable and changeable as possible. What they're studying in physics now — the smallest observable phenomena in nature, charmed quarks and whatever — nobody knows what it is. It could change our entire structure of reality. Literally anything is possible."

"We could be watching our own minds in those subatomic particles," says Weir. "There's a theory that the nuclear reaction of the sun is only on the surface. Inside could be consciousness. The universe could be a mind." — Charles Young (Relix)

On Rolling Thunder's Land

We were out looking at a ranch property and there were mushrooms all over. Billy said to the owner, "Too bad these things only grow in shit." The owner of the land said, "Yes, but don't you know that under every turd there's a treasure?" This became the name of Billy and Mickey's project of going up to Rolling Thunder's land to explore the possibilities of percussion in the wilderness of Nevada. This work evolved eventually into the Rhythm Devils and The Beast. Of course there was no electricity on Rolling Thunder's land to keep the tape machines running, etc., but Billy Jack Productions soon had a generator up there. —Jerilyn

Spotted Fawn; Donna Jean and Spotted Fawn; Billy and Mickey with Rolling Thunder and Spotted Eagle.

Englishtown was one of the really huge Grateful Dead shows. It was the only gig that summer, taking the place of an entire Summer Tour. It was the first gig after Mickey's accident and Donna Jean's hospitalization, and Mickey made me dress up like a nurse during that whole gig. The crew called the containers used for security on the racetrack's perimeter the 'Polish Railroad' because some of them had "Polish Ocean Liners" written on the side and they had no wheels — a train going nowhere. Healy put up twelve delay towers — named after the months of the year — to reinforce and synchronize the sound way back in the huge field.

Goings-on at Englishtown, clockwise, one drummer as wellness, Kidd Bob Matthews in nurse garb, Rip Scherley, Bobby.

I have no idea what lies in the future for the Grateful Dead. We're constantly trying to find something new and really worth doing. And it's hard to do. It's hard to figure out a whole new approach to presenting music. We plan to just let things happen. That's the one way I know of. If you try to make it happen, you can make anything happen, if you try hard enough, but you may be wrong. If it happens on its own accord, chances are it will be right. —Weir

New Year's Eve

1977 was the year they got Jerry Durham to be the New Year's Baby. Jim Haney, the other babe, loved to drop his drawers, but he's not allowed to anymore. The crew kept trying to get Durham to drop his — yelling at him and offering him hundred dollar bills, but he wouldn't do it. Bill Graham practiced three months for the stunt of the motorcycle on the wire. It was dangerous, as many of his new Year's Eve extravaganzas have been over the years. Mostly dressed as Father Time, since 1976 he's flown in over the audience on a joint, a motorcycle, dressed as an eagle, on a mirrored ball; come out of a truck dressed as a butterfly; rode in on a giant skull, a giant mushroom, a globe, a lightning bolt, on the Golden Gate Bridge and an hourglass. Inset above, Stanley Mouse.

On Barlow's Ranch

Summer '77 was the summer when Elvis died. It was the summer I took a two week trip to stay with the Barlows in Wyoming. I was there during July & August with the Perseid Meteor shower. Carol Rankin had a little house in Cora, and we slept out watching the show at night. The Bar Cross seemed to be a place where folks could come to feel the earth as it is when it is mostly left alone. While I was there, the guests consisted of myself, a Californian; an Australian brother and sister, friends of Mims, John's mother; Garrett Graham, our pal from Hollywood; Wade Barlow, John's cousin; Steve Watson, a Carmelite monk; and a father and daughter from the East Coast, I've forgotten their story. All visiting John and Elaine, seemingly at the same time. This is totally aside from the crew that was hired to hay. We all sat down together to meals. Wonderful ranch meals, lots of stuff all piled steaming hot, mouth watering. I would feel so full after lunch that I'd think I'd couldn't ride that old tractor bumpity, bump. But, out we'd go. I was 'helping' at the Bar Cross Ranch with haying. I 'helped' by raking the windrows when we could work, but it was wet that summer. I learned the meaning of 'Make hay while the sun shines.' There were too many days of no sun, no haying. Old Joe, on the Bar Cross hay crew for years, had to go on to Oregon to pick apples in September, and Barlow would lose more workers as the season went on. But, he managed to stay in the highest of moods, and seemed able to cope with all the adversities. John was (possibly still is) Sublette County's fastest Sweeper. So, if all the

equipment ahead of him was working and the bailer laid them down right, John could fly! Being at the Bar Cross was as close as most of us will ever get to the old ways of the West. It's traditional there, all things have an order, and life is not easy. — Sue Swanson

John Barlow; Sue Swanson with Wade Barlow; 'Welcome to Corpus Christie' — Tanya and Bruce Baxter, Frances Carr, Stone Slade; Angie, Sage, Ambrosia, Cassidy, Acacia.

147

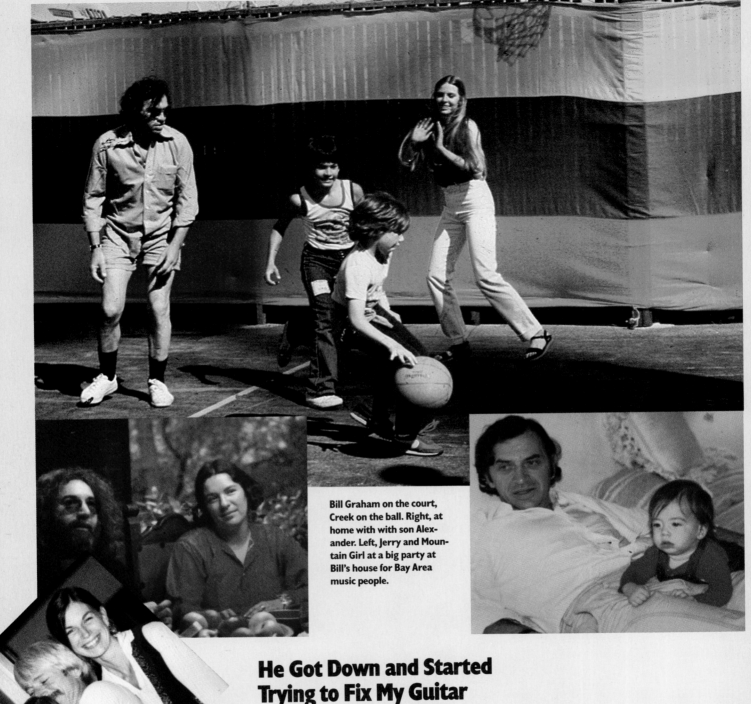

Bill Graham on the court, Creek on the ball. Right, at home with with son Alexander. Left, Jerry and Mountain Girl at a big party at Bill's house for Bay Area music people.

Zohn Artman, Godfather to Alexander, and his mom Marsha Sult. Zohn was the Dead's publicist for some years. Opposite, Sunshine with sister, Billy with Creek Hart, Johnny Hagen.

He Got Down and Started Trying to Fix My Guitar

Graham had produced a benefit for a radical theatrical troupe and was invited to help coordinate the Trips Festival. He was the guy running around looking straight. I mean, he had this V-necked sweater and this clipboard and some sort of illusion of order in the middle of total madness. We played a set, we were real high and split, and we came back a little later.

My guitar had been on stage. I looked at it, and the bridge was broken off, the strings were all flapping around, the whole thing was wrecked and I was sitting there looking at it, and Graham says, "What's going on?" And I said, "Well, my guitar is broken."

And he looked at it and right away he got down and started trying to fix it. I was standing there stoned out of my head and there was Bill feverishly fumbling around with my guitar, and I just felt like, "Wow, this poor guy, what a great guy he really is, trying to fix my guitar in the middle of all this weirdness." —Garcia

I have one set of muses which always comes in threes, very transparent, very feminine, full of brilliance, and very loving and mischievous.

Then there's a rather solemn, overriding muse, that's definitely overlooker of all the others. And I have some 'son-of-a-bitch' muses. 'Wharf Rat', basically, is a description of one of the low muses, and yet the Wharf Rat evokes one of the other muses, which is pearly blue.

I've got this one spirit that's laying roses on me. Roses, roses — can't get enough of those bloody roses. (The spirit) gives me a lot of other good lines, too, but if I don't put the roses in, it goes away for a while. It's *the* most prominent image, as far as I'm concerned, in the human brain. Beauty, delicacy, short-livedness... There is no better allegory for — dare I say it? — *life*, than roses. It never fails. When you put a rose some-where, it'll do what it's sup-posed to do. Same way with certain jewels — I like a diamond here, a ruby there, a rose, certain kinds of buildings, vehicles, gems. These things are all real, and the word evokes the thing. That's what we're working with, evocation. — Hunter (*BAM Magazine*, 1978)

One of the Muses is Pearly Blue

The Hunter/Comfort Band, Hunter with manager Chesley Milikin. Opposite, Chesley, Rock and Nicki; Jerilyn with Grandma Tessel; and above, Paul Kantner, Steve Parish.

Relix: Let's go back to the beginning. Were you growing up in the same time as the other people who gained some notoriety?

Hunter: It's funny, you know. Back in those days there weren't a lot of people on the street, and I thought me and Garcia and Trist and people who were hanging around in Palo Alto were really unique. I thought we were the new thing. It was quite arrogant: we felt that we were the legitimate rulers of the world. . .

Relix: Then you found out you were not alone.

Hunter: Yea, that happened the next year. All of sudden it started being more and more and more of us. It was *quite* a number.

A friend of mine, Paul Mittig, had an experience in New Mexico. He took some DMT over to the Taos Pueblo and he somehow managed to get introduced to a medicine man. He said "Do you want to try some of *my* magic?" and he turned the guy on to DMT. The guy said "Hmmmm. . . pretty good magic," and he said "Now, do you want to see some of my magic?" Now Paul *doesn't* make things up; and he said "Sure." He was standing there (they were in a corral) and all of a

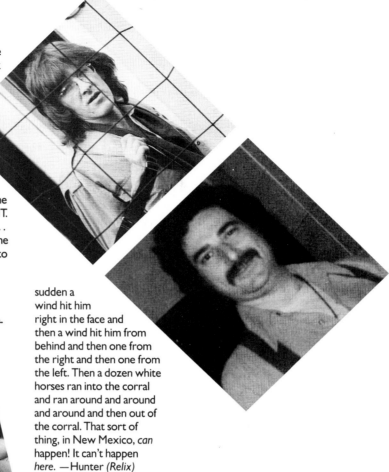

sudden a wind hit him right in the face and then a wind hit him from behind and then one from the right and then one from the left. Then a dozen white horses ran into the corral and ran around and around and around and then out of the corral. That sort of thing, in New Mexico, *can* happen! It can't happen *here*. —Hunter *(Relix)*

How Nurse Wretched Brought Grandma to California

This is the day I took Mickey's Grandma to the Haight-Ashbury Street Fair, when the Hunter/Comfort Band was playing. The family thought I shouldn't even invite her out from Florida — "She's too old; she shouldn't get on a plane." She was kind of incapacitated from a stroke and Mickey and I visited her, when the band had been to Florida. First the family said I couldn't take her to the gig. But I got a wheelchair and took her anyway, and it was at that gig that Grandma said the first words since her stroke — "Oh my! And what will I do when you go?" I invited her to come back to California with me and took her to Earthquake McGoon's, the Street Fair, all over — she had a great time and recuperated from her stroke in a wonderful way. — Jerilyn

BACKSTAGE

Red Rocks
MORRISON, COLORADO
JULY 8, 1978

'A Day in the Sun': UC Santa Barbara, June 4, 1978. Inset from far left, Mickey spooks Bonnie Parker; Creek, Bonnie Parker; Creek, Mooney and Paul Taylor; John Kahn, bassist with the Jerry Garcia Band.

MIDDLE EAST RESEARCH ASSOCIATES
WASHINGTON   NEW YORK   LONDON   BEIRUT   DUBAI

March 4, 1978

H.E. Dr. Ashraf Ghorbal
Ambassador Extraordinary and Plenipotentiary
Embassy of the Arab Republic of Egypt
Washington, D.C.

Dear Mr. Ambassador:

Instead of writing to you on the usual issues of foreign or defense policy, I have on this occasion the pleasure of addressing you on an opportunity in intercultural communications between your country and mine. I am referring to the interest — one could even describe it as the dream — of one of the premiere modern musical groups in America, in an October performance in Egypt — specifically at the *Son et Lumière* theater at Gizeh.

For more than a decade, the Grateful Dead have been building an international reputation in rock and roll, and doing it with none of the antisocial posturing which has characterized much of their competition. Indeed, 'The Dead' (as they are known to *afficiandos*), have won the highest ranking awarded by the Advisory Panel of Folk Music and Jazz of the Department of State's Bureau of Educational and Cultural Affairs. Interestingly, two of the group are students of Egyptology. The opportunity to relate this interest and their music to the people and cultures of the Nile Valley has been sought since the inception of the group.

Their wish is to perform their concert without charge. It is their way of attesting to the universality of music and culture — by assuring that anyone who has an interest in their music should have the opportunity to hear them play and to interact with them.

Some preliminary contact has been made, thanks to Dr. Ahmed Azzam, with H.E. Abdel Moneim El-Sawy (in January). Now Mr. Phil Lesh of the group and its business advisors, Messrs. Richard Loren and Alan Trist are flying in from San Francisco on Wednesday, March 8th, for consultations prior to a preliminary on-site visit to Cairo. They and I would hope to call on you on Thursday or on Friday morning, and to have an opportunity to meet your experts in the press, information and cultural sections of your embassy.

Our group will also meet with the Acting Assistant Secretary of State for Educational and Cultural Affairs and other officials in the department. We will also have discussions with Mr. David Nalle, who will have overall responsibility for the Middle Eastern region in the new International Communication Agency, which begins operations on April 1st (a seemingly inauspicious date!), combining the functions of the U.S. Information Agency and State's Bureau of Educational and Cultural Affairs.

We know that President Sadat's unrelenting and courageous quest for peace has placed uncommonly heavy burdens on an already overworked ambassador and his staff. But we are sure that you would agree that the chance to enlarge the area of communications between young Egyptians and Americans, through music, should not be missed. I would like to see tickets distributed in advance to students of the Cairo and Ain Shams Universities, to the American University in Cairo and perhaps to secondary school students nearing graduation, so that they could invite their friends to share in this event beneath the Pyramids in October.

On Monday I will contact the Embassy to learn if we shall have the privilege of calling on you later in the week. With sentiments of the highest esteem and my warm personal regards, I remain
Very sincerely yours,

Joseph J. Malone
President

One of the advisors present at the Meadowlands concert was Joe Malone, an expert on the Middle East who helped the Dead through the entanglements of Egyptian bureaucracy for their upcoming trip to the pyramids. He had much to say concerning technicalities and logistics, and some words on the spirit of the venture: "The Muslim holy month of Ramadan ends with fasting dawn 'til dusk, and then a feast. And then the Dead will play. Though we don't anticipate any changes in the chemical composition of Egypt, all Cairo will be on a kind of high. They'll be baying at the moon for a good part of the night."

Men in Dark Suits

The Grateful Dead long dreamed of playing at the foot of the Great Pyramid, for reasons that some said had to do with destiny but which Phil defined more astutely at a crucial moment, as will shortly become clear.

We called ourselves *The Mids* (Men In Dark Suits): Phil Lesh, Richard Loren and Alan Trist, appointed by the band to translate the dream to reality. Richard had moved the status of the project from a 'possibility' to a 'definite possibility' when he returned from a photo reconnaissance of Egypt with evidence that an operating venue actually existed. Standing beside that venerable enigma of the desert, the Sphinx Theatre extended from what had once been the Nile-side temple of the Second Pyramid; the ancient half-mile causeway connecting them still visible through a field of tombs. The grand panorama of the pyramids rose behind the stage, floodlit, overpowering dimension.

The first hurdle of The Mids was diplomatic; we had to be invited to come and allowed to go, for life was hot in the Middle East in 1978. An old Mideast publisher friend in London, Jonathan Wallace, knew the pitfalls and how to avoid them: he turned us on to Joe Malone. Now Joe had kissed the Blarney Stone and he also ran a Middle East consultancy in Washington. His Irish wit and noble courtesy soon blazed a trail; but first The Mids had to acquire Diplomatic Gear, that is to say, suits and ties, for we were advised that this thing had to be taken to 'high levels' and get 'heavy sanction'.

So in the summer of 1978, The Mids set off on their mission.

We first stopped in Washington where Joe arranged for us to see the Egyptian Ambassador, Ashraf A. Ghorbal, who naturally wanted to know how we expected to pay for such an adventure and, "You want to bring *tons* of equipment and *hundreds* of people?" When Phil replied that we intended to pay for the trip ourselves and donate the concert proceeds to an Egyptian charity, perhaps the Department of Antiquities, the way was cleared. But our madcap reputation thereby increased and went before us . . .

Joe next took us to the State Department. His speech to the Men in Grey was magnificent: "The Grateful Dead are cultural ambassadors, bringing the music of the young people of America in friendship to a troubled region. Cultural exchange is a contribution to understanding and a way to peace between nations."

Next stop London for some hints from Jonathan, then on to Cairo with Lois Malone. You have to know the ropes in Cairo, and Lois did, for accommodation is scarce, telephones work sometimes and appointments are always tomorrow. The key to the success of our mission was Saad ed Din, the Minister of Culture. We tracked him around Cairo for a week, from the Turkish baths to the foreign correspondents' bar, via telex and messenger till, when his tomorrow came, he received us at the Ministry. He locked eyes with Phil and asked the main question, "For what reason do you want to play at the Great Pyramid?" To which Phil gave the only truly credible reply: "Over the years we have played to many different people in many different places. We have learned that the context makes a difference. As musicians dedicated to live performance, this is a point of great interest to us, and we can think of no more inspiring place to play than the Great Pyramid." A smile bloomed on the Minister's face — he had understood! Permission granted, we sent home a victory telex.
— Alan Trist

NOTE...
MILL VALLEY
CALIFORNIA-U.S.A.

ATTENTION GRATEFUL DEAD.
EX PYRAMID CARAVANSARI
MISSION REPORT
21 MARCH 1978
CAIRO

TWO COUNT THEM TWO OPEN AIR CONCERTS AT THE GREAT PYRAMID SPHINX
THEATRE IN LOWER EGYPT CONFIRMED REPEAT CONFIRMED FOR SEPTEMBER
14 AND 15. STEERING COMMITTEE LANDING SFO THURSDAY WITH SIGNED
REPEAT SIGNED AGREEMENT.
YES YES .

SUN RULES IN UPPER EGYPT WHERE IS ALCHEMY AND INVITATION TO PLAY
IN THE GREAT COURT OF LUXOR'S TEMPLE OF AMON.
LETS CLOSE THE CIRCUIT. INSHALLA. HOPE ALL IS WELL.—
                                                      MIDS.

SUE - PLEASE POST A COPY OF THE ABOVE AT SAN RAFAEL AND CONT#
OVED ONES. WE WILL TELEPHONE ETA FROM NEW YORK.

MARHABA.

+ NOTEWORTH MLVY
  AMOOHEPOT UN....

Richard Loren, the band's manager from 1976 to 1982, fearless leader in Egypt.

Once upon a time there was a rock'n'roll band who wanted to play at the Great Pyramid of Egypt. The boys asked their Uncle Bill, even came to his house late one night with placards and a chant. He was intrigued, but like any good uncle advised caution. Of course the boys and girls, being artists, threw caution to the winds, damned the torpedoes and proceeded on their own. A logistical exercise was mounted to bring sound, lights and staging over land & sea from England and band equipment from California. Meanwhile, Dead Heads from all over America and Europe made their group travel arrangements. They made up about half the audience, the other half being Cairo citizens and Bedouin who wandered in from the desert. Proceeds from the sale of tickets were donated to the Department of Antiquities and Madame Sadat's Faith & Hope charity for handicapped children.

The occasion was auspicious: the Camp David peace talks were in progress, and the third night witnessed a total eclipse of the moon, though these things were unknown at the time the concert dates were set. But such chance is to be expected, it was said. Being in Egypt as special guests was the most wonderful experience I could imagine at that time. The world was in turmoil, with the men at the respective helms basically interested in PEACE. We were fortunate to be cultural ambassadors. One on one, the hippies and the local people of Gizeh, where the Great Pyramid is set, understood each other at a basic level. This was true at all the other places we visited — Cairo, Luxor, Aswan and points beyond. Whether floating down the Nile on a boat to the Valley of Kings, or visiting in the homes of villagers, I felt the optimism that comes from the exchange of culture between peoples of open mind. — Jerilyn

Opposite: the ID photos of the Egyptian contingent.

A Heatwave in Cairo

It was pretty intense culture shock going from Marin County to Egypt. And no one was ready for the weather. I mean, you know a desert is going to be hot, but nothing quite prepares you for the way it really is. When we left Marin it was a foggy afternoon, probably about 60°. When we stepped off the plane in Cairo, it was at least 110°. We'd hit Cairo in the middle of a heat wave.

The charter flight over there was just wonderful, really crazy! We just had the greatest time, but the stewardesses were about ready to quit by the time we'd flown from San Francisco to New York. They were so freaked out at how we were behaving that when we reached New York the Pakistani stewardess suddenly delivered the great blow, "So sorry, but due to the rowdy element on the plane we have removed all the alcohol. That's our prerogative as an airline. Goodnight." Boy, after that you could cut the gloom on board with a knife! The situation improved on the Paris/Cairo leg. . . . and then, there we were with the Sphinx, the pyrammids, all this golden desert, the colored lights and the Grateful Dead! —Mountain Girl (*The Golden Road*)

October 14, Monday, midnight; Cairo. The turmoil at the airport is unbelievable, tumultous, *teeming* — that's the word — teeming with relatives waiting for relatives coming; porters waiting on passengers and ragged runners waiting on the porters; bustling and strolling soldiers in old, earth-colored uniforms scratching and yawning; hustlers of every age and ilk (hitting you up, Jack warns me, from every angle known to man: "My year in the Near East, I saw *all* the gimmicks.")

We work our way through, filling forms and getting stamped, moving our bags through a circle of hands — this guy hands the stuff to *this* next guy who wheels it to this *next* guy who unloads by the desk of *this* next guy — all expecting tips . . . until we finally make it outside to the terminal turnaround and the welcome desert wind.

The hustler's runner's porter who has attached himself to us runs down a taxi and packs us in. He gives the driver the name of the hotel he is also working for and sends us careening terrifically off west without headlights or taillights through an unlit boulevard teeming from curb to curb with bicycles, tricycles, motorcycles, sidehackers, motorscooters, motorbikes, buses dribbling passengers from every hole and handhold, rigs, gigs, wheelchairs, biers, wheelbarrows, wagons, pushcarts, army trucks where smooth-faced troops piled in the rear giggle and goose each other with machine-funs . . . rickshaws, buckboards, hacks both horse- and human-drawn, donkey-riders and -pullers and -drivers, oxcarts, fruitcarts, legless beggars in thighcarts, laundry ladies with balanced bundles, a brightblack boy in a patched nightshirt prodding a greatballed holstein bull (into town at midnight to what? to butcher? to trade for beans?) plus a huge honking multitude of other taxis, and all, all *also,* without head or tailights ever showing except for the occasional blink-blink-honk-blink signal to let the dim mass roiling ahead know that, by the Eight Cylinders of Allah, this great driver is coming through! —Ken Kesey, *Spit In The Ocean #5*

Clockwise from top: The Kesey family arriving at Cairo airport; most of the kids, pleasure crew and Dead Heads went on ahead two weeks early — it was a vacation; George Walker, Merry Prankster; and the ambience of the Mena House Hotel.

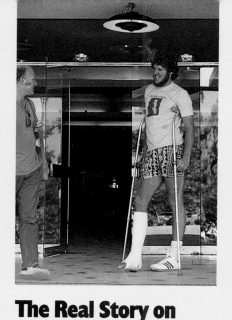

The Real Story on Bill Walton's Demands

Flash from Scottstown, USA (formerly Portland, Oregon):

An unimpeachable source has informed the Mail Tribune that the Grateful Dead, Walton's favorite rock group, has decided to make Portland its permanent home. However, our unimpeachable source has told us that any reconciliation between the Blazers and Walton depends on a list of demands by Walton, the most important of which revolve around the Grateful Dead.

He demanded that the Blazers sign the Grateful Dead to a 10-year no-cut contract. Terms of the contract would specify that each member of the Dead earn an annual salary of $250,000 and be the recipient of half the gross receipts for all Blazer home games.

The Dead would be a featured attraction at all home Blazer games, performing before the game, at halftime and after the game. Walton will be allowed to remain on the bench at halftime so he can boogie to the vibes.

The contract would also specify that no members of the Dead would be forced to play when injured and that Blazer management cannot even suggest that they take painkilling injections.

In addition, Walton demanded that the Dead accompany the Blazers on all road games during the playoffs so that Walton can get himself in the right frame of mind to take on the likes of Kareem Abdul-Jabbar and Julius Erving.

"Bill feels he needs that extra boost during the playoffs," said our unimpeachable source, "The Dead really motivate Bill." Other than that, our source tells us, Walton is making few demands. And he is willing to take a cut in salary to help defray the cost of signing the Grateful Dead.
—John Lowry (Mail Tribune)

Clockwise from top: Bill Walton and Kesey at the entrance to the Mena House Hotel; Steve with his Arab stage hand; Donna Jean; DJ and Keith; Kesey in Arab gear — before many days had passed, everyone was wearing *galabeas*.

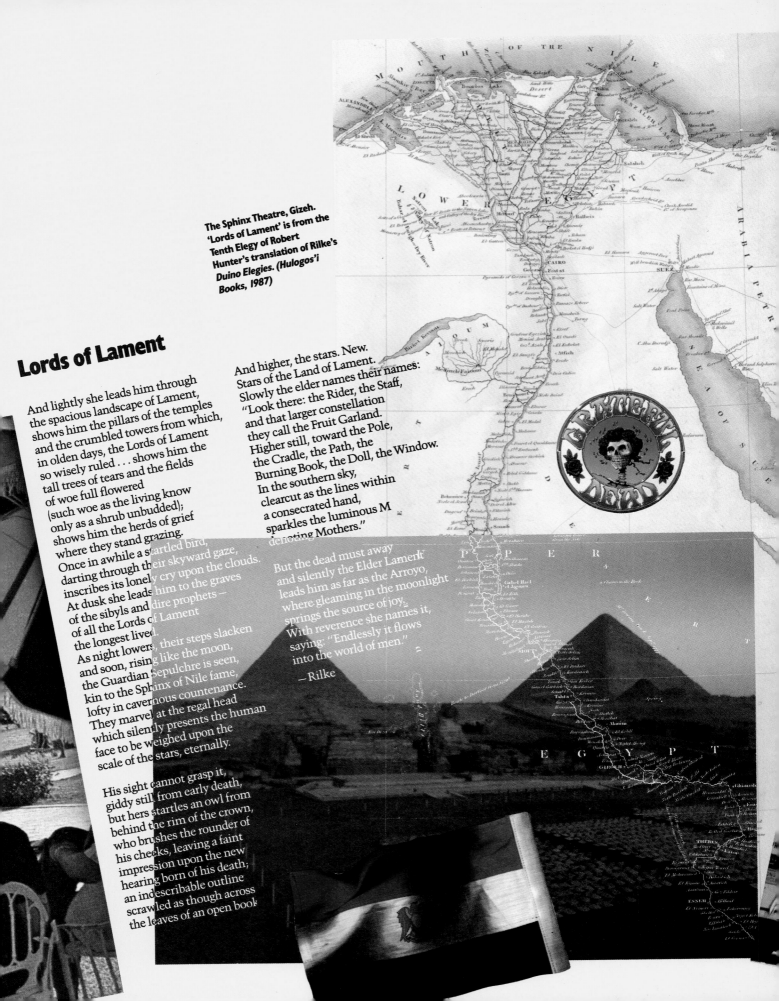

The Sphinx Theatre, Gizeh. 'Lords of Lament' is from the Tenth Elegy of Robert Hunter's translation of Rilke's Duino Elegies. (Hulogosi Books, 1987)

Lords of Lament

And lightly she leads him through
the spacious landscape of Lament,
shows him the pillars of the temples
and the crumbled towers from which,
in olden days, the Lords of Lament
so wisely ruled . . . shows him the
tall trees of tears and the fields
of woe full flowered
(such woe as the living know
only as a shrub unbudded);
shows him the herds of grief
where they stand grazing.

Once in awhile a startled bird,
darting through their skyward gaze,
inscribes its lonely cry upon the clouds.
At dusk she leads him to the graves
of the sibyls and dire prophets —
of all the Lords of Lament
the longest lived.
As night lowers, their steps slacken
and soon, rising like the moon,
the Guardian Sepulchre is seen,
kin to the Sphinx of Nile fame,
lofty in cavernous countenance.
They marvel at the regal head
which silently presents the human
face to be weighed upon the
scale of the stars, eternally.

His sight cannot grasp it,
giddy still from early death,
but hers startles an owl from
behind the rim of the crown,
who brushes the rounder of
his cheeks, leaving a faint
impression upon the new
hearing born of his death,
an indescribable outline
scrawled as though across
the leaves of an open book.

And higher, the stars. New.
Stars of the Land of Lament.
Slowly the elder names their names:
"Look there: the Rider, the Staff,
and that larger constellation
they call the Fruit Garland.
Higher still, toward the Pole,
the Cradle, the Path, the
Burning Book, the Doll, the Window.
In the southern sky,
clearcut as the lines within
a consecrated hand,
sparkles the luminous M
denoting Mothers."

But the dead must away
and silently the Elder Lament
leads him as far as the Arroyo,
where gleaming in the moonlight
springs the source of joy.
With reverence she names it,
saying: "Endlessly it flows
into the world of men."

—Rilke

The locals called us the 'mustached Californians' — that meant anything that had excess hair. They thought we were mighty strange. We didn't travel in big groups like other tourists, which they thought was weird, and they thought it was real weird that we liked to go to their homes and go out to the villages and dress like them.

There was serious sand at the Sphinx Theatre. Steve Parish caught some Egyptians rolling anvil cases end-over-end in it.

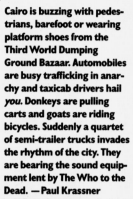

Cairo is buzzing with pedestrians, barefoot or wearing platform shoes from the Third World Dumping Ground Bazaar. Automobiles are busy trafficking in anarchy and taxicab drivers hail *you*. Donkeys are pulling carts and goats are riding bicycles. Suddenly a quartet of semi-trailer trucks invades the rhythm of the city. They are bearing the sound equipment lent by The Who to the Dead. — Paul Krassner

When the crew packed out from the gig, the recording truck got stuck in the sand. They sent a tractor, but it got stuck too — every piece of equipment they sent got stuck in the sand. They ended up using camels to pull them out. — Jerilyn

These guys were the official keepers of this corner of the Pyramid complex, and you had to pay them. Each of our crew had one of them assigned to him. These Guardians, as they were called, have been earning a living from tourists for hundreds of years, probably thousands. The jobs run in the families of Nazlet-el-Samman village. Their cry is 'Bakshish, Bakshish' and they're very persistent. — Sue Stephens

"We now return our souls to the creator and as we stand on the edge of eternal darkness, let our chant fill the void, that others may know: In the land of the night, the Ship of the Sun is drawn by the Grateful Dead. . ."

Setting up at the Sphinx Theatre, and inset, Jerilyn, Johnny Hagen and his double, the 'Hagen of Cairo'. Whether or not the alleged quote, left, from the *Egyptian Book of the Dead* is documented is a heavily debated but unre-solved question. Opposite, the Arabic translation of the Grateful Dead's bio in the concert program. Kelley's adaptation of Tutankamun's effigy.

Monday, September 4th
Flight: TWA #800
Dep JFK   7:30 p.m.
Arr Paris   8:30 a.m. (9/5)
Dep Paris   10:30 a.m.
Arr Cairo   2:30 p.m.

Tuesday, September 5th
Arrive Cairo.

Wednesday, September 6th
Check out site. Prepare list of parts needed.

Thursday, September 7th
Site preparation.

Friday, September 8th
Equipment Arr. Cairo 6:25 p.m.

Saturday, September 9th
Equipment clears customs.

Sunday, September 10th
Equipment available.

Monday, September 11th
Set up.

Tuesday, September 12th
Set up.

Wednesday, September 13th
Sound check – Sphinx Theatre.

Thursday, September 14th
Gig – Sphinx Theatre.

Friday, September 15th
Gig – Sphinx Theatre.

Saturday, September 16th
Gig – Sphinx Theatre. (Full moon). Equipment pack-out.

تتكون هذه الفرقة الموسيقية ، "جريتفل ديد"
من سبعة فنانين مرموقين حاولوا بنجاح
باهرين يتفاعلوا ابداعياً مع مستمعيهم ، وهذه
خاصية جوهرية من خصائلهم الفنية العديدة
جعلت وقع فنهم على النفوس وقعاً ابداعياً
خلاقاً.

موسيقاهم تجعلك الى قمم الروعة بحيث انها
تخلق مستوى جديداً من الوعي والجودة الفنية
في نفس المستمع .

انها تحض معها بذور الخلق والابداع الحقيقيين

وفي هذه المرحلة تصل الحواس بعضها الشئ
مع موهبة هذه الفرقة الموسيقية الامريكية
تصبح الانغام في موسيقى الجريتفل ديد"
شلالاً راشاً من الاحاسيس تنصب على
روح المستمع بشتى الالوان .

ان موسيقاهم تدفع بالرؤيا الفنية الى
ابعد مدى ، وتدفع بالاحساس الى أبهى
التجارب الروحية لتجسد بعد ذلك على
مزيج من التصاوير والتجاليب الرائعة .
ينتمي الموسيقيون أنفسهم الى خلفيات
فنية عديدة وهامة .

"جري جارسيا" : عارف جيثار
موهوب ، وهوى ظرار المغنيين الذين
اشتقوا العبقرية الموسيقية من منابع
غير محدودة العدد . تعتار روئيته الموسيقية

بالوان واختلاجات تخدف التصنيف .
"فيل لاش" : عضو آخر من الفرقة ، وهو
خبير مرموق في عزف الجيتار ، ومعرفته
بالموسيقى الكلاسيكية خبرته للموسيقى
الالكترونية من حيث تعمقه الاصيل فيها.
"بوب وير" : عازف ماهر ومغني وهو الذي
يدفع بالصبر والنغم الناعم من عبقرية
هذه الفرقة الى الاستهام والانتقال العميق
غناء "دونا جدشو" هو مزيج من العبقرية
والقوة الخلاقة .
و "كيث جدشو" يدخل على عدين العاملين
الوانا عنيدة من عزف البيانو والارض .
"بيل كروتزمن" و "ميكي هارت" بمغاورها
الموسيقى الخاص وفرط احساسيهما بالنغم
يخلقات نغماً جديداً حياً محبراً تبعتد طرقهم
وعندت بذلك ديناميكية حديثة في موسيقى
ال "جريتفل ديد" .

الكثير من مقطوعاتهم الموسيقية مستوحاة
من "روبرت هنتر" العتاق ، وهو الشاعر
الذي ترجم الاحساس في هذه الاغاني الى
لغة حية ونغم جميل .

جاءت فرقة "جريتفل ديد" من منطقة
خليجي سان فرنسيسكو . إنهم يكونون
فعلياً حياً بجوى عائلة الموسيقى . عندما
تستمع الى موسيقاهم تسمع تأثيرات

الغناء الشعبي الامريكي والجاز والبلوز
مزوجين بالموسيقى المقدسة والروحية
تسمع فيها "الرّاقاي" من حنايا ، و"الرّاقا"
من الهند . وكذلك تحس فيها بأمركلتهم
في عبقريتها وانضباطها وقوة فاعليتها الفنية
على عقل وقلب المستمع .

وفرقة "جريتفل ديد" هي فرقة "روك أند رول"
ايضاً ، تعبر عن امكانية الخلق الموسيقي على
المستوى الالكتروني ، مستعملة في ذلك
أرضهم . واحدة واجودة الامكانيات الفنية الالكترونية
ان هؤلاء الفنانين والخبرة التي يعيشونها
بموسيقاهم هي مستوحاة من التاريخ الادبي
لنهر النيل ، وأسرار كتاب الموت ، واساطير
أبي الهول والكرنك ، وفوق كل ذلك هي
مستوحاة من اعظم أثر شاهده تاريخ
الانسانية : الاهرام .

ان عليهم من مستويات موسيقية جديدة
والتجارب الفنية الجماعية هو الذي اتى بهم
الى أرض مصر . وهما تأمل هذه الفرقة أن
تبعث وتمزج التراث الانساني النفيس لا
حدود . ليمدا العرض بأتي معهم عارف العود
المرموق الموسيقار النبيل والمغني السوداني
الموهوب : "حمزة الدين" لبعث المهجات
الفنية ببعث من مقطوعاته الفنية الجليلة
التي ترجع اصلاً الى تراث وادي النيل القديم

وخبرة الدين" من الفنانين الذين استطاعوا
ان يتفاعلوا ويسهموا في الموسيقى العربية بأخلاط
انماط موسيقية ترجع الى تاريخ قديم جداً
في طيات عبقرية واصالة فنية فنية وعنده
المرشد الامريكية .

في القاهرة فرقة "جريتفل ديد" ستنساهم معكم
في احد الفئات الانساني والتقافة الواسعة
التي لا تحدها حدود ، باحثين من خلال ذلك
الى تجديد طاقاتنا لنصل بها الى أروع التجارب
الخلاقة .

فأهلا وسهلا بكم . ولكم من
فرقة "جريتفل ديد" الفنسحكي .

GRATEFUL DEAD

PRESENTS THREE CONCER
At the Sound & Light Theatre, Gi
on Thursday, Friday and Saturda
14, 15, and 16 September 1978
at 9:30 PM

Special Guest: HAMZA EL-DIN

A dirty Dean Martin and Jerry Lewis tape served as a preliminary sound check. Later, an American general complained to stage manager Steve Parish that a rock 'n' roll band performing here was a sacrilege to 5,000 years of history. Parish responded, "Listen, I lost two brothers in 'Nam, and I don't wanna hear this crap." The general retreated in the face of those imaginary brothers.

Bill Kreutzmann had fallen off a horse and broken his arm. The horse was unscathed but recommended that Kreutzmann be shot. However, as an Arabian fortune cookie pointed out, *In the land of the limbless, a one-armed drummer is king.*

Bob Weir looked up at the Great Pyramid of Gizeh and cried out this rhetorical question: "WHAT IS IT?!"

— Paul Krassner

One exceptionally fine evening three of us were sitting on a rooftop in a darkened village (the power was out in these small villages much of the time) facing the giant Pyramid which was framed by half a window in a wall that was half built. Nothing is completed in Egypt; no one is in a hurry. Our host was an exquisite Arab, sitting beneath the half window showing us the ritual of the Goza, an Egyptian water pipe. He spoke excellent English and our communications were quite high, but after I tried to tell him about redwood trees and how they are as tall as the Great Pyramid, I don't think he believed another word I said.
— Nicki Scully (*Sonoma County Stump*)

Prankster George practiced climbing the pyramid every morning in preparation for his tribal task of implanting a Grateful Dead flag at the very top. It was allowed to stay there for four hours, an international symbol of dedication and trophy.

GRATEFUL DEAD

168

We were down at the pool at the Mena House hotel one day — Billy and Mickey and Kesey were there, and George Walker, one of Kesey's good friends. Someone — I heard it was Garcia — had given Kesey a skull and lightning bolt flag to put on top of the Great Pyramid of Cheops, where there's this big long pole that represents where the tip of the pyramid would be if the top piece weren't missing. Down at the pool they were talking about how they were going to document putting up the flag. They had brought all sorts of video equipment, but it wasn't compact like it is today. The Pyramid's blocks are real big, not like steps, and you have to physically lift yourself up from one block to the other. So Kesey asked, "Has anyone got a movie camera?" And I said, "I do." So he said, "OK. Bernie, you're comin' with us!" I said, "Where?" And he said, "To the top!"

They made me climb up first so I could film everyone coming up. Once we were all up at the top, they had to climb all the way up to the tippy-top of this pole — a piece of wood with two or three struts, the thing was probably 10 or 12 feet high. But how were they going to do it? Finally this guy Kim stood at the bottom of the thing and George Walker climbed up on top of him and shinnied up the rest of the pole to tie the huge flag on. And we got the whole thing

I found myself compelled to come here at sunrise to greet the sun. Like most monuments in Egypt, the Sphinx faces the East, and the sun rises directly between the paws. I had brought with me twigs of the sacred sage which had come from the Dakotas to the Sun Dance at Davis following The Longest Walk this summer. This I placed under the left paw, as an offering from the native peoples of our country. I felt profound gratitude for being there. — Nicki Scully (Sonoma County Stump)

down on film. It was hilarious.

So there was the Grateful Dead flag blowing in the wind. And it was so beautiful. At the show that night they had a big spotlight on it. Cosmic stuff. And the next day we picked up newspapers from overseas and they all had reports on how the Grateful Dead planted their flag on top of the Great Pyramid. It was the same weekend as the Camp David Accords (negotiated by President Jimmy Carter, Israel's Prime Minister Manachem Begin and Egypt's President Anwar Sadat).

Unfortunately, by the third night, when the moon was in eclipse, someone

had taken the flag down — probably some Dead Head. — Bernie Bildman (The Golden Road)

Wave That Flag

It is only as I breathe in deeply before each *Om* while sitting in the tub-like sarcophagus at the center of gravity in the Great Pyramid that I am forced to ponder the mystery of who goes there to pee.

Outside, I ask a camel named R2D2 his theory on who leaves behind this universal odor of urine.

"I don't know," he replies, "and what's more, I don't give a dung."

"Why are you so bitter?"

"Well, if you must know, my testicles still hurt. My master squeezed my scrotum between a pair of bricks."

"Jeez, what a terrible accident."

"Accident, my hump! He did it on purpose so that in my painful response I would swoosh up enough water to last for twenty days. The lazy bastard!"

"Wow, I guess it's not easy being a camel."

"You ain't kidding, pal. These pyramids may represent the cradle of civilization to you, but to me they are simply reminders of five thousand years of oppression."

Beast of Burden

"Things haven't improved much for you, huh?"

"We have always been the victims of human chauvinism. Did you know that the first inter-uterine birth control devices were used in camels? My great-grandmother had pebbles put into her uterus to prevent her from getting pregnant on long journeys."

"Well, at least it wasn't permanent sterilization. I mean *you're* here, right?"

"Yeah, and I have the freedom to piss wherever I want."

"Except inside the pyramid."

"Listen, you seem like an okay guy, so I'll answer your question. It ain't sacrilegious visitors who take a leak inside the King's Chamber, it's just jaded guides. Hey, you wanna go for a ride now?"

"Sure, why not?"

"And the camel bends down, warbling a chorus of *I don't wanna be your beast of burden. . .*

— Paul Krassner

Riding camels and horses was a continuous pastime around the Great Pyramid. The horses are trained to do a kind of slow motion dance. Mickey and Jerilyn were intrepid horsepersons. Inset, Bill Graham, relaxed in Cairo. Paul Krassner, opposite, was a camel rider. Inset, Chuck Kesey.

Most recordings I have heard of African music have been technically poor, made on small machines by anthropologists, mainly as an afterthought. This trip gave us the opportunity to record this music — these elusive sounds from the 'other side' — in true stereo. The Saligeans, from Upper Egypt, were placed under shrubbery 30 feet away. These musicians take a long time in developing their ideas, which extend over many hours. There is no reason to hurry. The second group, Bedouins — wanderers from the North Country — sat on a stone porch and smoked while the Saligeans were finishing. They became so laid-back they decided to play where they sat. This required a change in microphones to the Newmann KM84s. The drumming and double-reeds created an eerie effect in the stone-enclosed porch and was reflected accurately with the larger pattern of the Neumann mikes. — Mickey Hart (BAM Magazine)

171

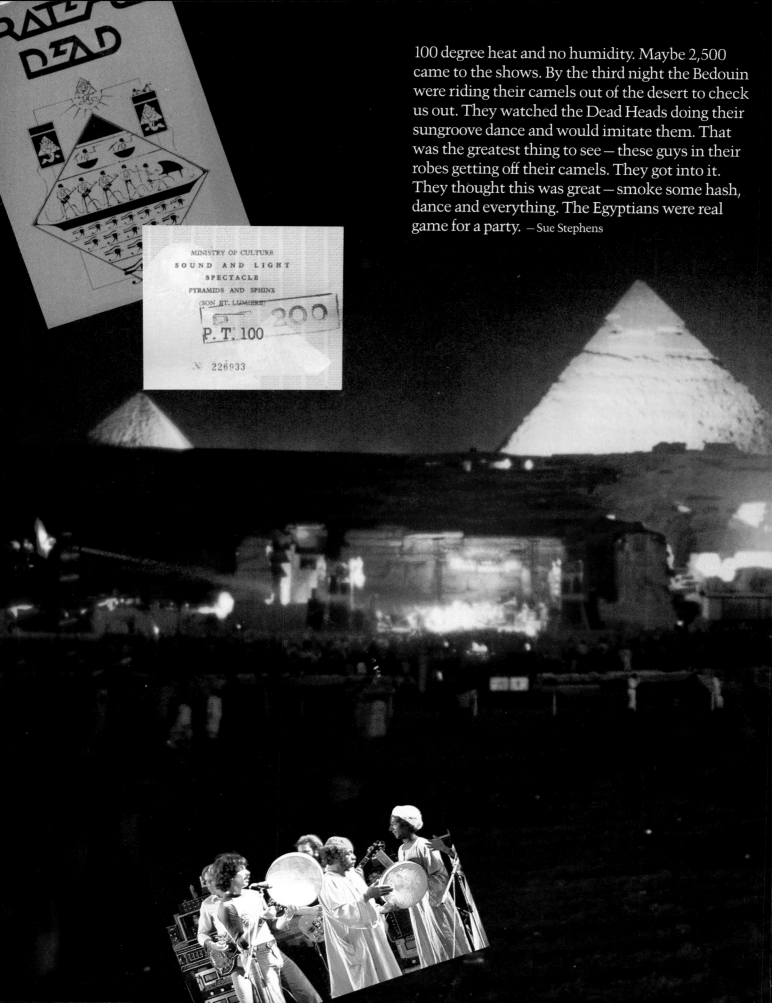

100 degree heat and no humidity. Maybe 2,500 came to the shows. By the third night the Bedouin were riding their camels out of the desert to check us out. They watched the Dead Heads doing their sungroove dance and would imitate them. That was the greatest thing to see — these guys in their robes getting off their camels. They got into it. They thought this was great — smoke some hash, dance and everything. The Egyptians were real game for a party. — Sue Stephens

MINISTRY OF CULTURE
SOUND AND LIGHT
SPECTACLE
PYRAMIDS AND SPHINX
(SON ET LUMIERE)
P.T. 100
№ 226933

You know, I've never danced in public before. I was never relaxed in front of a crowd. But the third night was one of the great experiences of my life — dancing to 'Sugar Magnolia' in front of the Great Pyramid. In my old age, if I remember major events in my life, this will be one of them. —Bill Graham

On the night of the third concert, manager Richard Loren had scheduled an eclipse of the moon. Hundreds of Egyptian kids were running through the streets, shaking tin cans filled with rocks in order to bring back the moon. But it took a rousing rendition of 'Ramble On Rose' to accomplish that feat.

Just before the Dead traipsed on stage that night, I had a feeling similar to the one Jerry Garcia had that time with Neal Cassady — that I was somehow involved in a lesson. It was as though the secret of the Grateful Dead would finally be revealed to me, if only I paid proper attention. And then it happened:

"Remember," I overheard Garcia instruct the band, "play in tune."

It was an outrageous event. The line between incongruity and appropriateness had disappeared along with the moon. The music was so powerful that the only way to go was ecstasy. I came out of my closet and danced. Someone described it as prayer. I may never dance in public again, but for that moment it was almost as if I had no choice. —Paul Krassner

had always been intrigued by the acoustical properties of the King's Chamber because of its size and shape, and because it doesn't conform to the physics formulas Western science has developed for determining the sound qualities of a given room. The King's Chamber in the Great Pyramid is essentially just a rectangular box. It's about 34 feet long, 17 feet wide, and 19 feet high. It's all polished stone, with completely perfect seams and edges. No building could be built that perfectly today. It's in the heart of the Great Pyramid, and its location in this mass of stone gives it a rigidity and resilience that is almost unfathomable. It seems as far away from people as you can get. Notes resonate in ways that defy the laws of physics.

The first night we went in there, we spent the whole evening singing in the room. We made up little choral groups and divided up into different vocal parts and just sang. The sound was incredibly rich and full, the King's Chamber has a rectangular coffer in it — about 7 x 4 x 4 feet — and it, too, had a particular resonance, so each of us took turns lying down inside of it and humming notes. When you found the resonant note, the softest you could hum would reverberate so much in that frequency that it would massage your whole body. And if you hummed at the level of a reasonable talking voice or louder, it actually hurt your ears.

It was about one-quarter mile from the stage to the Great Pyramid, and we had high-quality FM radio transmitters to span that distance. So, we put a transmitter down at the stage with a little antenna and sent the signal from there up to the outside of the Great Pyramid, where we had a receiver. We couldn't put the receiver directly in the King's Chamber

because it is deeply embedded in the stone structure, so from the outside we ran wires from a receiver into the Pyramid, up the Grand Gallery and into the King's Chamber, where we hooked the wires to a speaker. We also put a microphone in there, ran the wires back the same way, hooked it up to a transmitter on the side of the Pyramid and sent the signal down to a receiver onstage that was plugged into our recording console in the form of an echo return. The object, of course, was to send voices and instruments up through the radio link to the King's Chamber where it would play through the speaker there, be picked up by the microphone, and sent back down to the tape.

The Curse of Cheops

Unfortunately, the local cable we bought was inferior and was stomped on by the tour groups that tramp through during the day. After our hook-up in the King's Chamber was unsuccessful, some suggested that perhaps, cosmically, it wasn't meant to happen and that's why it

did not work. I don't buy that. I think it didn't work because from a technical end, we didn't quite have it all together. We were at peace with the gods and the authorities. There was no conflict or friction. None of us felt that we were transgressing any sacred rights or privacy. The Egyptians understood what we were doing and saw what our motives were. They knew this was the dream of our life. They saw the adventure in it, and it was exciting for them, too. It was like the cultural exchanges you read about in books, only this one was *for real*. — Dan Healy (*BAM Magazine*)

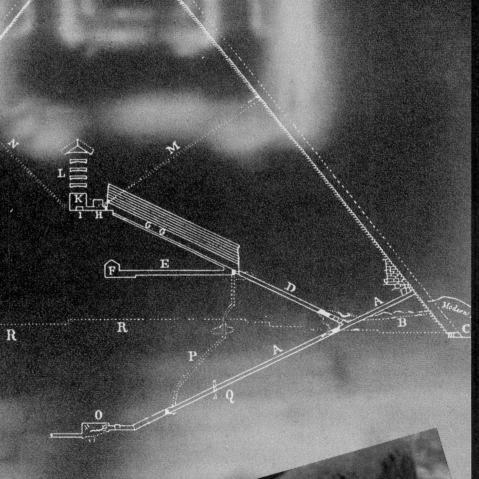

Caravan of Crazies

One of the highlights of the trip for me was the great camel ride we took across the desert after the final show. It was close to sunrise and Bill Graham rented every camel and horse he could find and we went in a huge caravan across the desert to a big tent village a few miles away called Sahara City. It's sort of the Las Vegas of Egypt. It was a full moon and we had just about everyone — at least a hundred people. There were taxis that went the long way, and motorcycles. As I remember, Graham and Mickey led the procession, with Mickey on his fabulous white horse. It was just huge, and it could dance and prance because it was really a show horse, and Mickey just had the time of his life galloping around on it. He looked like he was in some movie or something. — Mountain Girl

Most of the people who went to Sahara City got either a camel or an Arabian stallion. I'd ridden a horse earlier in the trip and had the life scared out of me. I'd never done it before, and the second I got on, mine bolted. I was thinking, "My God, after all this I'm going to die in Egypt!" But just as I convinced myself I was going to die, I got into the flow of it and it was just wonderful. Still, I was happy to get a camel for the night trip to Sahara City.

It was funny, because if you're an American woman, the Egyptian men all assume that you're loose. The guy who owned the camel I rode told me he wanted to marry me. But the real trouble started when we got to Sahara City around sunrise. The next guy just wouldn't leave me alone. He actually chased me all the way out to where Keith and all the other people from our group were. Everyone was yelling, "Leave her alone! Leave her alone!" He was serious. He was going for it! Finally, the only thing that succeeded in getting him off me was when Ken Kesey stepped out of the crowd and poured a bucket of beer on his head. — Donna *(The Golden Road)*

The camel park opposite the Mena House Hotel.

Ship of Fools

After the shows a bunch of us flew to Luxor in Upper Egypt, where the Karnak Temple is, and the Valley of the Kings with Tutankamun's tomb. We got special permission to go inside that. And we hired a train of donkeys and took a steep, rocky trail over the mountain to Queen Hap Set Shut's temple. We passed a village whose inhabitants were entirely devoted to grave robbing in those parts. These guys had been robbing tombs for thousands of years. Good jobs run in the family.

Richard had arranged a boat trip on the Nile. Ati, the boatman, spoke English and was like the Ambassador along the Nile. He knew everyone from Aswan to Cairo. When we were on the dock at Luxor getting ready to leave, Donna came over to me and said, "How soon are we gonna get there? Like I told Keith, he wanted to know, and I told him about half-an-hour." And I said, "More like two-and-a-half days," I said. We were going to Aswan! There were about 20 of us on the boat, including most of the band, and at night the deck was like sardines. All those people were sleeping on the boat under packing blankets, the scratchy kind — it was cold at night. We stopped at all the temples along the Nile. It was fun, it was great. At Aswan, Mickey went on deep into the Sudan and recorded the musicians in the villages. This is where Hamza el Din comes from. Hamza and a troupe of handclappers, singers and dancers opened the shows for the band.
— Sue Stephens

PROCESSED BY KODAK

Kodachrome SLIDE

Arriving at Aswan after a three-day cruise up the Nile from Luxor, Mickey, Hamza and Jerilyn had gone on ahead to Aswan and welcomed the new arrivals with drums from the balcony of the hotel, which overlooked the river.

Marag beckons me to the pole in the center of the square of limestone blocks. "Marag show you little Pyramid trick!" He has me reach as high as I can up the pole with a chip of rock and scratch a mark. I notice a number of similar scratches at various heights. "Now have a seat and breathe a while this air on top Pyramid. You will see."

I sit at the base of the pole glad for a breather. "How does it affect you, this magic Pyramid air?"

"It affect you to shrink," he says, grinning down from his scant five feet.

"Breathe deep. You'll see."

Now that he calls it to mind I remember noticing that most of the Pyramid scalers are indeed men of unusually slight stature. I breathe deep and steady watching the sun on the clouds. After five minutes or so he tells me to take one further breath and stand with my stone and scratch again. It's hard to tell, with all the marks of previous experiments, but it looks to me like I'm scratching exactly next to my first mark. I'm about to tell him his Pyramid air is just another piece of bull when I find myself flashing.

It's an old trick. I use it myself sometimes as a way to get an audience off cheap and easy. I call it the Dong-Dong. I tell them to take 15 deep breaths, hold the last and stand, and om together as the flash comes on. Hyperventilation. Every junior high kid knows it. But the business with the mark on the pole and the magic air was so slick I didn't have the vaguest recognition, even when I felt the familiar faint coming on.

I grab for support, impressed. But this is only the beginning, the necessary prep. Now he positions himself in front of me and stands hands on his hips, gazing upward. He's done all this before. He flaps a moment then, as the breeze stills, I look up and out of the hazy sky I see what he is waiting for. I see the thumb of God come down out of the hazy sky and settle on top of Marag's head, bowing him like a deck of cards until his face snaps down revealing another behind it, and another, and another, face after face snapping forward in an accelerating riffle—some familiar, from the village, the aouda, some famous (I remember distinctly two widely known musicians who I will not name in case it might bring them hamper) but mostly faces I've never seen. Women and men, black, brown, red and whatever, most of them looking at least past the half century mark in earthly years.

It's a large deck, numbering in the hundreds, and each face is alive, conscious, firmly aware of my onlooking and looking back at me to prove it. The faces are all individual and the expressions completely various—bemused; patient; stern—but besides their age there is one quality uniting them all: each face is entirely, profoundly, unshakingly benevolent.

It is a very good trick. —Ken Kesey, *Spit In the Ocean #5*

ضيف

They are delighted at our interest and excitement when they show us something. For example, a watchman led us to some huge granite slabs near where the Ship of the Sun had been buried. As he hit one of them with his open hand, it rang with a clear tone. He then watched us with delight as we went from slab to slab, discovering for ourselves that this was an ancient giant stone marimba of a sort. What music must it have played and how and for whom? — Nicki Scully (*Sonoma County Stump*)

Grateful Dead explore Upper Egypt: Jerry and David Freiberg at Karnak; going down to the tomb of Ramses; Mountain Girl and Richard on donkeys for the climb out of the Valley of the Kings to reach Queen Hat-Shep-Sut's temple.

Opposite, musicians in Hamza El Din's village, Tuska in the Sudan, where MERT, Mickey's 'mobile engineering and recording teams' (Jerilyn, Bret Cohen, John Cutler and the Nagra tape recorder) went after Aswan to record. A master tar maker displays the drum of the Nubians.

For many Egyptians, our music seemed to cause a sensory overload. They were in awe of it and weren't quite sure how to respond. I asked my friend Omar what he felt about the music and he told me, "It makes me feel like that man on TV who leaps buildings and breaks bricks with his hands." "You mean Superman?" I asked. He said, "Yes, yes . . . Superman!"

Some of the people looked at us as a finger on the hand of peace. They want peace more than anything in the world; they are not a warlike people at all. The Camp David peace talks were going on at the time of our visit and a lot of people looked at our presence as an extension of the goodwill that was spreading from the meetings across the ocean.

The final concert was the magic night. There was a full moon and a total lunar eclipse that evening which charged us even more with energy. We played as hard as we could and we peaked that third night, knowing all the while that this *wouldn't* be the last time we'd play there. We knew that if we played well we would *have* to come back. That's the difference between the Grateful Dead and most bands. We like to take the long overview which is why we didn't look at that as our *last* night in Egypt . . . it was part of our *first* trip to Egypt. It's a little like making love. When you make love slowly and it's good, you know there will be another time.

After the concerts, I prepared for a journey into Upper Egypt, I was accompanied by my good friend Hamza, who knew the area well; my engineer Bret Cohen, who was assisted by John Cutler; my assistant Jerilyn Brandelius; and Raafat Shoukkry, our cameraman with a 16mm camera from TV Cairo.

We packed the stereo Nagra recording machine, microphones, recording tape, and the movie equipment, and departed from Cairo to Aswan. My objective was to meet the people, play with them, and record their music. Not urban music, but folk music — music from the 'other side.'

As we started our trek into Upper Egypt, Hamza took me aside and said, "Now, Mickey, it is time for you to *surrender*. This doesn't mean to give up, to go fast or go slow, but to go with the natural flow of the desert. It is so big and you are so small. Soon, the loudest thing you will hear will be the sound of silence." Coming directly from an electric environment, this appears as some sort of pressure drop. When sounds do appear, there is revealed a new clarity to the beginnings and endings which are sharply etched in this new-found ambience — silence.

When we arrived in Hamza's village, called Tuska in Kom Ombo, he was greeted as a homecoming prince. He hadn't been there in four years, so all his brothers, cousins, aunts, and uncles were there in force. After the social graces of tea, handshaking and laughter, we moved outside into the courtyard of one of their homes and a cousin of Hamza's brought in a Cairo newspaper with a photo of Hamza and me playing our tars at the last concert. The men were happy to learn that I play tar, since it is their native instrument.

The desert is the tar's home, and in this dry air it speaks with a bell-like tone — crisp and sharp in its overtones. The tar is a single stretched skin, 14 inches in diameter with a four-inch laminated shell 1/4 inch thick. It looks like a

Recording in the Sudan

large tambourine without jingles. The drum has been used in Nubia since Pharaonic times and is even used by the women for such practical purposes as sifting grains. But only the men play it as an instrument.

One by one, the master tarists of the village showed themselves. First, the old blind tar maker of the village took my tar and felt the outside wood and skin, marveling at the uncommonly smooth finish. My tar was made by a friend of Hamza's in San Francisco and the craftsmanship is exceptional. After further checking the outside of the drum, the man began to scratch and sniff the inside of the skin to determine the type of skin it was. Then he played it, and the quickness of the drum surprised him.

He then handed me the drum with a gesture to play. This was a tough act to follow, but having studied the tar for three years with Hamza, I took a deep breath and started to play. After a minute, their faces lit up and the children started hand clapping; the women gathered around, the men brought out their tars and a party was underway. Each of the master tarists demonstrated his skills to me as they passed the tars around, and encouraged me to play with them. Individually, they greeted me and welcomed me as a drummer to their village through the language of the tar. At that point, the drums became the voice of The Spirit.

Recording the various types of music we encountered on the trip proved difficult, but ultimately rewarding. Success in these kinds of situations depends on having the right equipment, on mother nature, and a little luck. Each situation presented its own parameters. Just to be able to judge what kind of mikes to use and where to place them was a challenge.

All of this recording might not have been possible were it not for the existence of MERT (Mobile Engineering and Recording Teams) which was created specifically for the purpose of seeking out and recording ethnic music. MERT is for the preservation of quality music that would not ordinarily be recorded due to lack of interest and financial viability by major record companies. Its inception came in 1973 when Alla Rahka (an Indian tabla master) brought all of the Indian musicians traveling with the George Harrison tour to the Stone House in Fairfax (formerly the Ali Akbar Khan School of Music) for a night of playing for each other. This led to recordings of Ali Akbar Khan, Zakkir Hussain, Turk Murphy, the Inverness Music Festival, pre-recorded scores for the American Conservatory Theater, a new music show by Jerry Garcia and myself at the Palace of Fine Arts, sound effects for Lee Oskar's new album, work with Villiat Khan, Japanese Taiko drummers, Vincent Delgado's mid-Eastern group called Jazayer, Hamza's latest record, and much more.

Some of these tapes have found their way onto disc form and are distributed by Rykodisc, but mostly, they are preserved in my locker for posterity, not unlike fine vintage wines. Without MERT and the assistance of Bret Cohen, John Cutler, and Jerilyn Brandelius, the excursion to Upper Egypt could not have taken place, and we would have been unable to seek out and record this ancient music which holds a special place in my heart. (*The Music of Upper and Lower Egypt,* was issued by Rykodisc in 1988 as part of Hart's series, 'The World'.) — Mickey Hart ('As Told by Cookie', *BAM Magazine*).

Left, the Alexandrian musicians at Hani Sabat's house; the beautiful Nubians, Hamza's relatives; in the Sudan; and onward into Africa. . .

What are the pyramids themselves besides records
It really began before rock and roll
in some obscure corner of the american psyche,
there amidst the jazz and blues roots in africa, elvis,
schoenberg, sousa
and modern technology
the dead exploded
like a rocket
fully clothed in armor
from the brow
of zeus
What is in us that is finite is our knowledge of the infinite
What is in us that is infinite is our knowledge of the finite.
—Peter

SY OF THE
REPUBLIC OF
GYPT
ATUR PLACE, N.W.
GTON, D.C. 20008

October 10, 1978

Jerry Garcia
Grateful Dead
1073
Rafael, California 94901

Dear Mr. Garcia:

The accounts in both the Egyptian and the American
press, plus the reports that I have received re-
garding the success of your September concerts at
the Sphinx Theater, give me, as they must give you
and your colleagues, great satisfaction. It is a
historic "first" in the annals of modern music --
to play the Pyramids before thousands of fans, old
and new.

These concerts have become a unique chapter in the
story of Egyptian-American friendship and we are
pleased and gratified that the proceeds of the
ticket sales went to the Faith and Hope Society
and the Department of Antiquities. They will be
put to very good use.

My sincere congratulations and best wishes of
success to the Grateful Dead.

Yours truly,

shraf A. Ghorbal
dor, E. and P.

"IT'S NOT UNCOMMON," SAID ROBBIE TAYLOR, "FOR US TO SEE SAN FRANCISCO PEOPLE AT NEW YORK CONCERTS AND NEW YORK PEOPLE AT SAN FRANCISCO ONES. OFTEN PEOPLE WILL DROP EVERYTHING THEY'RE DOING TO ACTUALLY FOLLOW US AROUND FROM GIG TO GIG. ONE KID IN THE AUDIENCE LAST NIGHT SAID IT WAS THE FOURTH DEAD CONCERT HE'D ATTENDED THIS WEEK."

"THAT'S NOTHING," SAID JERRY, "WHEN WE PLAYED IN EGYPT, WE RAN INTO AMERICANS WHO'D MORTGAGED THEIR HOMES . . ."

The Greek Theatre, Berkeley, a favorite venue, during the day and at dusk. Inset, John Cipollina and Dan Healy.

Are the Dead Still a Militant, Vital Band?

The whole thing with the Grateful Dead is a challenge to get something new happening, even when you don't feel like doing anything new, or don't feel anything new lurking around the corner. We have to find something new in a given treatment of a particular song, or some totally new and unexplored territory in one of our jams. We try to go for that every night. To be together and responsive enough to do that sort of stuff, you really have to keep your wits fairly sharp and your chops together. The band has to be a working, functioning unit.

You always have to work at that, like they say you have to work at making a marriage work. — Weir

But are the Dead still a militant, vital band, or are they simply trading on past reputation?

"Well, I can tell you this," says Weir. "The son of a recent president of our country told my lyricist, who's a friend of his, that the Grateful Dead were more important to him than his mother and his father and everything that he'd learned in school.

"Of course my lyricist said, 'Surely you're outta your mind?' But he said, 'No, because these people showed me, more than anybody else, that there is another way.' We're committed to that ideal."

"How strong the foundation is," said Hart, "determines how strong the band will ultimately be. I don't know what every other band is built on but I know it's not built on what we're built on. We were all misfits in a certain kind of way musically and we sort of fit together in this odd puzzle.

That's one way of looking at it. And we appreciate each other's playing." (*The Aquarian*, February, 1979)

Bob Weir gestures during 'The Wheel'.

Francis, Gio and I went to a Grateful Dead concert. Bill Graham invited us to watch from the stage. The road manager sat us on some trunks in the shadows about six feet from the drummers. The music was amazing. It had physical impact. I could feel it and hear it, but mostly I was watching the whole performance. I was surprised to realize that these men were in their late thirties or early forties, Francis's age.

The lights kept changing and different things would come in and out of view. At the end of the set, we went back to the dressing room and Bill introduced us to Jerry Garcia. He reminded me of Francis, sort of portly with traces of gray in his black beard. He appeared to be a thoughtful, middle-aged man in the music business.

I met a friend in the hallway and was talking until I heard the music begin again. I went back to stage left and found that we had been moved to another position. I could see a different angle of the stage. It included the upper half of the guitarists and musicians in front. Slides taken during the Grateful Dead tour in Egypt were being projected on a huge screen above the musicians. There was a long sequence where just the two drummers played. The road manager opened the trunk we had originally been sitting on and passed out rhythm instruments to four or five people who seemed to be friends of the band. He moved a microphone to pick up their sound. At one point someone passed me a tambourine. I was too uptight to take it. I passed it to Francis. He shook it

awhile and then I tried it. It was surprising how heavy it was and how tiring it got to keep up a rhythm. Bill Graham came by every little while. He said, "Look at the audience, look at that, the crowd isn't crazy, it's just weaving, everyone is joined together. It's a sociological phenomenon. Somebody ought to study it."

Something about the evening reminded me of the evening inside the Ifugao priest's house, in the Phillipines, where we attended a religious ceremony. It felt like the same thing. The scale was different, but everyone being joined together by rhythms and images was the same, and instead of rice wine and betel nut there was beer and grass.

At the end of the last set

the band left the stage and the audience roared and clapped for an encore. Bill said to Francis, "Come on and see this. For fourteen years it has always been the same. They refuse to play an encore. I have to go back there and talk them into it. You want to see a performance? Come on and watch me." Francis went with Bill to the dressing room. About fifteen minutes later the band came back onstage for an encore.

We got home around three in the morning. We didn't go to sleep for a long time. — Eleanor Coppola (*Notes,* Simon & Schuster, 1979.)

The Coppola family, left, watching the Rhythm Devils during the Dead's second set, Winterland, October 24, 1978.

Joined Together by Rhythms and Images

MASQU...

GRATEFUL...
THE BLUES BROTH...
FEATURING JOLIET JAKE AND ELLWOOD B...

NEW RIDERS OF THE PURPLE S...

BREAKFAST AT DAWN

DECEMBER 31 · 8 PM

NEW YEAR'S EVE SUNDAY

Dear Winterland Fan,

This New Year's Eve concert with the Grateful Dead will be the last show at Winterland. We know there won't be enough tickets for everyone, so we have devised an innovative ticket distribution system.

Monday, December 10, tickets will go on sale at all BASS outlets. There will be no charge...

...Factory stores (except Irving Street and Hillock's (except Walnut Creek); ...more only); Eucalyptus ...d Reno only); BASS Ticket, ...Jeans in San Francisco, ...Hyatt Regency, Turf

...to buy Dead tickets ...and the outlet

...will keep a same-numbered ticket in a hopper. At 1pm today, each outlet will draw numbers to determine which people will be eligible to buy tickets (limit ... per person). The number of tickets available a... outlet will be based on the outlet's average a... of sales volume.

Between 1pm and 3pm today, you m... same outlet to see if your number... to buy your ticket. Winning nur... please do not call the outlets... after 3pm.

We hope this drawing... chance to obtain a... 415/TELETIX, 4...

Good luck, ...

Leave it to the Dead Heads to ultimately recover the stolen Grateful Dead ban- ners that vanished New Year's Eve. Mark Francis says that he and his fellow Dead Heads, the ad hoc Banner Recovery Team, tailed the suspects through the streets of San Francisco for two days before receiv- ing a phone tip late one night that led them to locate the banners in the hands of two young men, who "weren't Dead Heads at all," according to Francis. The banners were later returned to the Grateful Dead office by a member of Bill Graham's organiza- tion, and Francis is giving the thousand dollars in reward money to those that deserve it. We hope that's enough to cover the cars that Francis says they cracked up while pursuing the thieves! —(BAM Magazine)

186

Ten years ago this New Year's Eve, the Grateful Dead closed a chapter of rock 'n' roll history when they played the final concert at San Francisco's Winterland, a 5,000-seat arena that served as the de facto West Coast rock headquarters for a decade. The Dead played Winterland 62 times, by far the most of any band, and they almost always played well there. In many ways it was the perfect place for them during a period when their popu-their popularity in other parts of the country was beginning to reach hockey-arena proportions. Its dingy but labyrinthine backstage area easily accommo-dated the rambling Grateful Dead family and hangers-on, while out front there always seemed to be that extra ticket for the truly desperate. The consensus is that 12/31/78 was one of the best Dead shows ever.

The marathon opened with the New Riders, shifted into overdrive with the Blues Brothers, and then hit hyperspace with three long Dead sets covering the cream of their repertoire. After sunup, the band came out a final time and sang 'We Bid You Goodnight'. Bill Graham's weary troops handed out breakfast for 5,000, and then it was over. —Blair Jackson *(The Golden Road)*

Scenes from a New Year's Eve: Graham flying down on a giant joint at midnight; Keith in a sea of balloons; Lee Oskar (harmonica) and John Cipollina (guitar) join the band for a few tunes, and, inset opposite, John Belushi of the Blues Brothers.

Sardine Demographics

"Phew! It's *amazing*, isn't it?" marvels Donna, herself the mother of a five-year-old boy who is learning to play drums to the Dead's music. "The kids coming to the shows now are the same age that we were when we started getting into this other world. It is a younger audience now. The older fans still come, but they're content to hang out in the back. They've been seeing the Grateful Dead for years, so they don't have to be in the front rows anymore."

Or is it really, as rhythm guitarist Bob Weir ventures at a press conference following the Madison Square Garden shows, that the old-timers simply can't compete with the new generation of Dead Heads? "We see people passed out that can't fall down," Weir says about the sardine-can atmosphere at the front of the audience. And in one of his more serious tones, lead guitarist and Dead figurehead Jerry Garcia adds, "It's a bummer, man." — (*The Aquarian*)

The band invested in some new equipment for Mydland when he joined, even buying him a Sequential Circuits Prophet-5 when they discovered he didn't have one. Unfortunately, after working a while with it, Mydland decided the instrument wasn't right for the kind of music the Dead would be playing. "Everybody in general is into the idea of having synthesizer on the tunes. The problem is that the Dead's music is so spur-of-the-moment," he points out. "I might hear something that gives me an idea to change to a different program, but by the time I'd come up with it, they'd be off on something else. I don't like to be left back there trying to figure out what to come up with. It's not the kind of group where you can work things out in advance, like, 'Okay, here I go to 22.'" — (The Golden Road)

Keyboardist Brent Mydland Joins the Band

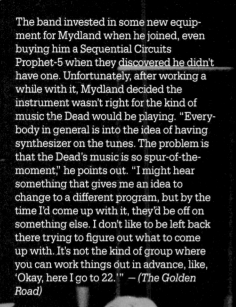

From far left, 'Rock for Life' poster from the benefit concert for Jane Fonda and Tom Hayden's foundation to end environmental cancer; Steve and Danny; Carrie and Marina Rifkin; *Heaven Help the Fool;* Willy John Cashman of FM Productions making a gongstand.

"The movie was already finished when Francis Coppola came to me . . . he told me it needed the heartbeat of the jungle and asked me if I would help him," recalls Mickey Hart. "What actually happened was that Francis came to see me through Bill Graham. A few days later, I get a call from one of his people to come down and watch the movie. It blows me away. I'm sitting there, figuring why would Francis want me to see the movie, and when it's over, he looks at me. I nod back to him because I can feel the colors and rhythms of the movie and I know immediately that I can put it into sound. I tell Francis that only under two conditions would I do the percussion. First, if he went over the movie scene by scene and told me exactly what he was trying to say and do, and, secondly, once we agreed on the type of format, that I would have complete freedom. Francis looked at me, and said, "Make it happen, Mickey."

For three months, Hart lived with the Coppola family. Hart assembled a percussion crew which could shake blood out of a stone. He called in Airto Moreira, the undisputed jazz king of percussion from Brazil, and his wife, vocal instrumentalist Flora Purim, to supply the sounds of the jungle. Hart invited his former student and now holder of a Julliard doctorate in classical percussion, Michael Hinton, plus fellow Dead drummer Bill Kreutzmann and Dead bassist Phil Lesh.

Unlike rock and roll, the instrumentation had to be capable of conveying anything from a whisper to a scream within the dynamics of supplying motion. Hart created the undercurrent of sound and fear of Kurtz's journey upriver into the heart of darkness. "We didn't use any traditional instruments like drum kits," Hart said. "We built all the instruments ourselves, probably over 200 in all, at the Dead studio, miked them up and then walked through the jungle. We built wind chimes, glass harps, scritches, tubalongs, and instruments of the future."

The glass harp was used as the sound signature in *Apocalypse Now* for Willard's dossier, a recurring thematic device used to heighten the suspense of the war intrigue set in Cambodia. A scritch, aluminum rods rubbed with glass that vibrates a high-pitched sound, was built to accompany the sounds of walking through the jungle underbrush. A tubalong, with its 31 notes to an octave, pounded out the passing onslaught of helicopters. "It's physics and mathematics and discipline," says Hart. "Sound is an incredible force that can transmit feelings through the physical extension of sound waves and their fractions in length and amplitude."
— Clint Roswell *(San Francisco Chronicle)*

Recording the *Apocalypse Now* percussion soundtrack. Left, setting up the instruments in 'jungle format' at the studio. Inset from left, Flora Purim, Francis Coppola, Francis and Mickey work it out and take a break, and the incomparable Airto. Below, Francis Coppola's 40th birthday and Easter party, right after the *Apolcalypse Now* wrap. Bill Graham and Zohn Artman arranged the events — the San Francisco Gay Marching Band, a plane trailing "Happy Birthday From One Yenta To Another" and a parachutist who landed right at Francis' feet, opened his flight suit, pulled out two glasses and a bottle of champagne. The Coppola family: Roman, Eleanor, Francis, Sofia.

Developing the Beast

Can you think of ways that your drum technique has changed in the last ten to fifteen years?

Kreutzmann: It's mostly changed because we've wanted it to change. We're always going for some new idea. Like Mickey has come up with a new idea for the drum solo where we've been doing something shown to him by a Japanese drum troupe called An-Deko-Za. They do Taiko drumming.

How would you describe that style?

Hart: It's like Martial Arts drumming. It's very Zen, very proper, very articulate. It's very emotional . . . and intellectual at the same time.

Kreutzmann: Another big change that's come about is that five, six years ago Mickey and I weren't able to line out exactly what we were going to do during the drum solo. Now we're in a place where we can actually discuss before a show how we're going to approach the solo. So instead of going out there and blasting out, we actually lay out a sketch.

Is that sketch strictly followed?

Hart: Hardly ever. We arrive at one way it could go. We'll start off with it usually. It'll lead us into the path. — (Relix)

Willy John, Danny Orlando and Mickey testing 'The Beast'; Opposite, Billy and Shelley Kreutzmann's wedding reception in Mendocino County, Robert Hunter.

Hunter's a very prolific lyricist; how do you decide what to turn into songs?

I don't decide. He'll give me maybe ten songs at a time. I'll take them and read through them, and look at them and look at them, and look at them, and sometimes I'll sit down at the piano and fool around a little. And one of them will start talking back to me, or maybe two of them, or three sometimes. All of sudden a line or two will start resonating . . . Hunter and I — our best collaborations are when we work together. That is to say, when I feed him a melody, and I say, okay Hunter, I've got this melody, and these changes that go like this.

We both agree that that's our best way to work.

So the songs which he gives me and that I eventually turn into music . . . they find me, and it really has to do with an emotional quality, it's not mechanistic. It's an emotional quality of the words, or something about the way a word sounds, or something about the meter, or something about the content. Sometimes I don't even know what it is. Sometimes the sense of the words doesn't occur to me until years later. I don't find it's in my best interests to try and analyze it, since it's fundamentally emotional.

It's hard to sing a song that doesn't mean something to you, and it's hard to have a song keep meaning something to you when you repeat it a lot of times. It's a testament to the power of a lot of those songs that I can still sing them and they still mean something to me. —Garcia
(BAM Magazine)

JERRY GARCIA BAND
CATS UNDER THE STARS

I've been playing for about twenty-five years. Right after my first drum lesson in high school I ran into my first set of drums, and another guy went out after his first guitar lesson and bought a guitar. That afternoon we played together. It was like instant love.

That's why I started playing music. To make people feel good, because it made me feel good too. That's what the Grateful Dead's all about — communication between the band and the audience.

They're really the seventh band member. There is some great power, be it God or whatever, that enters the Grateful Dead on certain nights, and it has to do with us being open and getting together with the audience. If we can do that, then it comes . . . and spreads everywhere.
— Kreutzmann

Dead Head News

Jerry and Phil are both playing custom-made guitars by Doug Irwin. Bobby still plays an Ibanez and Billy and Mickey are now playing Sonar rosewood drums and Zildjian cymbals. Brent plays a Hammond B-3 organ and Yamaha electric piano. The band has played four benefits in the last two years, each one emphasizing a different community problem: for Pacific Alliance's campaign against nuclear energy and for more solar development; for Jane Fonda and Tom Hayden's movement against Environmental Cancer; for SEVA's (Society for Epidemiology and Voluntary Assistance) campaign against cataract blindness and other eradicable diseases, beginning in Nepal; and for Joan Baez's Humanitas Foundation's direct aid to Cambodian refugees in Northern Thailand. The Dead's next benefit in the works is for the Committee on Worldwide Nuclear Disarmament, which seeks to gather support through education, starting with the Bay Area. On the Summer Solstice weekend, concerts are planned in Alaska (Anchorage and Fairbanks); there will probably be other summer festivals and weekend dates, but mostly the band will take a break from recording and touring until the fall and work on individual projects, some of which are now in progress. Mickey is working on a percussion-based record from the music he did with The Rhythm Devils for the film score of *Apocalypse Now*, soon to be released by Passport Records. Robert Hunter's new album, *Jack O' Roses*, which he recorded in England, and is distributed there by Dark Star Records, will also be released in America soon. We'll try to get more news out later. Thanks for your letters, advice, good ideas, helpful complaints, and artwork. (*Dead Heads Newsletter*, 1981)

From Left, John Kahn, Jerry's perennial bass player and musical associate in the Jerry Garcia Band; Bobby in a blue moment; Joan Baez and Mickey at the Cambodia benefit. Right, the cover to *Go To Heaven*, photo by Bob Seidemann with, inset, Willy John, Rudi.

"I remember telling Garcia once," Hunter recalls, "that there is a sort of charmed circle around the Dead, that we were safe as long as we directed our energies into the band. In order to achieve that kind of inroad into the consciousness of the times you almost have to feel you are magic. As cynical as I am now, and as childish as magic might sound, I still feel it and believe in it. I've seen the results of it — all over the world there are communities of people whose touchstone is the Grateful Dead. It's a vanguard of some sort of consciousness that has not yet died, a coming together of people who are vaguely anarchistic but peaceful and loving. I think the whole band feels this commitment to people . . . if the Dead were to break up, what would ever replace it?"

Hunter's concert artistry, apart from his reputation, is excellent. And, even though the '60s have come and gone, there is a large part of modern reality which Robert Hunter was heavily involved in creating. — Linton Robinson (*The Rocket*, January 1981)

If you're a fan of the Grateful Dead's, you'll go stark raving mad over the group's new album, *Go To Heaven*. If, on the other hand, the Dead is one band that you have been able to either take or leave, the new record may be just the thing to convert you. *Go To Heaven* has it all: Attractive songs, poignant lyrics and solid arrangements and instrumentation. It's a landmark album from the Grateful Dead, the most seasoned rock band in America — and quite possibly the best.

Musician Keith Godchaux, a former Stinson Beach resident who played keyboards with the Grateful Dead for eight years, died last Wednesday night in a Marin County hospital from injuries sustained in a traffic accident two days earlier on San Geronimo Valley Road.

The 32-year-old Seattle man, whose dreams of playing for the popular Bay Area rock band came true at age 23, had left the Grateful Dead in 1979 to form The Ghosts with his wife Donna Jean. According to Grateful Dead spokesman Rock Scully, the husband and wife team joined the Dead after Donna Jean dreamed Keith auditioned for and made the group.

Said Scully, "She came and told me about her dream and said Keith always hoped he would play for the Dead someday. She said her husband was perfect for the group." Scully arranged a try-out with Grateful Dead guitarist Jerry Garcia, the dream materialized and Godchaux joined the band for the tour that transpired into the *Europe '72* album. Godchaux took over full piano, organ, and synthesizer duties when organist Ron 'Pigpen' McKernan died soon after that tour.

He played on nearly all the Grateful Dead's records of the past 10 years, including *Wake of the Flood*, *Blues For Allah*, *Terrapin Station*, and *Shakedown Street*. He also played in Garcia's solo band, in performances of the Healy-Treece Band, a spin-off of Grateful Dead roadies and friends, and in the Heart of Gold Band.
— (*Point Reyes Light*, July 31, 1980)

NOBODY FOR PRESIDENT IN '80

Let's hear it for Nobody! Nobody for president! 'Cause Nobody's been with us a long time. As I explained to the native Americans — I empathize with their cause, but Nobody was here first. In fact, I *know* Nobody keeps all campaign promises. In fact, I *even* know Nobody is in Washington right now working for me . . . I firmly believe that Nobody should have that much power. I want Nobody to run my life. Nobody makes apple pie better than Mom . . . and you can go on and on endlessly, for Nobody, which we did. We would have these tremendous rallys with live rock and roll. In the middle of the rock and roll suddenly people would say, "Well, the Nobody motorcade has just been spotted and Nobody's headed this way." And everybody goes, "Oh, wow, wow!" And then Nobody pulls up in the back of an open convertible. Then Nobody speaks, and we use these little wind-up clicking, plastic teeth as a representative for Nobody. And it's always wonderful to see all the TV cameras pushing each other to get better shots of these clicking teeth.

My favorite Nobody story took place in 1976 in Kansas City, Kansas — the scene of the Republican National Convention. My friend, John Bryant, was there. He gave me a laminated press pass 'cause he had to go somewhere — far away. (Laughs) So I slipped off my clown gear, put on a three-piece suit (which I usually reserve only for Halloween), and slipped into the World Press booth and started typing up press releases . . . for Nobody. And giving them to the World Press 'cause they're right there, "Oh, thanks, I'll take that." So I'm spotted by this plain clothes Kansas City cop who calls the FBI and the Secret Service. They circumnavigate my clown ass, thrust me into a Lenny Bruce curtain call, and start patting me down; feeling this . . . bulge in my pocket. FBI agent says, "Is that a gun?" They whip it out. The plastic teeth start clicking in his hand. I said, "Quiet, our leader is speaking." He gives me back the teeth. He says, "Get out of here. You're too weird to arrest." — Wavy Gravy, aka Hugh Romney, *Old Feathers New Bird, The '80s Are the '60s Twenty Years Later* (Relix Records)

Wavy Gravy — Nobody, Hog Farmer, Clown, friend to children; Calico, Hog Farmer, friend to Dead Heads; Dave 'The Cutter' Turner, engineer, with Mickey.

Our trip was never to go out and change the world. I mean, what would we change it to? Whatever we did would probably be worse than the way it is now. We're just experts on a certain level, or saying "OK, so there isn't a whole lot available to you and there isn't a whole lot you can do about changing things around you, but you have yourself to work with and within that limitation you've got a lot that you can change — it's just a matter of taking that leap of faith and saying, Hey, the hell with the world. I'm gonna do what I wanna do and I'm willing to go for it." I think that we represent that possibility. Because here we are, still surviving, still following this intuitive path which makes itself up as it goes along in an almost magical way and yet it's no mystery. I just believe that if you get caught up in reality or society or any of the rest of those illusions, you're definitely gonna get nowhere. — Garcia

Fans spend 3 Days on Line to Buy Grateful Dead Tickets

Opposite, Bill Graham, Jerry Garcia, Howard Hesseman and Francis Coppola at the Bay Area Music Awards—Jerry received the award for Musician of the Year. Healy, Matthews, and Don Pearson of Ultra Sound in the basement recording room at the Warfield Theatre, San Francisco, where they recorded 15 Grateful Dead concerts the course of three weeks and later a further 8 weeks and later a further 8 at Radio City Music Hall in New York. Al Franken and Tom Davis from Saturday Night Live, below with kids, hosted the video simulcast from Radio City. Right, the first backstage Kids Room, the furnace room in the bowels of the Warfield Theatre — Mountain Girl is the big kid; and Len Dell'Amico, the Dead's video specialist, goes over the script with Al Franken.

...st, thank you for coming to spend an evening with The Grateful Dead. Wise decision.

When you step into the lobby, you'll see that much love and labor has gone into the creation of a 15-year retrospective of the Dead. We know that it'll flash you into times passed, and hope that you'll respect the fact that this memorabilia has been loaned to us by various members of the Dead, the artists, crew, families and friends; as well as much of our own stuff. Much credit must go to the responsible personnel that helped to put this thing together. Enjoy!

The Warfield is a theatre with seats, yet we know that many of you are gonna want to stretch and boogie—so, under the circumstances, and out of respect for the people around you, we ask you to avail yourself of the outer lobby areas when the bug bites. We'll have speakers in the lobbies, so the music will follow you. In return, we ask you to please refrain from standing on the seats and moving out into the aisles. This means a great deal to us, and we appreciate your cooperation.

We'd like to pass on to you the fact that the Dead could have earned in 2 nights at a large, indoor facility what it'll take them 15 gigs to earn here—and the fact that when all the mail had come in, we still had some 6,000 requests that we couldn't fill.

Reflections on the Warfield Run

These shows comprise the most important piece of work this company has ever done. After 15 years, we finally have some knowledge as to how to best deal with our fellow man. These shows are giving us the opportunity to handle a situation and give us a 2nd, 3rd and 15th chance to improve on the painting. The Grateful Dead and their audience allow us to be involved in this piece of theatre, and we have the opportunity to play director of the non-musical choreography, with 15 shots to make it better and better. When you realize how much better the third evening was than the premiere night, you get the picture. We're used to trying to hit a home run on one swing, and that's it. This is not the case here. To me this is a joyous piece of theatre. The boundaries are much more far reaching than I ever dreamed.

It's incredible when you realize that, given the opportunity, roughly 80% of the people coming to the event choose to sit most of the time. Strange, and all these years everybody's insisted that Grateful Dead fans always want to stand up. Well, here's an opportunity to prove that when you have the opportunity to do either, the Dead fan truly enjoys that opportunity and therefore sits and listens to what he loves, and only moves when the spirit moves him — not when he has to — only when he knows that he can go back to sitting down whenever he wants to. That, along with the sound in the lobbies, is the most important issue of this event, other than the magnificence of the music.

My hat's off to Peter Barsotti for the key to the whole gig — meaning sound speakers in the lobby to invite people in the lobby area to dance. This was the key to the entire event. Grateful Dead should consider lobby sound policy whenever it can improve the situation sociologically and environmentally. But, free form fornication in the foyer is firmly forbidden.

In general, the feeling of the building last night reached an all time high for me. It was clean, it felt relaxed, and I must say the public helped greatly in seeming to know what the rules of the game were. That's pretty much the extent of our role, and if we play it correctly, the rest is then left up to what the Grateful Dead do with what they do from the stage.

Something very strange going on — Mr. Healy and I have not frowned at one another since 2:49 p.m. on September 23rd. Isn't that wonderful . . .? While I understand Mr. Healy's need to calibrate the sound, we should do whatever we can to have sound on in the theatre when we open the doors to the public. Knowing Mr. Healy's attempt to strive for excellence, and his tenacious pursuit of nirvana sound, we must allow for, and give in to, The Quest.

I'll take this moment to thank the entire staff for having been so instrumental in making this Dead run at the Warfield a most memorable occasion. It is a testimony to the qualitative merits of the Grateful Dead, the respective artists, families, and music. It is also a testimonial to the 35,000 persons who've come to spend an evening with us here these past three weeks — the way in which they've respected what's been put here for them to enjoy.

I've had the good fortune to be involved in some fine times these past 15 years, and none of them, none of them, have given me more pleasure than these past 15 shows, with all of you and the Grateful Dead. I've always felt that the proper function of a professional producer is to create an environment which is conducive to the positive expression of both the artists and the patrons. If all the elements are there, the result will reflect the respective input of all parties concerned. I've also always felt that the next best thing to being an artist is to be somewhat involved with the art, and that's where our good fortune comes in. In the end, it's just not possible to explain to others the delicious feeling of knowing that you've been part of a situation wherein, for whatever length of time it may last, you just know that everything that's coming out is positive. Everyone gains. Everyone's pleased with the results. Other than good health and a good mind, that's where it's at. I'm extremely proud of this accomplishment on behalf of our company, and I commend you one and all for helping to make this exceptional experience possible. — Bill Graham

From left, Dan Healy, Brent Mydland, opposite, Bobby and Otis, Mickey and Glups, Mydland, Lisa and Jessica superimposed on one of the many posters celebrating Dead benefit concerts; this one by cartoonist Nutzle for the Campaign for Economic Democracy (Jane Fonda and Tom Hayden).

Grateful Dead

In celebration of the Grateful Dead's 15th anniversary, the group and Bill Graham have donated to charitable organizations all the proceeds from the final night of the Dead's sold-out, fifteen-night run at the Warfield Theatre in SF. The $27,500 raised by the show included the sale of special $100 tickets put on sale October 8 to help raise money for the organizations picked by the Dead and Graham: The organizations were considered based upon their immediate need of money for specific projects. The groups chosen were: the Haight-Ashbury Free Clinic/Rock Medicine Dept., California Coalition Against the Peripheral Canal, the Abalone Alliance of Northern California, the Planet Drum Foundation: Big Mountain Defense Fund, the Goodman Building Artists Cooperative, and the American Friends Service Committee. Bravo to Bill and the Dead for their generosity!

Here's a trivia item for all you hardcore Dead Heads that our research department dug up: during the Dead's Warfield run, the group played a whopping 93 different songs! That has to be some kind of record. — (BAM Magazine)

Foundation Established for Former Rock Group's Road Manager

The Grateful Dead's newly formed philanthropic foundation has been named in honor of past road manager and crew member Donald Rex Jackson of Pendleton, Oregon.

One of the foundation's board of directors is Larry 'Ramrod' Shurtliff. Also among the directors are former Trailblazer Bill Walton, Grateful Dead guitarists Jerry Garcia and Bob Weir, promoter Bill Graham, Dead manager Danny Rifkin and lawyer Hal Kant.

Mike Hagen, who now lives outside Athena, got to know Jackson in the '60s in Southern California. He remembers Jackson as a tall, spirited young man, who could ride a horse 'like the wind.' Jackson was a rider with the Umatilla Sage Riders which formed in 1948. He moved to California in 1968, but returned often to visit, says his mother.

The Rex Foundation "will be making contributions to creative endeavors in the arts, science, education, and in the areas of social change and healing." — *(East Oregonian)*

The Rainbow

With a band as great as the Dead, criticism becomes almost redundant. It's a bit like trying to prove that Bach was the greatest composer of his era, or that Charlie Feathers is a more significant figure musically than Carl Perkins. You either know it already, or you don't know what I'm talking about.

Despite the clouds of sweet 'erb that have turned the atmosphere into a re-run of an old-fashioned London pea-souper, you will rarely find an audience more in tune with the music, more likely to respond with immediate enthusiasm to a felicitous instrumental phrase or change in dynamics, more totally aware of what's going on.

The relationship between the Dead and their audience transcends all the usual biz trappings of stars up there and worshippers down here, for while there is no doubting the fans' devotion, it is more a communion between equals, a true folk relationship in the sense that Garcia, Weir and the rest are speaking for the audience rather than *at* them.

And, it is interesting to report, the audience is not several thousand relics from the '60s. These young men and their incredibly beautiful ladies were perhaps eight years old when Pigpen died. One reason for this young audience is the continual freshness of their music, whether they are rerunning an old warhorse like Willie Dixon's 'Little Red Rooster', playing newer material which shows they have been listening to reggae and soul, or following an unravelling yarn into labyrinths of almost atonal melody.

They are masters of the segue, moving smoothly (but not at all mechani-

Previous page; the band onstage at the Greek Theatre with a Courtenay tie-dye backdrop; inset, Wavy Gravy and the Kid's Chorus, Loretta Lemon, Kristine at Ambrosia's graduation, Stacey Matthews, Cole Cantor-Jackson.

From top, the Rhythm Devils at the Marin Civic Center Auditorium, Billy, Airto, Michael Hinton and Mickey; John Belushi and Jerry; Phil; John Kahn and Jerry performing an acoustic show in Eugene, Oregon, 1982.

Opposite, Al Franken and Tom Davis returning to New York after a hard New Year's Eve with the Dead; Mickey and young drummer Kingsley Melton. Left, Billy, Mickey with tar, and the Flying Karamazov Brother rehearsing at the Second Decadenal

Field Trip at the Oregon Country Faire site, Veneta, Oregon, 1982. Backstage: Airto, Craig Chaquico, Phil, Ainsley Dunbar, Paul Kantner, Billy, Flora Purim, Mickey and Grace Slick.

cally) from one mood to its almost opposite, carrying us all from one area of their mythology (part private trip, part collective consciousness) to another, so that one listens not to individual tunes in the sequence — just as, despite their frequent brilliance, one is not so conscious of any particular solo — but to an organic whole, the sum of which is so much greater than its parts. This was typified by the way they closed. Having built up a near frenzy with a couple of closing rock 'n' rollers (including 'Not Fade Away')

a lesser band might have attempted to top that peak, leaving the crowd dissatisfied, the evening unconsummated. Instead, they returned for a valedictory gospel tune which was very obviously a true closer, as intimate as a post-orgasmic embrace. The shouts for more from

the audience died down as the lights came up and they filed out, not with the obedience of a crowd which has been manipulated, Nuremberg-wise, but more like old friends who have met for an all-too-brief reunion, who part with warmth and a strength gained from each other, back into the world outside.

The autumn night felt not so cold, the city lights not so harsh, after five hours plugged into the Dead's life support system. — Karl Dallas (*Melody Maker,* October 18, 1981)

Grosses

Grateful Dead Concert Grosses: Boutwell Auditorium, Birmingham, Ala., April 28, $9.50 top, $30,847 ($50,760 potential); Fox Theatre, Atlanta, April 29, $9.50 top, $36,062 SRO; Greensboro (N.C.) Civic Center, May I, $8.50 top, $53,831 ($129,594 potential); Hampton Rhodes Coliseum, Hampton, Va., May 2, $8.50 top, $81,799 ($103,500 potential); Baltimore Civic Center, May 5, $9.50 top, $90,791 ($118,713 potential); Recreation Hall, Penn State U., State College, Pa., May 6, $12 flat, $45,708 ($60,000 potential); Barton Hall, Cornell U., Ithaca, N.Y., May 7, $8.50 top, $67,770 SRO; Civic Center, Glens Falls, N.Y., May 8, $9.50 top, $64,953 SRO. Civic Center, Hartford, May 10, $10.50 top, $156,946 SRO; Cumberland County Civic Centre, Portland, Me., May 10, $9.50 flat, $88,160 SRO; Boston Gardens, May 12, $10.50 top, $148,325 ($159,080 potential); Nassau Coliseum, Uniondale, L.I., N.Y., May 14-16, three shows, $10.50 top, $554,288 SRO. — Variety

NBC TELEVISION STUDIOS · RADIO CITY · RCA BUILDING · NEW YORK

WELCOME TO "SATURDAY NIGHT LIVE" WITH FRANKEN AND DAVIS AND THE GRATEFUL DEAD

DOORS CLOSE 11:00 PM

SAT. 18 APRIL 1981

205

The Dead is Livelier Than Ever

The open-air beauty of UC-Berkeley's Greek Theatre provided a perfect setting for Saturday's concert by the Grateful Dead, as the band played straight through the end of the afternoon into the dark of the evening.

Performing in front of a giant, colorful mosaic-like backdrop, the Dead turned the massive Greek Theater into an intimate parlor. The stage was festooned with wreaths of flowers and various bits of Grateful Dead emblemology. Sound and lighting worked marvelously and the Dead played to beat the band.

Improvisation lies at the heart of what the Grateful Dead does. Not only does the band perform an entirely different program every night, but each selection is drastically altered each time it is performed through instrumental inventions. Some songs contain as many as five separate instrumental breaks and sometimes lead mysteriously into whole new songs.

The music is a delicate synthesis of American music styles and traditions — jazz, country, blues, folk and electric rock — constantly kaleidoscoping into an ever-changing arabesque of musical patterns. The ultimate creation contains some majestic powerful passages and some mundane, boring sections. Such is the price of improvisation.

The whole Grateful Dead concert experience — from the retrograde partisan crowd to the sophisticated sound system, the challenging nature of the Dead's musical inventions to the anti-show biz presentation where the band just stands around aimlessly between numbers — is a unique institution in rock. While the band has codified and regimented the program to a degree, it remains an experience based in surprise, adventure and the luck of the draw. Saturday night, everybody went home winners. —Joel Selvin (*San Francisco Chronicle*, September 14, 1981)

Have you ever worked for the authorities? Would you ever consider playing to support a political candidate?

Never. We draw the line at that. Who's that cool, really? Nobody, certainly no politician. We've been hit on by all kinds of them, candidates, gurus, holy men. All kinds of power freaks have hit on us at one time or another to raise money for them or to get on the bandwagon and sell their trip. It's our responsibility to keep ourselves free of those connotations. I want the Grateful Dead experience to be one of those things that doesn't have a hook. We're all very anti-authoritarian.

So your main responsibility is to your audience.

Sure. Of course, we want to give them their money's worth, but we also want to avoid putting them in positions of harm. There are some places in America where we can't play because of the friction between the local authorities and the audience. We've had the experience of,

basically, acting as bait. The first couple of times we played Nassau Coliseum on Long Island, the police busted about 100 people. They took advantage of the situation. We have to try to make sure that doesn't happen.

Do you still get hassled by the law?

It's an ever-present danger. I have a feeling this whole Reagan era means a

tightening down from the top, so we're always on guard. We try to be as cool as we possibly can. The world is still not that safe for people like us. But I don't think any law enforcement agency sees us as a real menace.

That's interesting, because ten years ago you were perceived as a menace to public health and safety.

Well, we might still be. It's just that nothing's ever come of it. No major disasters or anything; our audience comes out for a good time and that's it. We've had countless sheriffs and chiefs of police giving us points because they've dealt with our crowd, and they know the difference between our crowd and other crowds. I mean, maybe I'm wrong. Maybe they have thick dossiers on all of us and they're just waiting for us to make a false move. But I don't think so, I think we've won the fight against our '60s image.

Club Le Front. The band's rehearsal hall and recording studio exists in a zone of never-ending sleaze near the waterfront in San Rafael. UltraSound, from left: Don Pearson, Mike Brady, Clark Scott, Howard Danchik, Bernie Granat, Geoff Peters and 3 guys from Morpheus Lights, Dan English in front.

But that image was cultivated. The skulls and the Hell's Angels and . . .

Well, let me put it this way: We didn't make any effort to *avoid* scaring people. But we didn't think we'd scare them as much as we did. It all seemed pretty normal to us.

Were you surprised by the power of the images you put forth, by the power that other people invested in you because of them?

Well, one of the things about the name, right from the beginning, was that it has a lot of power. It was kind of creepy. People resisted it at first. They didn't want us to be the Grateful Dead. It was too weird. But that response has sort of

flattened out. It was so obvious what was happening back in those days. Like the Black Panthers. I mean, what happens when a bunch of black guys put on berets and start packing submachine guns? They're going to get killed. You can't do that in America. You can't wave guns in the faces of the biggest guns in the world. It's suicide. That's obvious, but how could you say it? Like, all that campus confusion seemed laughable too. Why enter this closed society and make an effort to liberalize it when that's never been its function? Why not just leave it and go somewhere else? Why not act out your fantasies, using the positive side of your nature rather than just struggling?

Just turn your back on it and split — it's easy enough to find a place where people will leave you alone. You don't have to create confrontation. — Garcia (*Playboy*)

Next page, Nicki and Rock dancing in the New Year, 1982/3. Inset, from left, just married, Mr. & Mrs. Donna & David MacKay; Bobby 'Sky' Steinbrecker prankster filmmaker. Stanley Mouse with Dava Sheridan; "Set up like a bowling pin, knocked down, it gets to wearing thin . . . ." Above, Wavy Gravy with his one-stringed instrument, the *iktar.*

Bill Graham in his office. "You may not know me, but this laminate will get me in anywhere. I don't leave home without it."
Captain Kennedy, Commander of the Denver Vice and Drug Control Squad, stands by his favorite confiscated 'trophy' with 'pride and joy'. Inset Bobby and the Midnites, Hal and Jesse Kant.

it gets lonely
in the high pines
& lonelier when
you finally get
to town
all that
goodness you
done stored up
be gone
in about 15 minutes
so you gotta go
through all that
sickness
& all that joy just
like pig did
wonderin'
what the fuck
am I doin' here & why?
when you damn well know
it's because we all love
each other

Robert M. Petersen

10. WHO ARE THE GRATEFUL DEAD AND WHY DO THEY KEEP FOLLOWING US?

St. Dilbert was walking in the market one day when up staggered a Bozo to ask his opinion of whether the king, who had been caught with his hand in the exchequer, ought to abdicate, be deposed, have his hand cut off, or be given a medal. With very little pondering, the Dilbert is said to have replied: "You Bozos slay me. You pick a king who best represents the sum of your individual lamenesses to rule you, and then complain because he has a *big red nose*."

While considering this reply, the Bozo smelled smoke, and looking down realized that the Dilbert had, once again, placed a lighted match between his toes. — Hunter

Denizens of Front Street. From left, Steve, Kidd, Robbie, Brian, Joe Thomas, Paul Roehlk, Willy Legate, Ramrod. Inset, Paul Roehlk, the Grateful Dead's truck driver until his untimely death in 1986 from cancer. Bernie Granat tuning The Beast.

G.D. PRODUCTIONS INC.
BOX 1065 SAN RAFAEL, Ca. 94915

Courtenay tie-dying for the Greek Theatre backdrop. One reason for commissioning the huge stage tie-dyes was the 'rackety' acoustics of the Greek Theater — they built a plywood backdrop which was ugly, so they covered it with the tie-dyes. Inset, David Nelson, John Dawson and, left, Jerry with John Cipollina.

Mayor Dianne Feinstein, Bobby Weir, Bill Graham and Huey Lewis at a press conference about a benefit for the City.

Before there was music for entertainment, there was music for transportation, music that alters your perception, music that might be called ecclesiastical, or religious. We have a connection, a link, to the real old music, the archaic music. That's one of the great strengths of the Grateful Dead. —Hart

This is about *Dead kids*. Some might say we were *born Dead*. We showed you all the grown-ups in our lives, now how about us and some of our friends. Nobody ever really asked us what it was like growing up with those weirdos. Whether we liked it, hated it or just didn't notice. I always noticed that everyone around me was crazy but, hey, it was fun.

I always remember all of us grouping up before the gigs at the Henry J. Kaiser Auditorium. We'd go in the back behind the stage and there was another theatre there. And right behind this was a big room with red carpeting and a bunch of dressing rooms. Big dressing rooms. We would always play football, or soccer, or wiffel ball, or keepaway. We had a blast. — Cole Cantor-Jackson

Backstage Out of Harm's Way

A thousand lights, a hundred thousand wires, a million birthday parties happening at once . . . the air alive with ozone, sweat and reefer smoke . . . astrologers, magicians, a hot tub on a truck, people shooting pool, video games, spilled beer, the working press, and wandering throughout—doctors, lawyers and their clients, musicians and painters . . . people serving food and drink. Amidst this seeming chaos, a small group of dedicated clowns and jugglers (thinly disguised as baby sitters) see to it that the band's most cherished guests, the kids, are kept from harm's way as often as possible . . . NO SMALL TASK . . . rest assured . . . a hundred children clapping with one hand . . . and how many angels can dance on a pin?

This function is assumed by the Hog Farm and other friends of the band . . . no amount of prose could describe the workings of this clan . . . dada bodhisattvas each and all . . . This is simply to thank them for everything one hundred and eight million times. —Peter

It's hard to talk about the Grateful Dead's family without invoking a litany of the children's names . . . Zion, Trixie, Sunshine, Creek, Annabelle, Ambrosia, Breeze, Bodhi, Starfinder, Marina, Sage, Justin, Stacey, Jubal, Rudzo, Taro, Whip, Amber, Redbird, Raina, Didrik, Ivan, Ruben, Omar, Julia, Christina, Anne Winter, Cassidy, Luke, Debbie Doobie, Strider, Pearl, Orion, Jessica, Joshua Tree, Elric, Ruby, Graham Hamilton, Eva, Kate, Acacia and Joe . . . maybe that's enough.

INSERT YOUR KID HERE

The family Dead — and their family extended around the world — are what is left of the counterculture that was turned off in the '50s and '60s, turned off by a patriotism that turned out to be a bloody, bullying battle-rag, by a winners vs. losers free enterprise system that tightened the chains on the already enchained, by the ideal of thrift that turned out to be greed, by the ideal of frugality that turned out to be meanness, by a work ethic that turned out to be rapacity and a coronary, by a faith that became a hard sell, by a purpose that became a trample.

They are having a good time in a bad-time world. They are having a good natured hour — three hours — on a bad natured planet. They are having the nearest thing we see these parlous days to good clean fun. They are able to let themselves go, and not just harmlessly. Their friendliness is consummate. Their openness is consummate. Their acceptance is consummate.

The Dead have marshaled the truants, piping them, if to no lasting good, at least to no immediate wickedness — and that, in an immediately wicked world, is super-great stuff. The Dead Heads are the part-time grasshoppers, dancing while the full-time ants, here, there, everywhere, make industrious headway making bigger and better means of inflicting indiscriminate pain. The truants are not dropouts from the rat race, they are non-droppers-in.

Why are the Dead Heads different from all hordes that ever were? Why don't they fight and brawl and trash and tear the place apart and make miserable mischief in the streets? Why do they do nothing at a Dead concert but enjoy themselves unconfined? Why are they mannerly? Harmless? Innocent? The answer has got to be a magic chemistry that produced the Grateful Dead and says something to a world stoned on suspicion, hostility, war, and woe. — Milton Meyer (*The Progressive,* 5/83)

GRATEFUL DEAD
SANTA FE 1983

A Good Natured Hour on a Bad Natured Planet

Santa Fe, New Mexico — who forgot the roof? Inset, from top: Billy and Bobby; Peter Barsotti of Bill Graham Presents with Justin Kreutzmann; Harry Popick. Opposite, Wavy Gravy in the Santa Fe campgrounds with Paul Krassner.

The campground just south of the Downs at Santa Fe is filling with vehicles from all over the United States — vehicles plastered with Grateful Dead stickers and filled with hippies and dogs and kids — but filling in an orderly way. They are the fans — Dead Heads — who have come from Virginia, New York, Illinois, Kansas, Colorado, Washington and California. They have come from all over, just to be a part of this, many trailing after the band as it makes the 1983 western tour.

They need a safe place to sleep, and so a safe place, a campground, has been provided . . . by the Hog Farm, a group fully as unique as the Grateful Dead and

their fans. The Hog Farm is an 'extended family', the Hog Farmers say, and playing host for Dead Heads is one of the many things they do well. They came together in the late '60s around a small core of writer Ken Kesey's LSD-inspired Merry Pranksters, and have evolved with their skills and interests right along with the times.

Down the road a bit is a big con-

verted school bus, painted with Grateful Dead symbols. The interior is crowded with bunks and tables and chairs, as any bus that houses six people ought to be. Up front in the kitchen area is a girl in her early 20s selling avocado, tomato and sprout sandwiches for a dollar apiece. The dollars add up, and help

get the bus from concert to concert.

Milling about among the vehicles and people are tie dyed t-shirt sellers and tie-dyed hat sellers, Grateful Dead button sellers and bumper sticker sellers. It is a small, transient, but throbbing community, one that will grow up and pass on in a weekend. It is not only the band that brings it all together, but the lifestyle as well.

As evening descends on the campers the bonfires are lighted and peaceful crowds begin to collect around them. There is very little hype there, no social posturing, just a bunch of humans gather-

ing around a warm spot, talking, joking, singing or just staring into the flames.

"It is a joy for us to provide these services so that this may occur," Wavy Gravy says. At one time there were no campgrounds for the traveling Dead Heads, and they were forced out into the hostile streets when the last tunes died away. But the Dead themselves took pity on the Heads and moved to have the campgrounds provided. "These places make statements in creative anarchy," Wavy Gravy says. "You see that without anyone being in charge these little communities spring up." — Howard Passell (*The Santa Fe Reporter*, September 14, 1983)

Still Wavy After All These Years

Wavy took up his *iktar*, a one-stringed instrument of Muslim origin, and started to sing: *Wouldn't it be neat/if all the people you meet/have shoes on their feet/and something to eat?/ Wouldn't it be fine/if all human kind/has shelter?*

"They're going to bury me a hippie," he said. "Peace

and love, man. I believe in it. I'd bet my life on it." And the song goes on: *Wouldn't it be grand/if we all lent a hand/so each man could stand/on a free piece of land?/Wouldn't it be swell/if people didn't sell/their mother . . . Earth?*
— Kevin Lollar *(Marin Independent Journal)*

For the past year or so, during the guitar 'space' part after the Rhythm Devils, I've been able to do a lot with the sound. I have synthesizers in my booth, and we sort of play together. A lot of the equipment is home-brew stuff. Again, it's an experimental process for me. It's a huge 'breadboard', which is an electronics term for a temporary circuit that you put together to verify an idea. We've been doing stuff for quite a long time, but now it's gone further and the band is pushing me more: "Hey Dan, do more of *that!* I heard the tapes of the other night — what was that thing you did?" It's gotten to be a lot of fun, and I've realized that there's a lot more dimension to what I can do.

I have about six different kinds of delay systems that are basically all the popular varieties you find in recording studios. I also have three or four pieces of custom equipment designed by John Cutler and myself. There's a thing I've got now that allows the sound to be controlled by a computer. The sound can move around the room, and as it moves it turns inside out and upside down, like those computer graphics on TV where they can turn things all around and show you the inside and outside of things all in one motion. I can now do the aural equivalent of that.

For audience taping, I use an AKG stereo microphone — one of those two-mikes-in-one that was developed in Europe for recording classical concerts; a matrix box that I built for the figure-eight thing — MS — and then I have a Beta hi-fi PCM video deck that gets the board mix onto the video band, and then on the beta hi-fi track I put the audience MS mike. Then I can take that back to the studio and take this new analyzer we've got and it will compare the notes and the impulses of the music and regulate the delay so I can play back and mix the room mikes and the board mix. It's beautiful to hear.

When we start the spring tour, we're going to have a whole new trip. There'll be that system, plus we've also recently acquired this marvelous piece of very complicated audio analysis equipment that uses three computers. In addition to measuring the amplitude of the various musical notes, it measures the notes' arrival time, the reverberance in the hall, all sorts of things. I think where it's all leading is that in a couple of years we should be able to go into a hall and completely eliminate the echo. We can do that now on a good night — the room will just vanish and it's you and the music.
— Dan Healy (*The Golden Road*)

On A Good Night the Room Will Vanish

A shared moment of recognition of something intangible. This is the stuff, the heart of the Grateful Dead "experience." And the end result is perhaps nothing stronger than . . . happiness.

In California: the Dead Live On

An unbeliever claims that only 10,000 people in the entire world are followers—cultists, really—of the durable and idiosyncratic rock band called the Grateful Dead. What gives the band its undeserved appearance of popularity, he adds with exasperation, is that Dead Heads, as these fans call themselves in what should be apology but probably is boasting, are so zonked on Dead music that they all show up for every concert, no matter where on the planet it is played.

"I don't know," says J.R., 25, an engineering student from the University of Massachusetts. "I missed some concerts this year." He is standing in a very chilly line outside the Civic Center auditorium in San Francisco, where in something like five hours the Dead will go onstage. J.R. is making what sportswriters call a great second effort to get serious about college, he says, his first effort having been stopped for no gain by, in part, too many Dead shows. The reward he gave himself for industrious scholarship this semester was to hitchhike across the continent, with little cash and no tickets, to attend all three sold-out concerts in San Francisco. He has managed to score tickets somehow and now is a happy man.

It can be argued that there are at least 37,351 Dead Heads, because that many attended an outdoor concert at Saratoga, N.Y., last summer. But even 37,351 is a statistical flyspeck in the megahyped world of rock music. The fact is that in almost 20 years of playing, the Dead have never managed to record a song that sold enough copies to make it as a hit single. They have had fair success with albums, but their ecstatic, visionary offshoot of rock spins with improvisation, and the necessity to nail things down in a studio version tends to fossilize the band.

What the Dead have managed, however, are those 20 years of playing, with most of the same early-'60s rebels and LSD voyagers who started the group. The original keyboard and harmonica player, Ron McKernan, known as Pig Pen, died of hard living in the early '70s, and the present keyboardist, Brent Mydland, is the only relative newcomer. Otherwise the Dead are still Mickey Hart and Bill Kreutzman on drums, Phil Lesh on bass, Bobby Weir on rhythm guitar and, first among equals, Jerry Garcia on lead guitar.

One of the striking qualities of the Dead Heads' obsession with the band is that although it is highly personal—the fans think they can sense how Bobby and Jerry feel during any given song—it is remarkably unintrusive. The Dead Heads don't seem to know or care what bandsman is dating or divorcing whom.

One result is that the fans, knowing nothing important to the contrary, can go on assuming that the Dead live in a warm, funky, '60s time warp that has not really changed since the days when they jammed at the Acid Test roisterings of Ken Kesey and his Merry Pranksters. Playing in a rock band for 20 years is probably a good way of staying in a time warp, and if your legs go first, as with boxers and third basemen, you do not pick guitar with your feet. But the stranger truth is that the Heads have a '60s warp of their own. While most of the band members are

The Heads enjoy the ritual of celebration; inset, Lead Guitarist Jerry Garcia

From left, Dan's eye view with, inset, Phil and his 'rain hat'. Phil, a racing car enthusiast, in the cockpit with 3-time world champion driver Jackie Stewart. The Dead, and Dead Heads, make *Time Magazine*.

After a visit to India in 1985, Mickey Hart invited the Gyuto monks to the United States to record their unique chanting.

They are the Dalai Lama's personal chorus. Like the Pope's choir in the Vatican, they sing for their religious leader as well as their king (who are both personified in a single individual: the Dalai Lama).

Enrolled as buddhist monks they begin their clerical training at the age of four, and spend the next 20 years qualifying for this

The Gyuto Monks

highest honor. Rather than singing single notes as Western musicians do, they are capable of several notes simultaneously (forming chords) . . . and as they sing the last words of each stanza, they close their mouths and three or four harmonic overtones can be heard echoing the first after they stop singing.

Two thousand people witnessed a musical event unrivaled in Western history, and like Bill Graham says, "They not only are the best at what they do, they are the only ones who do what they do." — Peter

Inset from left, Merry Christmas from the Winslows, Sandy with Popeye, Amber Blue with 'Buzz', Joe with 'Harpo'; Solar, Billy, Rikki, Nickel and Christina; Russ, Janet, Jeremy, Rene and Gina Knudsen; The Kesey clan on the barn stoop, Pleasant Hill, Oregon.

223

Just like Grandma Moses
Just like Auld Lang Syne
Play the change, however strange
And get it right this time!

It's been a hard haul
20 as the crow flies,
When your back's to the wall
Got to play it as it lies

Let there be music, dance and the beating of drum
Drop whatever you're doing and come on the run
Twenty years later the groove is just starting to click
It's all variations on some impossible lick

Come hear Uncle John's Band
Playing to the years
Come along or go alone
Like an avalanche or a rolling stone

GRATEFUL DEAD

Twenty Years So Far

Wave that flag!
Wave it while you can
Long as you keep coming
You got a band

Thanks for 20 years of being
an audience which is the envy
of every other rock and roll band alive.
Fuck 'em if they can't take a joke!

Write if you get work.

Spare change?

Don't touch that plug!

Cassidy

"I don't know *how many* people were living at the ranch," Eileen Law says. "People were in every room and out in the barn. You had to have seniority to reach bedroom. I'd sleep in haystacks sometimes, with the horses and all these other animals."

Eventually, Mickey decided he wanted his ranch back and asked most of those living there to leave, so Eileen moved in with Bob Weir and his lady friend, Frankie, in a small house in the tiny West Marin town of Nicasio.

"That's where Cassidy was born," she says of her daughter, whose father was Rex Jackson, a Grateful Dead crew member until his death in a car crash in 1976. "Weir wrote the song at the house during that period. I lived in a tent behind Weir's and I'd go out there and practice my breathing exercises. I'd hear Weir playing these beautiful riffs in the house. Later I think he asked Hunter to write some words

for the tune, and he was going to write something about a card game, and I said, 'No, no, that's not what that tune is about.' Around that time, John Barlow came out here on his motorcycle, and the next thing I knew, he and Weir had this song, which was about my daughter, Cassidy, and had parts about Neal Cassady, too." Ironically, Cassidy wasn't named after Cowboy Neal at all, but after the character in the popular film of that year, *Butch Cassidy & the Sundance Kid.* "I decided on it before Cassidy was even born because I thought it sounded good for either a boy or a girl. I don't think she's

ever really liked the name, though."

Cassidy began going to Dead shows from birth. "I took her as a newborn," Eileen says. "Like the other kids, she sometimes would sleep wrapped in blankets in equipment crates during the shows. Other times I'd hold her all night and then not be able to move my arms the next day."
— Blair Jackson
(The Golden Road)

Everyone in the band is working on different systems that are customized to suit their own needs. So Bob and I have been working to get my setup so it has a lot of flexibility. Like in a lot of other bands, if the keyboard player's going to come in with a synthesizer part, he just pushes a button and there's the sound at exactly the volume he wants, and it's the same every time. But with the Grateful Dead I can't necessarily do that because I'm not sure if the song is going to be the same way the next time we do it. And we change everything around so much that one time I might want one sound on a song, and another time something different. I'm going for colors usually. I'll be playing piano and might sneak some strings in or something like that. I need that kind of flexibility, so we're developing a system that works for me playing in the Grateful Dead. — Brent Mydland *(The Golden Road)*

Harry Popick, monitor man, and Patti Harris, manager of Grateful Dead Merchandise; inset, Eileen Law, who keeps Dead Head communications running, and her daughter Cassidy; below, the 'Dead Head Wall' at the ticket office covered with decorated envelopes — Steve Marcus, manager, and Frankie Acardi square off.

"These musicians can combine and improvise on things and it's earthshattering, time-stopping, anything that's wonderful that you can think of. It's music made by humans, but an elusive quality does manage to manifest itself at the concerts. You can stick your tongue out and lick what's going through the air." – Paul Grushkin

We can raise the sail, but we can't make the wind come. "Raising the sail" is preparing to be moved. Spirit is the wind, the sense of musical well-being, of being together. This is a unanimous process. —Hart

They follow us around because they're looking for the same answers in the music that we are. We tend to draw a different kind of person —someone with an advanced sense of adventure. —Weir

Right, Taro Hart, drum puppy: "Train them young and train them right!" From left, Bob and Stacey Matthews; Brent; Nicki and Acacia; Wavy Gravy, Billy at Susana Millman's wedding to Dennis McNally, Grateful Dead publicist and official historian; Steve and Marilyn Parish.

"This is great! A happening thing! I love the people here! I love the *energy!* I live on a bus. We call it the Magic Bus!"
Another Dead Head guarded her movie carefully:
"Get your own facts!" she scolded. "I'm not going to give you mine. I can't speak for these people. You should be covering El Salvador — something *real.*"
This isn't real!?
"No," she said. "This is fun."

The reason we have poetry is to say the oblique things. Anybody can sit down and say that a terrible thing happened because of the war in Vietnam and two halves of one generation were split because some of them went and some of them stayed, and that we've had a difficult time reapproaching one another and being brethren again. But the point is to get into the inner realities and use myths and to go back to something that's old and deep in human experience, like Jacob and Esau. The literal references may elude you, but you've been brought up in a culture where those references are kicking around and they still resonate in the back of your head whether you know them or not. There's also the possibility that somebody might go out and *read* the story of Jacob and Esau, which is fine with me. The point is to say it and use the symbols that come to you and then let the meaning take care of itself.

Community is something really important to me, if for no other reason than because I come from a very small town in an isolated place. I come from a place where even my enemies would help me out if I were in a certain kind of trouble, because there's a bond we all share. But America, for whatever reason — and I think corporate policy has a lot to do with it — is erasing the idea of community, and people need that desperately.

So the Dead Heads have done something wonderful. They've done a little conceptual blockbusting and realized that you don't have to do it in one place. It doesn't have to be out in the middle of a cornfield somewhere. It can be anywhere in America, and they just take it

on the road. People get to know each other and they help each other out. It's one of the things that makes it possible to do this for all the frustrations involved — because you want to go on supporting that. We're doing some pioneering work in how to create communities and keep them together in the future. Rather, I should say *the Dead Heads* are doing it; I don't think we — the Grateful Dead — have that much to do with it on that level. We have the same relationship to their community as corn does to a small town in Iowa probably.

I was watching the New Year's Eve gig and it was clear to me how *tribal* it felt. Good communities are tribes. They have rituals and myths and those kinds of deeper realities that light up everyday reality and give it some substance. I felt like I was looking at a tribal ceremony, and I liked that.
— Barlow *(The Golden Road)*

Conceptual

Blockbusting

"There's a better way. There has to be education, and the education has to come from the poets and musicians, because it has to touch the heart rather than the intellect, it has to get in there deeply. That was a decision. That was a conscious decision." — Hunter

Grateful Dead lyricists Robert Hunter and John Barlow. Phil and son Graham Hamilton. Bobby with Andrea Salter of Fantasy Records and Barbara Whitestone.

Anarchy at its Finest

We were terrible business people! We made mistakes from the outset (as managers of the Carousel Ballroom in the '60s). We opened up with the Dead and the Airplane, and the place was crammed to the gills. The next weekend, we didn't have anyone, and then we opened up again the following weekend. Well, if you're trying to establish a place as a draw, that's death. We didn't keep the momentum going. At either the second or third show, we had so few people show up that instead of charging admission, we went around Haight Street passing out tickets, and then when people got there we gave them free food and free ice cream. Free *everything*. We turned it into a party.

And it was *fun*. It totally changed the atmosphere. And it gave us the reputation of being street people, which is what we were. We had a great love for this place and gave our lives to it for that period of time. Everyone did. Everyone cared *a lot* about each other, and the care was genuine and it showed.

To me it was freedom, true freedom. You can do anything here and it's OK, as long as you don't hurt anyone. That's the kind of anarchy that shows that people at their basis are good; they don't need constraints to *make* them good. So that's what we were experimenting with there. I think that's what all of us in the Haight were experimenting with. The Carousel was the epitome of anarchy at its finest. A lot of people found it scary. But I think a lot of people in San Francisco found it to be exactly what was going on, and very important to them, and exciting, warm and wonderful.

I have a lot of faith in the resiliency and street savvy of the Dead Heads. I also have a lot of faith in their gentleness. In fact, that's what I have the *most* faith in — that nonconfrontive, noncombative attitude. And the more that can be shown as the hip attitude to have, the better off we are. — Jon McIntire (*The Golden Road*)

Jon McIntire with Goldie Rush, Willy Legate; inset, Tangerine, Mickey, Sara, Taro and Mary Hart.

Wary of Exploitation

I told Eileen that on that very morning someone supporting Walter Mondale asked me if I thought the Dead would let them use their list for a mailing. "That doesn't surprise me," she says. "We get a lot of that. Someone from the Gary Hart campaign called up and wondered if they could use names from New Jersey awhile back. But we don't let the list out. We've had friends ask us to use it because they're starting a business or something, but we don't even let them use it. I'm really against letting those names out because I respect the privacy of the people who have joined Dead Heads. They didn't join it to get mail from politicians."

That sort of integrity runs deep in the Dead organization and is unquestionably a by-product of the era in which the Dead scene was spawned. The group was wary of exploitation by profit mongers in the '60s, and today they carry their hip business ethic into every aspect of the operation that they can, maintaining a distance from the straight business world philosophically while attempting to use their business savvy to meet their own ends. — Blair Jackson *(The Golden Road)*

Opposite, The Crew: Steve, Kidd, Ramrod, Paul Roehlk, Harry, Billy Grillo. Inset above, Luke Badger Raizene, Laird Grant, Esq. and below, Bobby Petersen, David "X" McQueen, Laird and Alan Trist at the graveside of Page Browning in Pleasant Hill, Oregon.

The Thunder Machine is a remnant tool of the Acid Tests. You could crawl up inside it and beat on it, or beat it from the outside. It was wired. Ron Boise was the sculptor. It's a survivor, still in use. Here, Kesey is with co-driver Zane Kesey. Decorations at Kaiser Auditorium, Oakland, St. Valentine's Day, 1986.

Yet none of this matters, for the Dead have forged a symbiosis with their audience that, no matter how naive some may find it, is simply unequaled and probably unshakable. In fact, the Dead and their audience practically form their own self-sufficient fellowship—an alternative commonwealth that boasts, among other things, its own pop press (made up of several Dead-related magazines, its own radio program, syndicated as *The Grateful Dead Hour*, hosted by David Gans), its own computer-linked database system (in which Dead Heads not only trade fans' notes and debate ethical issues but also pass along their concerns directly to various band members) and its own worldwide network of tape collectors, who, with the band's blessing and cooperation, record all the Dead's performances and share them with other obsessive archivists. The Dead maintain one of the largest staffs of any pop act around and bypass conventional ticket-sales systems (and reduce scalping) by selling fifty percent of their tickets through their own scrupulously organized mail-order system.

If all this sounds vaguely utopian or communal minded, well, that's precisely the point: the Grateful Dead and their audience function—and thrive—almost entirely outside the conventions of the mainstream pop world. Consequently, the Dead—a band rooted in the ferment and romanticism of the 1960s—somehow epitomize the two most prominently contradictory ideals of 1980s pop culture: they are not just a raging cult fave but also a smashing mass success.

II. THE NEW DAWN

GRATEFUL DEAD

January 28, 1987
San Francisco Civic Auditorium
San Francisco, California
BACKSTAGE

GRATEFUL DEAD

January 29, 1987
San Francisco Civic Auditorium
San Francisco, California
BACKSTAGE

Yet despite this achievement, the Dead are an object of indifference and, just as often, outright ridicule. That's because the band never seemed to have let go of the ideals and styles that it first laid claim to in San Francisco's Haight-Ashbury scene in the mid-1960s, and much of its audience can still seem obsessed with that period as well. At least one critic has described the Grateful Dead as little more that "nostalgia mongerers . . . offering facile reminiscence to an audience with no memory of its own."

It is a charge that nearly every person in or around the band is familiar with, and clearly it rankles. "It's mortifying to think of yourself as a nostalgia act when you've never quit playing," says Robert Hunter. "We're looking at an audience of nineteen- or twenty-year-old kids. Can you have nostalgia for a time you didn't live in? I think some of our music is appealing to some sort of idealism in people, and hopefully it's universal enough to make those songs continue to exist over the years."

John Barlow, a cattle rancher and writer who lives in Wyoming and is the band's other lyricist, has an even stronger reply. "I find it sort of curious," he says, "that there's a pejorative attachment to the fact that there are people who refuse to let go of a certain time and place — especially when the values that that time and place represented were the best that we've seen in our lifetime. These are soulless times now, and I don't see anything wrong with people who want to fix themselves on times that were a lot more enriching. But the real point is that that doesn't represent the audience at all."
— Mikal Gilmore (*Rolling Stone*, 7/16/87).

Everything has exceeded my expectations so much that I have a tendency to think that anything I might have done consciously to change things would have served to make things smaller. My own vision was never large enough to imagine that the Grateful Dead would become what it has become. — Garcia

Sheer Innocence . . .

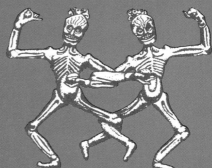

Fervent Loss of Self

Rock music has never seemed that interesting to me. But when you see a room with 8,000 young people for five hours going through it to the beat of these boys, and when you see 8,000 kids all going up in the air together . . . Listen, this is powerful stuff! And what is it? The first thing I thought of was the Dionysian festivals, of course. This energy and these terrific instruments, with electric things that zoom in . . . This is more than music.

It turns something on in *here* (the heart). And what it turns on is life energy. This is Dionysus talking through these kids. Now I've seen similar manifestations, but nothing as innocent as what I saw with this bunch. This was sheer innocence. And when the great beam of light would go over the crowd, you'd see these marvelous young faces all in utter rapture — for five hours! This is a wonderful, fervent loss of self in the larger self of a homogeneous community. This is what it's all about!

It reminded me of Russian Easter. You go to the Cathedral at midnight and you hear *"Kristos anesti!"* "Christ is risen! Christ is risen!" It's almost as good as a rock concert! It has the same kind of life feel. When I was in Mexico City at the Cathedral of the Virgin of Guadalupe, there it was again. In India, in Puri, at the Temple of the Jagannath — that means 'the lord of the moving world' — the same damn thing again. It doesn't matter what the name of the god is, or whether it's a rock group or a clergy. It's somehow hitting that chord of realization of the unity of God in us all. That's a terrific thing, and it just blows the rest away.
— Joseph Campbell *(The Golden Road)*

Left, noted mythologist Joseph Campbell *(Hero With A Thousand Faces, The Masks of God, The Skeleton Key To Finnegan's Wake,* etc.), in one of his last appearances before his death, shared a San Francisco dais with Garcia and Mickey Hart at a university symposium entitled *Ritual and Rapture: From Dionysus to the Grateful Dead,* praising the Dead as worthy successors to the Eleusian Mysteries and proclaiming them "the antidote to the atom bomb."

Q: What did the herd of militant horses demand for breakfast?

A: Hey, now . . . !

The origins of the kids room are shrouded in the inky depths of chromosomal amnesia. But wait . . . Rifkin remembers me and a kid under the stage at a Day on the Green with the Grateful Dead and the Beach(ed Men) Boys. The date was June 8, 1974.

I'm sure we shared some bubbles and makeup and it kinda caught on and started snow balling . . . with the Hog Farmers fillin' in the holes, working in cahoots with the band and Bill Graham Presents. (Kiddie care at regular rock 'n' roll concerts is usually quite chaotic or totally non-existent.)

We created the kids room as a safe haven for the kids of the cabal. A space of wonder and joy with an ever expanding palate of stuff to explore: puzzles and games and glitter and glue and bingo for prizes, and jugglers and clowns and a legion of face painters that double as laps and soft lovin' shoulders.

The years have slipped by like bubble juice on linoleum. Camp Winnarainbow appeared on the Hog Farm horizon and lots of kids-room-kids became campers and brought back circus skills like juggling and unicycle riding and clowning (I call camp "Survival in the 21st Century" or "How to Duck With a Sense of Humor") and it all goes into the mix.

The bigger kids help the little kids with their bingo card then slip away to teen world and big time video games . . . and to rock 'n' roll.

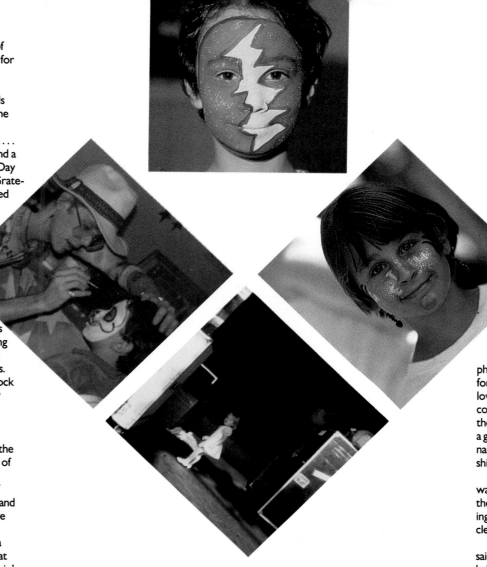

The Kids Room

The Hog Farm gets photos of dead presidents for what once was a labor of love. It helps pay for our country land plus each year the Rex Foundation gives us a generous grant in Pigpen's name for our camp scholarship program.

Meanwhile, the next wave comes crawlin' thru the kids room door searching out bristle blocks and clean diapers.

It was Paul Foster who said, "Out of the mouths of babes comes dribble." And yesterday's dribblers are tomorrow's camp counselors and role models in the grand kids room of life.

— Wavy Gravy

A Eulogy for Robert M. Petersen

Bobby Petersen would not applaud a long and tepid eulogy. He was a street poet, first, last and foremost, who recorded what he saw in lucid verse, which is his living memorial. He played a dangerous game with life and left some damned fine work behind.

Bobby was heading north to finish compiling a book of his poetry when his number came up, so there is more to be heard from him; at least from that part of him which extends into the world beyond his friends and family.

In the words of Rimbaud: "The task of a man who wants to be a visionary poet is to study his own awareness of himself. He must seek out his soul, inspect it, test it . . . learn all forms of love and suffering; search until he exhausts within himself all poisons and preserves their quintessences. He must endure unspeakable torment, where he will need the greatest faith and superhuman strength, where he becomes among all men the great invalid, the great criminal, the great outcast — and the Supreme Scientist! For he attains the unknown! And if he finally loses the understanding of his visions, he will at least have seen them!"

The voice of Robert M. Petersen will endure, for those with ears to hear, crackling through the static of our generation like the sound of a faraway radio.
— Robert Hunter, January 1987.

like those before me here
i will come
sing

      & disappear

leaving only
broken sandals & imperfect
tools

    name
    forgot

    or just
    maybe

      never

        spoken

— Robert M. Petersen

I think if you take *In The Dark* and put it in some other decade, it speaks to that decade just as clearly. And it's equally nonspecific. I mean, if you really listen to it carefully it doesn't say anything that pins it to the '80s. It's stuff that pins it to *this* world, though. That may be the difference — we're finding that living this long of a time in this world and surviving it, there's some things that you start to be prepared to talk about. —Lesh

"It was a year which saw the Dead getting respect and attention from some fairly unexpected quarters, as magazines from *People* to *Forbes* examined their 22 years of overnight success."

Opposite, Bobby Petersen and his son, Didrik; Didrik's wife, Kirsten; and Phil at the mike of *Rex Radio*, dedicated to the forefront of music, aired by KPFA in Berkeley; Above, Club Dead abounds throughout the country, this one in Eugene, Oregon, put on occasionally by Downtown Deb who also broadcasts *Dead Air*, a local

Grateful Dead radio show; Patti Harris, Diane Geoppo and Eileen Law take care of business in the Grateful Dead office.

Most people make money on the records, and take their losses on the tours.
Garcia: That's true. Exactly. With us it's been just the other way around.
It's been more fun for us . . .
Garcia: Well, it's been more fun for us too. But we're definitely mortal. What would really be helpful would be for there to be half a dozen other Grateful Deads playing.
— Mary Eisenhart (*BAM Magazine*, 12/18/87)

Garcia: The way we approached the *So Far* video was like multi-track recording, the same way you do it with music.

Dell'Amico: One of the differences, though, is that in audio recording all the tracks are one tape. We'd go into these post-production places and have seven one-inch machines going for playback with different things on every machine.

Garcia: Once you start having images and you put them to music, you start to say, "Wow! That looks great! Let's try this!" It's mainly a matter of slipping the pictures back and forth in relation to the soundtrack.

Dell'Amico: In the one-inch editing room, we'd have the lists and keep track of the images we wanted to look at that way. So let's say on 'Playing in the Band' we wanted to create a ballroom. We'd take a group dance shot and lay that down and do a silhouette of it. Then we'd say, "Well, let's blow out the foreground and put in a lava-lamp floor that's moving. Now we'll take this dancing couple from this tape, do some jazz on them, and put them over here."

The idea is that instead of laying it out from a strictly cerebral starting point, which is not realistic because it's not based on anything, and then trying to execute something that's

already been decided, it's more like you sculpt it as you go.

Garcia: It's a natural process. When you put pictures and music together, magic things happen. Sometimes you don't know why it works, but it works.

DellAmico: Some of the people at the post-production places thought we were crazy. They're used to harassed and harassing clients who are losing their minds and uptight and abusive. So we come in and say, "What we want to do is *play*," and they're thinking, "Oh my *God!*" The client isn't the slightest bit prepared. They don't know what it's going to cost." But when they learn that you mean it, that you want everyone to relax and stop worrying and just do it for fun — boy, by the second day they were just flying! At the end of each day the technicians would say things like, "You're getting more for your money than anybody we've worked with."

Garcia: In places like that, people want 30 seconds of dynamite. They're spending their top dollar to get it and so they're very goal-oriented. Our way of working is more process-oriented. And once you flash on the process, it takes a while for the operators — the guys who are working for us — to say, "Oh, I see what these guys are trying to do." And then *they* start making suggestions. They get to actively join in creatively and suddenly they're not guys who you're telling what to do — they're people with ideas.

The *So Far* video is the Grateful Dead way of doing things, which turns out to be expensive, difficult and unrepeatable. If we went back to do this again, we'd come out with a different finished version. We couldn't repeat it.

If you're going to do something, it's important — for me, at any rate — to shoot high, even if you miss. It's a matter of art to be able to convert those images of war and violence from shocking reportage to cathartic epiphanies, to use a phrase coined by Larry Lachman at the Post Group. The idea is to sit there and say, "Yeah, this is getting me pretty weird. This is working!" (laughs) We were after the idea of electronic mind altering and consciousness altering. And on that level I think it's pretty successful.
— (*The Golden Road,* Summer 1987)

Cathartic Epiphanies

Bill Graham and Jerry; images from the *So Far* video; and, opposite center, Trixie and her dad.

. . . and there is only the band and the audience shouting Buddy Holly's old and timeless lyrics: "Love is love and not fade away/Love is love and not fade away." "Not fade away," the crowd shouts to the band. "Not fade away," the band sings back. **"Not Fade Away!"** the crowd yowls, leaning forward as one . . .

Drug use is a kind of cul-de-sac: it's one of those places you turn with your problems, and pretty soon, all your problems have simply become that one problem. Then it's just you and drugs.

It's a black hole. I went down that black hole. Luckily, my friends pulled me out. Without them, I don't think I ever would have had the strength to do it myself.

I am not a believer in the invisible, but I got such an incredible outpouring. The mail I got in the hospital was so soulful. All the Dead Heads—it was kind of like brotherly, sisterly, motherly, fatherly advice from people. Every conceivable kind of healing vibe was just pouring into that place. I mean, the doctors did what they could to

keep me alive, but as far as knowing how to fix it (diabetes)—it's not something medicine knows how to do. And after I'd left, the doctors were saying that my recovery was incredible. They couldn't believe it.

I really feel that the fans put life into me . . . and that feeling reinforced a lot of things. It was like "Okay, I've been away for a while, folks, but I'm back." It's that kind of thing. It's just great to be involved in something that doesn't hurt anybody. If it provides some uplift and some comfort in people's lives, it's just that much nicer. So I'm ready for anything now.

The truth is, time pays off. Longevity is real special when it comes to playing music, because pretty soon you have a relationship with the other players in the band that is beyond intimate. It's closer than any other relationship you have in life. I know these guys better than I know anybody. And they still have that capacity to surprise me musically; I have to stay on my toes to keep up with them. At the same time, if I have an inspiration, they're

all ears. They'll follow me down any dark alley. Sometimes there's light at the end of the alley, and sometimes there's a black hole. The point is, you don't get adventure in music unless you're willing to take chances. —Garcia (*Rolling Stone*, July 30, 1987)

"When it seems like this night could last forever, And there's nothing left to do but count the years, I will walk alone by the black muddy river And believe in a dream of my own." —Robert Hunter

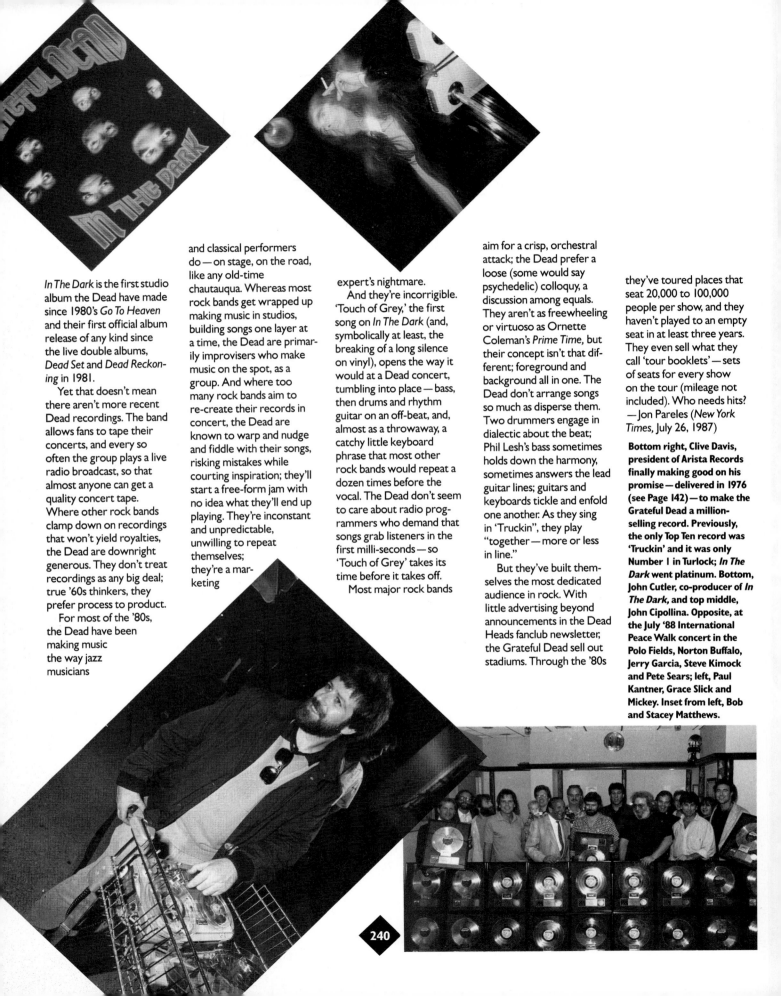

In The Dark is the first studio album the Dead have made since 1980's *Go To Heaven* and their first official album release of any kind since the live double albums, *Dead Set* and *Dead Reckoning* in 1981.

Yet that doesn't mean there aren't more recent Dead recordings. The band allows fans to tape their concerts, and every so often the group plays a live radio broadcast, so that almost anyone can get a quality concert tape. Where other rock bands clamp down on recordings that won't yield royalties, the Dead are downright generous. They don't treat recordings as any big deal; true '60s thinkers, they prefer process to product.

For most of the '80s, the Dead have been making music the way jazz musicians and classical performers do — on stage, on the road, like any old-time chautauqua. Whereas most rock bands get wrapped up making music in studios, building songs one layer at a time, the Dead are primarily improvisers who make music on the spot, as a group. And where too many rock bands aim to re-create their records in concert, the Dead are known to warp and nudge and fiddle with their songs, risking mistakes while courting inspiration; they'll start a free-form jam with no idea what they'll end up playing. They're inconstant and unpredictable, unwilling to repeat themselves; they're a marketing expert's nightmare.

And they're incorrigible. 'Touch of Grey,' the first song on *In The Dark* (and, symbolically at least, the breaking of a long silence on vinyl), opens the way it would at a Dead concert, tumbling into place — bass, then drums and rhythm guitar on an off-beat, and, almost as a throwaway, a catchy little keyboard phrase that most other rock bands would repeat a dozen times before the vocal. The Dead don't seem to care about radio programmers who demand that songs grab listeners in the first milli-seconds — so 'Touch of Grey' takes its time before it takes off.

Most major rock bands aim for a crisp, orchestral attack; the Dead prefer a loose (some would say psychedelic) colloquy, a discussion among equals. They aren't as freewheeling or virtuoso as Ornette Coleman's *Prime Time,* but their concept isn't that different; foreground and background all in one. The Dead don't arrange songs so much as disperse them. Two drummers engage in dialectic about the beat; Phil Lesh's bass sometimes holds down the harmony, sometimes answers the lead guitar lines; guitars and keyboards tickle and enfold one another. As they sing in 'Truckin'', they play "together — more or less in line."

But they've built themselves the most dedicated audience in rock. With little advertising beyond announcements in the Dead Heads fanclub newsletter, the Grateful Dead sell out stadiums. Through the '80s they've toured places that seat 20,000 to 100,000 people per show, and they haven't played to an empty seat in at least three years. They even sell what they call 'tour booklets' — sets of seats for every show on the tour (mileage not included). Who needs hits?
— Jon Pareles (*New York Times,* July 26, 1987)

Bottom right, Clive Davis, president of Arista Records finally making good on his promise — delivered in 1976 (see Page 142) — to make the Grateful Dead a million-selling record. Previously, the only Top Ten record was 'Truckin' and it was only Number 1 in Turlock; *In The Dark* went platinum. Bottom, John Cutler, co-producer of *In The Dark,* and top middle, John Cipollina. Opposite, at the July '88 International Peace Walk concert in the Polo Fields, Norton Buffalo, Jerry Garcia, Steve Kimock and Pete Sears; left, Paul Kantner, Grace Slick and Mickey. Inset from left, Bob and Stacey Matthews.

240

You have to have enough access to the fingerboard so that you're not hung up about where you are. In other words, 'What key am I in? What scale interval am I at?' You need to be able to let that go past you, to be able to get a good sound regardless of the structure's mathematics. So much of the guitar is patterns. But if you look at it right, patterns start to melt into each other; pretty soon you can hit anything from anywhere. The quality of consciousness that you put into a note also has a lot to do with it. You can play any note in any context, and if you play that sucker like you mean it, it's going to sound good— almost. The note that comes after it, and when it comes, and how smoothly you play it, and how much expression, individuality,

you can give to it — that also has a lot to do with it. Like, choosing to give a note a really rich vibrato or a real dry attack. Or having a slow opening and a long sustain. The personality of the note has as much to do with its appropriateness as the setting does.

If you're two octaves above whatever instrument is playing the chords, you can play almost any note and it will work as an extended part of the chord. If you're in the same octave, then it will work because it darkens or brightens the chord like an

interior voice. It's like playing two hands in the same octave on the piano; it really clangs. If you spread it out more, it sounds prettier, though the darkness is sometimes real interesting.

The rhythm is the final part of the equation. The way you release notes, their value, and the holes you leave have a lot to do with the strength or the power of your playing. When the

band is pulsing along, punching eighth notes — where you can think of any note as one — I like to do things like play a figure that's maybe seven beats long starting, say, on the end of beat four. You create this incredible tension, and the next thing you play is either going to

Personality of the Note

increase the tension or you're going to find yourself back at a new one. It's like a jigsaw puzzle where all the pieces are white and all the same. —Garcia *(Guitar Player Magazine)*

A Touch of Grey

Every Friday morning, the programming brass at MTV get together to screen the videos that have arrived during the week. Generally, they watch only a minute or so of each clip; bang, bang, on to the next one, please. But on the fateful Friday that the Dead's 'Touch of Grey' videoclip was screened, the assembled group demanded to see the whole film, applauded lustily after the showing, and then proceeded to screen it a couple more times during the day. Not bad for the band's first foray into the field. It went on the air the following Friday and it's been in the network's rotation ever since.

The man behind the Dead's hilarious send-up of standard rock concert videos — in which puppet skeletons belt out the Hunter-Garcia anthem 'Touch of Grey' before transforming into the band near the end — is no stranger to either the Dead world or rock videos. Gary Gutierrez, of San Francisco-based Colossal Pictures, is best known to Dead Heads for his psychedelic animations sequence at the beginning of the Dead Movie and the unusual opening for CBS' recent revival of *The Twilight Zone* (which was accompanied by theme music by the Dead).

When Gutierrez told Arista Records about his idea they flipped for it. The skeletons were obtained from a medical supply firm on the East Coast and altered by Gary Platek, an independent effects specialist, and were jointed so they could be manipulated as puppets. The six band members were photographed in front of a grid from different angles and in close-up so the puppet makers could make skeletons to the players' precise measurements. Exact duplicate guitars were built, and, of course — the clothing had to be perfect too — right down to Phil's wrist sweatband.

The actual shoot took place the second weekend in May at a venue the Dead had never played before — Laguna Seca raceway in Monterey. The videomakers built scaffolding above the Dead's lighting rig to accommodate three puppeteers, one for each guitarist; the Billy, Mickey and Brent skeletons were controlled by rods rather than wires. — Blair Jackson (*The Golden Road*)

...olinas — Several dri...
...reported a skeleton jumping
out in front of cars being
driven around the lagoon.
After officers checked the ceme-
tery and reported there was
no evidence of a missing
skeleton.

Hell in a Bucket

The Devilettes, the ladies from Grateful Dead offices and friends at New George's in San Rafael on their way to hell. From left, Sue Stephens—do not pass GO! Bobby trod on the tiger's tail, but it didn't seem to mind. Len Dell'Amico, director of the video; Willy Legate; The Rhythm Devils, Billy and Mickey.

I don't feel that close to the center of whatever this culture is. Like I say, I live in the Grateful Dead universe, its which has its own parameters, its own goals. For me it's very narrow. I don't mean narrow in the sense of limited horizons. I mean narrow in the sense that the way I experience the Grateful Dead and this culture is: the Grateful Dead is like a door and you pass through that, then another door, and so on. The door frame and the wall and the room beyond are the rest of the culture. I'm seeing it from the wrong end of a telescope, so to

From top, left to right: Kristine and Elric; Frances, Ramrod and Ambrosia; Dan Healy and Rudson; Mickey, Hal Kant, Bill Graham, Jerry, Barlow, Maruska, Bobby, Bill Walton and Ramrod in front; Justin, Billy and Stacey Kreutzmann; Maruska, Ramrod and Dick Latvala; Dennis McNally and Paul Grushkin; Harry, Patti, Frankie, Eileen, Basia, Mary Jo and Andrea; Danya Veldfort and Willy, Opposite inset, Jean Carl and Rosie McGee Ende; Rudson; Jerry and Bob Dylan.

speak, with the Grateful Dead in the extreme foreground. The Grateful Dead translates to me as my community, my friends, the people that I care about. The kind of first-line political stuff is the stuff you touch with your hands, the people that you see eye to eye with and deal with. Then everything beyond that is some sort of wild rumor you either believe or don't believe. And I have no direct evidence of it. So it's tough for me to talk about that world with any degree of confidence. — Garcia (The Golden Road)

244

What do you think the Dead Heads are finding? Why did it work with you guys and not with all these other people?

Well, a lot of it is because it *is* us, it's not me. For me it's easier to believe a group than it is a person. That's certainly one of the things that makes the Grateful Dead interesting, from my point of view — that it's a *group* of people. And the dynamics of the group part is the part that I trust.

It stands to reason that you have a lot of fans among us 40-year-olds, but a whole bunch of kids that are just discovering rock and roll, period, are getting into being Dead Heads. How do you account for that?

I just think that there's a certain kind of kid for whom we say something. And it's been that same person in each generation. Back when we started it was the people who were our age, and we've been picking them up younger and younger every decade.

It was never my intention to say, this is the demographics of our audience. I was delighted the first time that people didn't *leave.* Everything above and beyond that is pure gravy. So when *anybody* likes it for *any* reason, great . . .

On that show last night *(Sergeant Pepper: It Was Twenty Years Ago Today),* somebody says, we won. It's over, and we won. They don't know it, the Reagan era is over; they don't know . . .

They're dying off, and we're still here.

The point is, it happened, there was a revolution, and we won. And

It's Over and We Won

he's right, and a large part of this is the expression of, yeah, we did win, here it is.

The thing of just having fun, having adventures, having something to bounce off of, having something that's the background music for your life, which is always great no matter how close you are to it, or how far away you are from it. All of those functions get fulfilled, and hopefully the whole little society that's out there now, the new Grateful Dead marketplace out there, and all that stuff, these all represent alternates — these are all extensions of the American idea. The American experiment.

For us, there never was a debate. It was over from the very beginning. The very first acid trips, the very first excursions into psychedelia revealed — whatever there is, there's more than we've been allowed to believe. We don't know what it is, we can't describe it, we just suspect its existence, but we know, beyond the shadow of a doubt, that there's more than anybody ever let on. We know that.
— Garcia (*BAM Magazine,* December 18, 1987)

The Night of the Living Dead

Dylan came on shortly after 6 pm at Autzen Stadium, Eugene, Oregon, on July 19 for the Dead/Dylan concert, in long jacket, jeans, cowboy boots, headband and beard. From the first song through to the last, he came through with singular power and authority, with a miraculously energized Garcia crackling along on guitar behind him.

Thanks to Grateful Dead sound engineers, Dylan's cut-through-the-crap voice came through more strongly and clearly than I've ever heard it on record, allowing the audience to appreciate his inimitable mastery of ironic nuance.

The Grateful Dead pitched in with some backup vocal harmony from time to time, but mostly they just got behind Dylan and cooked. One member of the band said before the tour that the Dead would be the best that Dylan has ever played with. They made a strong case Sunday afternoon with some full-throttle playing.

When Dylan finished his set, the nonstop dancers finally stopped and did what nobody had seemed interested in all afternoon — simply touching each other. There was a whole lot of huggin' going on. But there also was a lot whis-

tling, clapping and cheering — enough to bring Dylan and the Dead back for encores.

Garcia went first with 'Touch of Grey', a Robert Hunter song that is rising fast on the charts and becoming a Dead Head favorite with its refrain: "I will survive, we will survive."

Dylan came along right behind that, as is his wont, with a word to the wise about survival in 'All Along The Watchtower'. He couldn't have picked a better way to leave the modern-day descendants of the Merry Pranksters.

Bob Dylan's abundant life is the stuff of legend, and now he is joined on stage by the world's premier touring band, the Grateful Dead. This is not just a rock show, this is a modern American folk phenomenon, timeless in its appeal and unparalleled anywhere. *Soundcheck,* Spring 1987

"There are many here among us who feel that life is but a joke. But you and I, we've been through that, and this is not our fate. So let us not talk falsely now, the hour is getting late." — Paul Denison (*Eugene Register-Guard,* July 20, 1987)

The Grateful Dead onstage with Bob Dylan at Robert F. Kennedy Stadium, Washington, D.C., July 6 & 7, 1987. Below, "I know you," Dylan and Olatunji, label mates at CBS in the '60s, meet again at the Dead's rehearsal studio. Inset, the Lesh family.

With 'Noosphere', (a piece of contemporary, classical music composed for Kent Nagano, conductor of the Berkeley Symphony), Lesh is returning to an older side of his musical identity. His first and formal training was classical. At age eight he started playing violin. At twelve, he began playing violin and trumpet in Berkeley Young People's Symphony. After graduating from Berkeley High, he went to UC Berkeley, the College of San Mateo ("they had a jazz band"), and Mills College where, in 1962, he studied music

with Luciano Berio and composed an ambitious piece for four orchestras called 'Foci'. His influences were Ives, Stockhausen and Coltrane.

Lesh: The process of composition is essentially the same for any composer. You have an idea that defies description so you compose it.

Alice Polesky: *But do you hear it?*

Lesh: You don't hear it at first. You perceive it first. You *are* it, you know what it is, you're experiencing it. Later you translate it into actual sound. You perceive what is consecutive simultaneously. There's no hearing, no feeling. It's a structure. Shoënberg called it the 'grund gestalt', the basic shape. . . . It's mostly long sequences in time. Sequences of sound. As the layers peel off from this

soundless sphere, the sound enters. It's like a backwards supernova. You have this singularity which reveals nothing except itself: It's a unity, you have to unroll it, unfold it.

Is this peeling away the entire process?

Lesh: No, then you have to arrange the pieces in a chronological sense, since music takes place in time. You can't play the whole thing at once. It would be like someone flashing a blinding white light in your eyes and saying, "That was my painting." In the process of peeling it off, you end up

The Arabo-Dickensian Western Dead Gang during the shooting of 'Throwing Stones', the band's third MTV video in 1987 in support of *In The Dark*. Inset from top left, Bobby's mug shot, Brent Mydland and Lisa; Felicity silences Bobby; Michael and Frankie; "Gotcha," Michael Peri. Below, Maureen Hunter; the band with Dylan.

with the sequences. In Mozart's case, his genius was so great that he peeled off an entire movement in an hour. In my case, I peel off a section or a little segment at a time, and sometimes they don't come off in chronological order; they're not linear, so I have to rearrange them.

How has the rock music you have been playing eased its way into 'Noosphere'?

Lesh: If anything, just a freedom of phrasing, not so much on the beat as concert music. I'm trying to liberate it from the down beat, in other words.
— *Berkeley Monthly*

Balloons fall at midnight, Father Time enters on the Globe and the crowd goes wild at Kaiser Auditorium, Oakland, 1987/88. That year there was a national TV broadcast and during the breaks Tom Davis hosted some stylish guests: Mountain Girl as 'Future Lady', Justin Kreutzmann interviews Dead Kids, Cooking with Jerry, Mickey works the Spock mind meld on Jerry. John Cipollina with Natalie. John, a great musician from the Quicksilver days through Zero and the Dinosaurs, spent many a New Year's Eve jamming with the Grateful Dead. He was a friend to many and his death in the Spring of 1989 was felt in musical circles around the world.

New Year's Eve Come and Gone, My Oh My

Escena De Bella Ternura

Fue hace muchos, muchos años. Entonces, hacia 1966, una serie de jóvenes americanos que no gustaban ni del fútbol ni del béisbol descubrieron el ácido bajo el sol de California. Así nacían los *hippies,* la psicodelia: así nacía Grateful Dead, su grupo más representativo y el único fiel a sus orígenes.

Pero nadie vaya a creer que la presencia de los Dead en Barcelona, el pasado lunes, y en el Palacio de Deportes, fue un viaje hacia tiempos más floridos. No; todo aquello era real, ocurrió en nuestro tiempo y así debe entenderse. Eso sí, resultaba curioso percatarse de que todavía existen *hippies* que visten como tales; resultaba chocante ver a gentes disfrazadas de muertes agradecidas, con su guadaña y todo; resultaba emocionante ver a esas familias (papá, mamá y los niños) con sus macutos a un lado y la expresión arrobada. Habían venido de lejos ('Del cielo, del cielo', decían unos), habían surgido de la vuelta de la esquina, pero allí estaban todos, dispuestos al trance. No hace falta explicar como el *chocolate* era principalísima materia prima, no es posible describir tanta escena de bella ternura, pero sí constatar que allí no sólo había la tirada pereza del *colocado,* sino una suave marchita que finalmente conduciría al personal a lo largo de unas tres horas y media de concierto. Muchas horas y mucho concierto.

Poco a poco, aquellos trinos desgalichados fueron dando paso a una verdadera avalancha de notas que lo llenaban todo, de canciones típicas que iban adquiriendo mayor y mayor peso hasta lograr lo que es el alfa y el omega de este tipo de cosas: la vibracíon.

Ellos, los Dead, no estaban muy contentos de su música, pero sí de un público que les recordaba su San Francisco soleado. Y hacia allá vuelan ahora, como unos reyes magos de la alucinación, unos dulces pero enérgicos provocadores de sensaciones. Y, como los reyes magos, volverán. —J.M. Costa (Barcelona, 1981)

Iko Iko, the Grateful Dead celebrating Mardi Gras, an annual event. Other goings on about town: Robert Hunter was accompanied by Tom Constanten at a poetry reading in San Francisco. Poster artists Wes Wilson, Alton Kelley, Stanley Mouse, Victor Moscoso and Rick Griffin at the Poster Artist's Benefit. Ramrod and Frances, Bob Bralove and Cameron Sears at the March 1988 BAMIES, when the band won five awards. Jerilyn celebrates the book.

SAVE THE RAINFORESTS

RAINFOREST ACTION NETWORK

On Tuesday, September 13, 1988, Jerry Garcia, Bob Weir, and Mickey Hart from the Grateful Dead; Dr. Jason Clay, the director of Cultural Survival, Peter Bahouth, the chairman of Greenpeace USA, and Randall Hayes, the director of the Rainforest Action Network, held a news conference at the United Nations to alert the world's press to the fact of the vanishing rain forest and what this means for life on this planet. The conference followed a benefit the Dead had done for the Rain Forest Coalition at Madison Square Garden in New York. "With us, the whole notion of doing good is a little suspicious," said Garcia. "We've been working on it for years and we've discovered certain things — like you have to follow the money to find out if it's actually doing any good. We mostly deal with close-to-the-bone, grassroots, low scale, direct action stuff. No bureaucracy. We're looking to advance the idea."